THIS IS A UNCOREC
W0017004

*I want to thank Lois Morse for the help and encouragement she gave me. A true friend.*

# Enduring Times

**BETTY GODFREY**

This is fiction based on a true story. Names, places and incidents, any resemblance to actual persons living or dead is used fictitiously. People, businesses, companies, churches or locals has been changed and is entirely coincidental.

© 2020 Betty Godfrey All rights reserved. No part of this publication may be reproduced, distributed, or transmitted in any form or by any means, including photocopying, recording, or other electronic or mechanical methods, without the prior written permission of the publisher, except in the case of brief quotations embodied in critical reviews and certain other noncommercial uses permitted by copyright law.

ISBN 978-1-09830-049-4 eBook 978-1-09830-050-0

# Chapter One

Jennifer woke up hearing the rooster crow. Unlike most people, she loved this sound. She yawned, as she stretched her arms and said, "It is such a beautiful morning." Her husband, who was still sleeping, grunted and turned over. While she dressed, she could hear their three children giggling in their rooms. She knew they would soon want their breakfast and she hurried to the kitchen.

The children came down full of energy, and dug into their eggs and bacon. Andrew finished first and said, "I'm going out to feed the rooster."

"Wait for me," said Margaret and Cassie, as they drank the last of their milk.

Bill came rushing down. "I forgot. I have an important meeting this morning."

He worked at Jennifer's father bank in town. Although Bill and her father got along well, he demanded promptness. Jennifer quickly put his breakfast on the table and poured the coffee. Gulping it down, he looked at his pocket watch and said, "Gotta go," then kissed her goodbye.

Jennifer watched him walk to his car through the kitchen window. Bill was six-foot-tall, with a slender body and muscular arms. She loved him so much. "He's my pillar of strength," she thought.

Jennifer poured a cup of coffee and walked out to the porch. She inhaled the beautiful scent from her garden as she sat in her rocking chair. "What a beautiful day for Andrews's birthday party," she thought. "I can't believe he's five-years-old. Time passes so fast. Margaret is three and Cassie's almost two." She sighed, "My life is complete. I'm the happiest woman alive."

Jennifer went to the kitchen to make Andrews birthday cake and she heard the children fighting. She looked out of the window, Andrew was hitting Margaret. Jennifer ran out and grabbed him, then noticed his arms felt hot.

She kissed his forehead. "You're burning up, no wonder you're so cranky."

Jennifer called their doctor, then bathed him in cool water.

Andrew squirmed and cried, "Mommy its cold, its cold."

She lifted him out of the tub and wrapped a towel around him as Margaret asked, "What's wrong with Andrew? Why is he going to bed so soon?"

Cassie tried to crawl up on the bed with her brother, but Jennifer took her in her arms. "Andrew isn't feeling well. The doctor is coming to see him. Go downstairs with your sister and watch for him."

Doctor Forman pulled up to the house as the children shouted, "He's here mommy, he's here."

He examined Andrew, then patted his head, "I'm leaving you some magic pills." He lifted the child's head and gave him a pill with some water. "Go to sleep now. You'll feel better when you wake up." The doctor led Jennifer out of the room as he said, "He has an ear infection and a fever of one hundred and one. High for such a little tyke." He handed Jennifer the bottle of pills. "Give him one every four hours. Keep cool clothes on him until his fever breaks."

"Will he be all right?" asked Jennifer

"These pills should take care of it. I'll be back in the morning. Call me if you need me."

Jennifer opened the ice box and chopped off a chunk of ice, placing it in a basin.

"Why are you doing that?" asked Margaret.

Cassie climbed up on a chair and tried to put her hands in the water. Jennifer took Cassie's hand and led both girls to the kitchen table. She poured each a glass of milk and gave them cookies.

"Sit here, while I call your Grandmother."

Bill's parents, Nellie and William, lived next door on their farm. When Jennifer told them that Andrew was sick, they came right over.

"Would you mind taking the girls over to your place? It would be a big help," asked Jennifer.

"That's what we planned to do," said Nellie. "Come on girls, let's go play at our house," said William. "We'll call Andrew's friends and tell them the party is off."

Jennifer took the basin of ice water upstairs and felt Andrew's body. He still had a fever. She wiped his body, then placed a wet cloth on his forehead. Kissing his cheek she whispered, "Please God help him get better."

It was 5 p.m. when the front door opened and Bill called out, "Babe, I'm home."

"I'm upstairs," said Jennifer, "Andrews's sick."

He ran up to his son's room, "What's wrong with him?"

Tears filled Jennifer's eyes as she said, "He has a fever of a hundred and one."

Bill touched his son's face. "My God, he's hot as fire. Did you call the doctor?"

Jennifer's voice quivered, "Yes, he said, his ears are infected. He gave me medicine to give him. He's coming back in the morning." Jennifer leaned back in her rocking chair, by the bed and closed her eyes. "I feel exhausted." Bill rubbed her shoulders and Jennifer yawed, then said, "I didn't have time to fix dinner."

"I'm not hungry. I'll just sit here with you."

After a few hours Bill said, "Why don't you go to bed and I'll stay here with Andrew."

Jennifer stretched, "No. I'll be all right. You have to work tomorrow."

"No. I'm off tomorrow, it's a bank holiday." He put his arms around her and led her out of the room. "You can relieve me in the morning."

Bill sat by Andrew's bed, listening to his son's heavy breathing. He wrung out the cloth in cold water and gave him the medication. Andrew seemed to be breathing easier. It was 3 a.m. and Bill felt tired. His eyes were burning so he closed them for a few minutes. He suddenly woke up and looked at his watch. "My God, its 5 a.m., I've been asleep for two hours."

Bill felt Andrew's head, it seemed cooler. "Good, the fever broke. He looks peaceful." Almost too peaceful, thought Bill. He placed his face to the child's lips and couldn't feel his breath. Panic rushed through him as he felt for a heartbeat. "Oh my God, I can't feel it." Bill picked Andrew up as he screamed, "Son, wake up! Please wake up!"

His voice woke Jennifer and she rushed to the room. "What's the matter?"

Bill was in the rocking chair, cradling Andrew in his arms, rocking back and forth. "Don't leave us, son. Please, don't leave us."

Jennifer knelt beside him. "Tell me what's wrong?"

Bill whispered so low she could hardly hear him, "He's dead. I fell asleep when he needed me."

Jennifer rushed to the phone and called the doctor, "Come now! I think our son is dead."

Doctor Forman found Jennifer and Bill on the living room couch, huddled together with Andrew in their arms. "Please let me have him," he said.

Bill kept saying over and over, "It's my fault. I let him die."

"It's not your fault." said Doctor Forman. "Listen to me; it's not your fault." The doctor had delivered Andrew and his heart felt heavy as he took the child. "It's no one's fault, he was very sick. Sometimes a fever that high is too much for a small child and the Lord takes them out of their misery."

Bill jumped to his feet and screamed, "If I hadn't gone to sleep, he would still be alive."

Doctor Forman handed the child to Jennifer. "Don't blame yourself. He was a very sick child."

He filled a syringe with a sedative and put it in Bill's arm, then led him to the couch.

Jennifer cuddled Andrew and tears poured down her cheeks. "My first born baby is dead."

Doctor Forman handed Jennifer two pills, "Take these, they'll calm you down."

Jennifer wiped her eyes. "I'll take them later. I have to tell Nellie and William."

Doctor Forman took the boy from her. "You take those pills now! I'll tell Bill's parents, then I'll call the undertaker."

Nellie and William rushed over and put their arms around Jennifer. "I can't believe our grandson is dead. What can we do to help?"

"Just keep our daughter's over at your house, I can't handle them now." Jennifer's body shook violently, as she cried.

Nellie held her, trying to comfort her. "That's it honey, cry, get all the tears out. William and I will take care of our granddaughters, don't you worry."

———————————

St Regis Catholic church was filled with friends and relatives. Caroline, Jennifer's sister, walked down the aisle of the church and sat next to her. "How are you holding up?"

Jennifer looked around, "Where's Mother?"

"She's not coming."

"Why couldn't she forgive me and come?"

"The service is starting, we'll talk later," said Caroline.

When the mass was over, friends and relatives came to the cemetery. Jennifer and Bill stood in the front row.

Father Donahue officiated the service then concluded, "Andrew has gone to heaven and is sitting at God's side looking down on us." The Priest made the sign of the cross and picked up a handful of dirt.

Bill ran towards the grave pushing the priest away. Sobbing, he threw himself on the casket and shouted, "There is no God. If there was, he would never have taken my son."

Francis pulled him to his feet and took him to William's car. "Come on Bill. Let's go home."

Suddenly Cassie and Margaret scrammed, "Mama, Mama." Everyone turned to see what was wrong. Jennifer was on the ground, unconscious. The children sobbed, "Is Mamma dead too?"

Caroline knelt by her sister. "Jennifer wake up! Wake up!"

Francis ran to them. "Please God, don't take my daughter too." He picked Jennifer up, carried her to his car and drove to Nellie's house. He laid her on the bed, placing a blanket over her. The guests were arriving from the cemetery and Francis reluctantly left to help Nellie.

———————————

Jennifer woke up but kept her eyes closed, reliving the scene at the cemetery. I thought Bill was strong enough to handle the funeral. I was surprised at his reaction. Now, I know I have to be strong for both of us. Jennifer thought back to the night six-years-earlier, when she was a student nurse at the Nursing Academy. Bill picked her up in his black model T Ford and they went to dinner.

That was the night they got engaged. As they were driving home it started to rain, as lighting slashed the sky. "I can't see a darn thing." Bill opened the window and stuck his head out. "Okay now I can see the road to your house, it's just ahead." Bill wiped the fog from the windshield and drove on.

When he started to turn up the road Jennifer said, "Let me out here."

Bill stopped, "Why! You'll get all wet."

Jennifer flung open the door. "I don't want you to drive to my house. If mother sees you,

I'll be in trouble."

"You mean she doesn't know we've been dating for two years?"

"No, Caroline and I are not allowed to date. That's why I always arranged to have my Father meet us and bring me home."

"You mean we've been sneaking around all this time?"

Jennifer jumped out of the car and before Bill could grab her, ran up the dark road like a scared rabbit. Thunder rumbled in the dark sky and Jennifer ducked when the tallow lightning slashed near her. The rain turned the dirt into oozing mud that swished over her white ankle high shoes. It splashed on the hem of her white uniform.

Gasping for breath, she finally reached her house and as she ran up the steps. She prayed, "Please God, let mother be asleep!"

Jennifer wiped her muddy shoes on the mat and reached for the doorknob. The door sprang open and her mother grabbed Jennifer's long auburn hair and dragged her into the hallway.

"So you finally came home." said Freda

"Let go of me." Jennifer pulled away and swept her hair from her face. "I told you I would be late."

Freda's long black hair hung down passed her shoulders and with her black flowing robe she looked like a witch. "Refresh my memory."

Jennifer saw the anger flashing in her mother's eyes and she looked away. I worked late at the lab, then Lisa and I had dinner."

Freda's eyes looked piercingly into Jennifer's. "Yes, go on."

"Then Lisa drove me home."

"You're lying. I called the Academy and you weren't there. The janitor said everyone left hours ago."

Jennifer's hands trembled as she unbuttoned her coat and placed it on the banister. "I'm, going to get a glass of water."

Freda pulled her back as she started to walk away and Jennifer tripped and fell on the floor.

"I'll tell you where you were," said her mother. You were out with that good-for-nothing Bill Rennie. She reached under Jennifer's dress and tugged at her underwear.

Jennifer pushed her away. "Stop it."

Freda held her down as she ripped off Jennifer's bloomers. "I want to see if that no-good bum got into these pretty things. If you let him touch you, I'll send you to a convent."

Jennifer huddled against the wall gazing up at the crystal chandelier. The twinkling crystals mesmerized her, as they cast a glimmering reflection on the ceiling. She felt like she was floating away. A muffled sound snapped Jennifer out of her trance and she saw Caroline crying, as she leaned over the bannister in the upstairs hallway.

Caroline's pale distorted face peered down as she cried out, "Stop it! Stop it mother!"

All our life mother has been mean and controlling, thought Jennifer. I can't take it any longer. Courage sparked inside her. She banged her fist on the floor and shouted, "I won't let you turn me into a sniveling coward." She tried to stand but the heel of her shoe caught the hem of her uniform and she fell back down.

Freda let out a hideous laugh. "Looks like you're too weak to stand up. You must have had a hell of a night."

Jennifer clamped her teeth in anger as she grabbed the hall table and stood up. She lunged at Freda, grabbing her lacy underwear

"Yes I was with Bill, but he didn't get into my bloomers as you so crudely put it. I'm twenty-one and you can't stop me from seeing him."

"That's what you think." Freda grabbed Jennifer's arm, twisting it behind her back.

"You're a good catholic girl and I'm keeping you that way." She forced her daughter up the spiral staircase to her bedroom. "Open the door and turn on the light." She pushed Jennifer in the room. "If you ever see that bum again, you'll regret it. I'd rather see you dead than married to that man." She slammed the door and Jennifer heard the lock snap.

"Don't lock me in," cried Jennifer. She banged on the door sobbing, until her fist hurt.

Jennifer pulled the rosary beads from under the neck of her uniform and held them tight. The beads were ivory and rosewood with angel faces carved on them. A small cross hung in the middle. Her mother had given them to her when she made her holy communion, they always relaxed her. Jennifer took off her mud-stained uniform and unbuttoned her muddy shoes. She placed them by the door; the maid would clean them tomorrow. Jennifer put her nightgown on, then pulled the rosebud spread off the bed and crawled in.

She thought of the wonderful night she had with Bill, then gasped. "Oh no, I left my ring in my coat pocket. If mother finds it, she'll throw it away. She heard a knock on the French doors that led to the balcony and she sat up quickly.

"Are you asleep?" whispered Caroline.

Jennifer opened the door and gave her sister a hug. "No, come in."

"Shush, talk softly. I don't want mother to hear us."

"I'm so glad you're here," said Jennifer.

"I wanted to make sure you're all right. I hated watching mother torture you. She is so mean and hateful." Caroline sat on the bed. "Why were you so late?"

"Bill took me to a fabulous restaurant to celebrate my birthday, we had a wonderful time. I love him, he's such a gentleman."

"If he's such a gentleman, why didn't he drive you home? You were drenched."

"Bill gave me a ring for my birthday."

Caroline gasped. "Mother will lock you in your room forever when she finds out."

"She won't, unless you tell her."

Caroline shook her head. "I won't, but if she finds out, you'll be in deep trouble." Tears ran down Caroline's cheeks. "Neither of us will ever get married. She won't let us."

Jennifer put her arms around Caroline. "Don't cry. I know how much it hurt when she broke you and Jack up."

Caroline wiped the tears away with the sleeve of her nightgown. "I still love him. I'll go get your ring." She went back in her room and peeked into the hallway.

Caroline could hear Freda snoring as she crept down the dark stairs. Carefully stepping over the ones that she knew creaked, she made her way to the pantry. Caroline reached into the pocket of Jennifer's coat and found the ring.

"Good! I found it. Now, I have to get upstairs before I get caught." Caroline felt thirsty and opened the icebox and reached for the milk. The pantry light suddenly came on.

"I thought I heard someone down here," said Freda sharply.

Caroline stayed calm, as she poured a glass of milk. "I felt thirsty."

Freda stared at her for a moment then said, "Well hurry back to bed."

Jennifer could hear her mother's slippers, slapping against the steps and she prayed that Caroline found the ring.

Caroline knocked on the balcony door and pushed the ring under the door. "Happy birthday."

Jennifer slid the ring on her finger and crawled in bed. She turned on her side and whispered as she fell asleep, "I can't believe I'm engaged."

---

Caroline sat on the bed, watching her sister. The guests were leaving and Nellie was cleaning up the kitchen. She brushed Jennifer's hair from her face. "Wake up Jennifer."

Jennifer opened her eyes and smiled. "I'm awake. I was just thinking about how I met Bill and our life together."

———————

Nellie kept the girls at her house, giving Jennifer and Bill time to cope with their loss.

Jennifer knew she had to snap out of the morbid mood and start coping with life. She went in to the bathroom and started to run the water for a bath, but stopped when she heard a thumping noise coming from Andrew's bedroom. Jennifer opened her son's door.

Bill was banging his head against the wall shouting. "If I hadn't fallen asleep, my son would be alive."

Jennifer pulled him away and wrapped her arms around him. "Stop it, you'll hurt yourself."

He pushed her out of the room and slammed the door. "Leave me alone." Bill sat in the chair, and rocked back and forth staring into space.

Jennifer sat on the glider on the porch and felt grateful that Bill's parents were taking care of their daughters. Jennifer went into the kitchen, and prepared dinner, then took a plate upstairs to Bill.

She knocked, then opened the door. "I brought you something to eat."

"I don't want it."

"You need to keep your strength up," said Jennifer. "You haven't eaten in days."

"Dam it, I don't want it."

Jennifer went back to the kitchen and threw the plate in the sink. "What can I do? How can I help him?" She walked to the wicker rocker on the porch, and sat watching the scattered clouds, that glowed with a pinkish blue. Jennifer laid her head back and thought, "It's hard enough for me to get over Andrew's death, but how do I get Bill to realize our life has to go on." Tears streamed down her cheeks, as she closed her eyes trying to blank out the sorrow. Then she thought of her mother. That brought back memories.

To make sure I didn't see Bill again, Mother took me to and from school every day for three weeks. Then, on the Wednesday morning of the fourth week, Freda was still in her robe when I came down for breakfast.

"Why aren't you dressed?" asked Caroline.

Freda took a sip of her coffee, "I don't feel well today. I'm letting Maurice take Jennifer to school."

Jennifer stifled a smile. "That's fine." She was happy to know her chauffer would be driving.

Bill had been sneaking into school around lunch time to see her; they met in the janitor's closet. When Jennifer got to school, she couldn't wait to tell him the good news. At lunch time, she checked to make sure no one was around then entered the janitor's closet. She hugged him as she said, "Mother didn't bring me to school today; maybe she's getting tired of the early morning routine."

"This sneaking around is nonsense, I'm engaged to you and we can't see each other!"

"Except in the closet," laughed Jennifer.

"Why should we put up with this? Let's get married."

"What! That's impossible; Mother wouldn't allow it."

"She can't stop us, if we run away. We could go to Maryland. I'll arrange everything."

"But what about Caroline? When mother realizes I'm gone, she'll take it out on her."

"We'll only be gone a week, then Caroline can live with us."

Jennifer leaned back against the wall and didn't answer.

"I thought you loved me? Don't you want to be my wife?"

"Of course I do but I'm afraid."

"Then it's settled. I'm going to talk to my supervisor and see if I can take my vacation starting Monday. If he agrees, we'll leave Friday night."

"Thursday night mother always plays cards with her lady friends. I could pack then.

Oh now, I'm getting excited."

The next morning Jennifer could hardly concentrate and when lunch time came she rushed to the closet. Bill was there and he grabbed her and kissed her as he said, "We can leave tomorrow. I'll pick up your suitcase tonight, then we'll leave on your lunch break."

"This is happening so fast. I hope mother doesn't catch us."

"Don't be nervous, everything will go smooth, I promise Just think, soon we'll be married and your mother can't break us up." Jennifer peeked out the door to make sure no one was in the hallway. Bill kissed her. "See you tonight."

———————

As soon as Jennifer heard her mother leave, she went downstairs and headed toward the cellar to get her luggage. She decided to get a cookie first. She was in the kitchen and just bit into a cookie when the door opened and her mother walked in.

"I thought you'd be upstairs studying?" said Freda.

Jennifer quickly grabbed a glass. "I wanted to get a cookie and a glass of milk. Aren't you playing cards?"

"I forgot my reading glasses. Why are you acting so jittery?"

"I thought you left and I didn't know who was coming in the house."

Freda picked up her glasses from the table. "Good night dear, study hard."

Jennifer waited until she heard the car pull away, and then wasted no time getting her suitcase out of the cellar. She placed them on her bed and started to pack.

Caroline came in the room and asked, "What are you doing, cleaning out your closet?"

"I tell you a secret. Swear that you won't tell Mother."

Caroline raised her right hand; "I swear I won't breathe a word."

"Bill and I are getting married."

Caroline's mouth opened in shock. She stared at her sister, "Mother's going to be furious."

Jennifer put her lacy underwear into the suitcase. "Bill and I love each other and we're not going to give her a chance to break us up."

"Are you sure you know what you're doing?"

"Yes, this is what we want, but I am nervous. You look upset. I thought you'd be happy for me."

Caroline's hands shook as she reached for her sister. "Mother is going to be angry and take it out on me."

"I'm sorry." Jennifer hugged her sister. "Come with us, and then she can't hurt you."

"Wouldn't that be cozy?" Caroline forced a laugh, "You, me and Bill in one room, on your wedding night." "I'll swear to mother I knew nothing about it." She carefully folded Jennifer's dresses, placing them in the suitcase. "I wish Jack and I had done this."

At 10 p.m., Bill tapped his horn and Jennifer and Caroline carried the luggage down the stairs. Bill was on the porch when they opened the front door.

"Hi Babe, hi Caroline, everything ready?" He kissed Jennifer, and then picked up the suitcase. "It's all arranged and I'll see you tomorrow at lunch."

They waved as he drove away, and Caroline asked, "Why does he call you Babe?"

"It's his pet name for me." Jennifer laughed at the expression on Caroline's face.

"That's a funny name, what's the matter with Jennifer?"

"He says I'm…" Jennifer giggled. "I'm his pretty baby."

Caroline laughed. "Come on Babe, we better get to sleep before Mother comes home."

———————————

Jennifer couldn't sleep and as soon as it was daylight she quickly dressed and went downstairs. The aroma of cinnamon filled the air and fresh bums sat on the table.

Jennifer bit into one. "Hmm…they're good,"

Freda was in her robe reading the morning paper. "You seem happy this morning."

Jennifer ate her eggs quickly and picked up another bun. She kissed her mother on the cheek. "Goodbye Mother."

Freda patted Jennifer's hand. "I'm glad you've come to realize that I know what's best for you. Have a good day and we'll talk when you come home."

Jennifer worked on her lab assignment, trying to keep her mind off the time. She leaned across the table to look into the microscope and knocked a glass tube over and it fell on the floor.

The Professor looked up. "Jennifer, can't you be more careful!"

She bent down to pick up the broken pieces. "I'm sorry, I don't feel well."

"Don't try to clean it up. You might cut yourself." He walked over and put his hand on her shoulder. "Sit down; I'll get the janitor to sweep it up." When the lunch bell rang he pointed to the door. "Go get some hot soup; if you don't feel better, go home."

"Thank you professor." She walked calmly out of the room and stood by the bulletin board. As soon as the hallway cleared, she ran out to Bill's car and they drove away.

"I have the train tickets to Elkton Maryland, a hotel reservation and a judge lined up to marry us."

"You thought of everything." Jennifer unpinned her nurse's cap and threw it on the back seat. She reached over and kissed him. "I hope nothing goes wrong."

"It won't." He held her hand. "We'll be on the train before anyone realizes we're gone."

Bill parked the car at the train station, and took the luggage out of the trunk.

"I better get a porter. I can't carry all these and they're too heavy for you."

Jennifer picked up her suitcase. "I can carry mine,"

When they were on the train, Jennifer let out a deep breath. "We made it, I wish I could see mother's face when she finds out I'm gone."

Bill laughed, "All hell's going to break loose when she hears we eloped." He held her hand and Jennifer could feel his warmth and strength. She brought his hand to her lips and kissed it gently. Bill smiled then laid his head back on the leather seat and sat quietly wondering what she was thinking about.

"Penny for your thoughts?"

"I didn't sleep last night and I'm worried about Caroline."

"Are you sorry you're doing this?"

"Of course not, I want to be with you for the rest of my life."

---

They had been back from their honeymoon three days and were staying at Bill's apartment in town. Jennifer had just arrived home from Carnegie Nursing School and cooked dinner. Bill brought home a bottle of wine and they were ready to sit down for dinner when they heard a loud knock on the door.

The latch rattled as a harsh voice called out, "Jennifer, Jennifer, it's your mother, open the door."

"It's a good thing I locked the door," said Bill.

Jennifer opened the door and Freda burst in glaring at Bill. "How dare you take my daughter off without my permission?" She turned to Jennifer and sneered, "I'll bet you're pregnant, that's why you ran away like some trollop?" Freda grabbed Jennifer's arm. "You're coming with me; I'm having this mock marriage annulled."

Jennifer yanked her arm away. "Let go of me. Father Donahue sanctioned our marriage in church Sunday."

Freda moved quickly, she grabbed Jennifer by the shoulders and pushed her toward the door. "I don't care if he did; you're coming home with me."

Bill stepped in front of Freda. "Let go of my wife; she's not going anywhere with you."

"Oh yes she is and there's nothing you can do about It." Freda tried to push Bill away. "I won't have her married to cheap trash like you."

He clenched his fists at his side. "Mrs. May, I've never hit a woman in my life, but so help me God; if you try to take my wife, I'll lambaste you."

Freda could see the fury in his eyes and released her hold on Jennifer. "Stay and be his harlot, but mark my words, you'll regret the day you married him." Freda slammed the door as she left.

Jennifer yawned and stretched as she thought, I'll never forget that day. It was a Friday, June 6, 1914, and Bill was so strong and protective. Jennifer thought of that day and hoped her mother's words would not come true.

A thumping sound snapped her out of her thoughts as Cassie and Margaret came up the porch steps.

"Mama, are you all right?" they asked.

Jennifer looked at her sweet daughters and smiled. "Yes, I'm fine sweethearts. Does grandma know you came home?"

Margaret hugged her. "Yes, but we don't want to stay there anymore. We want to stay with you."

"Grandma says you're unhappy because you miss Andrew," said Cassie. "We miss him too, but we miss you the most."

"Grandpa said he's in heaven looking down on us," said Margaret. So why can't we see him?"

Jennifer hugged them and took Cassie on her lap. "My God, you're so little, you don't understand. I've been so deep in my sorrow that I've neglected you."

Margaret touched her nose to her mother's. "How come you never tell us stories anymore?"

"Come inside and Mama will read you a fairytale right now. You don't have to stay at Grandma's house; Mama's going to take care of you from now on."

When the children were in bed, Jennifer went in Andrew's room and stood behind Bill's chair. She started to rub his shoulders as she softly said, "I know how much you loved your son, but our daughter's need our attention, even more now. We have to get on with our lives for their sake."

Jennifer put her arms around him, but he pushed her away and stood up. "For God's sake, leave me alone!"

He ran down stairs and out to the car. "Bill, where are you going?" She ran after him, but he drove away. Francis drove up the driveway as Bill came barreling down, almost side swiping him. He shook his head in confusion as he walked up on the porch. "What's wrong with him, he's driving like a mad man."

Jennifer put her arms around her father and laid her head on his shoulder. "I don't know what to do with him. I tried talking to him, but he screamed at me and ran out." She wrung her hands together and paced back and forth on the porch. "I know he's upset, but I am too. I've lost Andrew and now I'm losing Bill."

Francis patted her gently on the shoulder. "I'll go look for him; maybe I can get him to listen to me."

Francis drove around for hours, searching all the local speakeasies, but Bill was nowhere to be found. He went home and called Jennifer. "Sorry, honey, I had no luck, but I'm sure he'll be back soon."

Jennifer lay in bed counting the chimes as the clock struck midnight, then she heard Bill's car in the driveway. "Thank God he's home."

Bill staggered up the steps, and fell in bed reeking of alcohol, his clothes, wrinkled and stained. Jennifer breathed a sigh of relief, and undressed him. After she covered him with a blanket, she went in Andrew's room to sleep. She couldn't sleep and thought about their past.

Jennifer remembered Bill was an only child, raised on a farm, but never cared for farming. That's why he went to work at my father's bank, that's where I met him. Jennifer remembered how excited everyone was, when she got pregnant with Andrew. Nellie invited my father and sister over to celebrate.

William poured everyone champagne and held his glass high as he said, "Here's to Jennifer who is carrying our first grandchild. We love you both and we are giving you ten acres of our farmland so that someday soon, I hope, you can live close to us."

Bill couldn't believe what he was hearing. He put his arms around William. "Thank you so much dad. We weren't expecting this."

My father was not to be out done as he stood up to say, "Well you might have a lot of land William, but I own the bank in town. I'm giving them enough money to build a house."

William laughed, "Figured you'd have to top me."

Jennifer laughed to herself, then sighed thinking. Everything about my life had been perfect until now. I've lost Andrew and my husband is going out of his mind. In my sorrow, my mother won't forget the pass and forgive me.

# Chapter Two

Bill woke up the next morning when the phone rang, sending a sharp pain through his whiskey soaked brain. He grabbed the phone. "Hello."

"Bill, this is Francis. Are you coming to work today?"

"No, I don't feel well."

"I've been paying you full salary while you've been out these past four weeks, but I can't do it any longer."

"I can't make it today."

"Your work is piling up. If you don't come in, we'll have to replace you."

"How can you be so cruel? It was your grandson who died."

"Snap out of it. He's gone and there's nothing we can do about it. I want you to come to work now." Francis slammed the phone down.

Bill sat with his hands over his face waiting for the pain to pass. He tried to remember where he had gone last night, but his brain was too fuzzy. He got dressed and went downstairs to his study, poured a shot of bourbon, downing it in one gulp. The house was quiet and no one was home.

He fixed a bowl of cornflakes, but after the first bite he gagged and threw the dish in the sink. "God, I feel awful," he said as he started to get dressed.

Bill entered the bank through the side entrance; he didn't want to talk to any of the employees. Walking through the hallway he felt the thick, blue, wool carpet under his feet. Heavy cherry wood chairs, upholstered in a soft gold, sat against the walnut paneled walls. He had forgotten how elegant the officer's section had been decorated. Bill touched the shinning brass sconces that hung on the walls that provided a muted light. "I don't remember these," he mumbled.

He walked past his secretary's desk and she looked up. "Good morning, Mr. Rennie."

Bill walked into his office ignoring her greeting and shut the door. He sat at his dark walnut desk staring out of the window, wishing he could have a shot of bourbon. The phone rang and waves of pain shot through his head and he grabbed it quickly. "Yes?"

"I have several messages for you, would you like me to bring them in?"

"Just hold them until I call you."

"Oh, Mr. May wants you in his office right away."

"Eh, tell him I'll be in shortly."

Bill picked up a pencil and made funny designs on his desk pad as he tried to get the courage to see Francis. He straightened his tie, and walked to his father-in-law's office. "Sorry I took so long, but I had a few things to take care of."

Francis was sitting behind his desk writing and never looked up. Bill admired the desk, it was almost as wide as the room, from the finest mahogany wood. The oval legs were circled with lions that had been carefully carved.

Francis continued to sign the papers. After a moment he looked up. "You look hungover."

Bill turned his face away. "No, I think I'm coming down with a cold."

Francis sat back in his swiveled black leather chair and smiled. "Glad you're back. I need the report on the Castaway account." Francis stood up and walked close to Bill. "Can you have it ready by the end of the week?"

"Yes, I'll have it ready."

Francis studied him for a moment. "The board needs to decide if they qualify for the loan."

Bill couldn't look Francis in the eye; he glanced out of the window. "Don't worry; it will be on your desk by the end of the week." Bill stood up, I'll start working on it now. He walked out of the room and instead of going to his office; headed for the speakeasy on the corner.

———————————

Bill worked every day on the Castaway account finishing it a day early. Francis was impressed. "That was fast work. Let's go over to the club and have lunch, it's on me."

Bill bit his lip, as if in thought. "No, I better not. I have a project I have to complete, maybe next time." He watched Francis leave and when he was in his car; Bill made a beeline to the speakeasy across the street. "Bartender, let me have a shot of Vodka please."

Mike the bartender poured a shot and Bill downed it in one gulp. "Whoa, take it easy. It's lunch time."

"Pour me another."

"You're getting to be a regular. You're here before lunch and after work. When do you eat?"

"Right now, give me a ham on rye." Bill ate half the sandwich, then went back to work.

Jennifer looked at the clock, Bill was late. She fed the children, then cleared the table and wiped the counters until they glistened. To keep her mind off him, she cleaned out the ice box, throwing away dried up leftovers until Bill finally walked in at 8 p.m.

"Where were you? I was worried about you."

Bill shrugged his shoulders. "I'm sorry I'm late, but I had a busy day."

She watched him hang up his coat on the brass rack in the hallway; he seemed sober. It had been six months since the night he came home drunk. Jennifer put her arms around his waist and kissed him. "I'm glad your home, I kept dinner warm for you."

"Thanks, I'm hungry."

He sat at the table and Jennifer put his plate on the table "Why don't you put the girls to bed after you eat? They'd love you to read them a story?"

Bill looked sadly at Jennifer. "I can't, it reminds me too much of Andrew."

"They don't understand why you're ignoring them."

He banged his fist on the table. "I can't do it." He pushed his plate away and went to his study. "I have some work to do for the bank."

Jennifer stared after him, and then decided to put the children to bed instead. When she came down his door was still shut. She waited in the parlor hoping he'd come out, but finally she went to bed.

In the morning Bill dressed and went down for breakfast. "Good morning Babe. Did you have a good night sleep?"

"Yes I did. I never heard you come to bed last night. Did you work late?"

"Yes, till midnight. I got a lot accomplished." After he finished eating, Bill kissed her.

"Goodbye, I have to get going. I'm late."

That afternoon Nellie and Jennifer went shopping with the children. When she returned, she baked a cherry pie and roasted a chicken, hoping Bill would be home on time for dinner.

It was past 6 p.m. and he hadn't come home, she fed the children and put them in bed. The longer she waited for him, the more frustrated she felt. By 9 p.m., she was angry and threw his dish in the sink. Jennifer went upstairs and set up the ironing board, heated the iron in the fireplace, and started to press the children's clothes.

The front door opened and Jennifer heard strange voices. "Who's down there?" When no one answered, she went down to investigate. She gasped when she saw two men standing by the kitchen sink. They looked tough and dirty and had a drink in their hands.

"What are you doing in my house? Get out."

"It's all right Babe, they're with me"

"Thank God you're here. Who are these strange men?"

As Bill staggered over to her, he splashed his drink on the floor. "Guy's meet my Babe." His words slurred. "We were just talking about you." Bill put his arm over her shoulder. "Babe, this is Harvey and Nick, my good pals." Bill gave her a slobbering kiss. "How about fixing us something to eat?"

"What! It's 10 p.m. You don't expect me to cook something this late?"

"Ah, come on Babe. We're hungry." Bill took a gulp of his drink and sat at the table. "Come on guy's, join me."

Jennifer thought, "If I feed them maybe they'll leave." She took the leftover beef stew from the icebox and scraped it into a heavy skillet. As she racked the hot coals in the stove, Nick swaggered over. His reeking odor made her sick to her stomach. His beady eyes leered at her and he reached out to grab her.

Jennifer stepped out of his reach, "Get away from me."

Nick moved closer, forcing her into the corner, and grabbed her by the waist. "Hey, Bill, you got yourself one good-looking bitch." His whiskers scraped Jennifer's cheek as his whiskey spittle showered her face. He grabbed her head and tried to force Jennifer's lips to his. "How's about a little kiss, sweetie?" Jennifer pulled her face away, and he grabbed her buttocks and squeezed hard. "Nice ass. I'd like to have some fun with you."

Jennifer slapped him, "Get away from me you pig. Bill, help me. Make him stop." Bill had passed out; his head resting on the table.

Harvey laughed. "Her old man can't help her, he's passed out."

Nick forced her body up against his and laughed in her face. "I like a woman with spirit."

With a quick movement Jennifer brought her knee up and hit him hard in the groin.

"Get away from me."

Nick doubled over with pain and groaned. "You bitch! I'll kill you for that."

Harvey darted at her. "I'll fix you for hurting my buddy."

Jennifer screamed, "Bill, wake up and do something. Please help me!" Jennifer grabbed the hot skillet from the stove and swung it at Harvey. "Don't you dare touch me?" The hot stew flew in Harvey's face as the skillet hit him on the side of his head.

"Son of a bitch." He staggered, and fell on the floor.

Jennifer raced up the steps and stood in the back of the hallway, waiting to see if they would follow her.

Nick rubbed his crotch as he groaned, "Jesus Christ man, she almost killed me. You can't let that bitch get away with that."

Harvey shook Bill awake. "Your wife almost killed us. Get up there and show her who's boss or I will."

Bill stared at the men. "What! What are you talking about?" He was in a drunken stupor.

The two men pushed him toward the steps. "You heard me, get upstairs and bring that wife of yours down here. We want to show her whose boss," said Nick.

Bill staggered to the steps and in a hoarse voice called out, "Babe! Get down here."

When she didn't answer Harvey looked up at her. "Get down here before I drag you down by your hair."

Jennifer could feel her heart beating and her muscles quivered as she moved to the head of the stairs. Bill started up the steps and the men were standing at the bottom. The hall light beamed on her like a spotlight as she stood with the hot iron in her hand.

She glared down at him. "Don't you dare take one more step, if you do I'll hit you with this hot iron. "She swung it back and forth. "You get those drunks out of my house now."

The hate flaring from her eyes almost sobered Bill and he stopped. "Guys, it's time to go home."

Harvey grabbed Bill's arm. "No! No we want her down here."

Bill shook his arm loose. "My wife wants you out of the house."

Jennifer shook the iron at them. "Get out now."

Nick headed toward the door. "We know whose boss in your house. She sure got you tied to her apron strings, you're pussy-whipped."

Harvey pushed Nick out the door. "Ah shut up," "You're just mad because she crushed your balls. Let's go back to the bar."

Bill closed the door and leaned against it for a moment, wondering what had happened, but too drunk to care. He walked to his study and collapsed on the couch.

---

Bill woke up when he heard the children running down the stairs laughing. He went to the bathroom and stared at the red face in the mirror. Bloodshot eyes stared back at him and his head throbbed. "God, I look awful." Bill threw cold water on his face and flashes of Jennifer pleading for help went through his mind. He sat on the side of the tub and put his face in his hands and scenes from last night flashed through his head.

"Oh, my God, I was so drunk last night, and I couldn't protect my wife."

He hurried down to the kitchen and his daughters were on the floor, playing with their dolls.

Margaret called out, "Daddy, will you play with us?"

Bill picked up Cassie, and took Margaret's hand. "Where's your mother?"

"She's outside hanging clothes," said Margaret.

Bill patted her head. "Let's go see mama."

When they went outside, Margaret ran to her mother. "Daddy's going to play with us."

Bill went over to Jennifer and tried to put his arm around her. "Good morning."

Jennifer moved away and continued to hang up the laundry.

The children climbed on the swings and Bill pushed them as he sang, "Oh she floats through the air with the greatest of ease, the daring young girls on the flying trapeze."

"Sing it again daddy," Margaret said, each time he stopped.

After lunch, Jennifer wiped their little smudged faces. "You haven't seen Grandma today. Why don't you go visit?" They ran out the door and she started to wash the dishes.

Bill walked up behind her. "I owe you an apology. I never should have brought those men home. I'm sorry."

She felt him move closer and turned and put her hand out. "Don't come any closer. I don't want you touching me. You let that horrible creature kiss me and you did nothing, nothing at all."

"He did what! Please forgive me. I was so drunk, I didn't realize what was happening."

"You're not the man I married. The man I married would never allow anyone to touch me." Her eyes blazed. "You're nothing, but a drunk."

Tears filled his eyes. "I'm so ashamed. I thought I was dreaming. I heard echoing in my ears and everything seemed hazy, like it wasn't real."

He moved closer to her and she backed away, "I said, don't touch me."

"I'll stop drinking. I promise. I love you so much."

Jennifer pushed him aside and stared at him. "You blame your drinking on the death of our son, but you're not the only one grieving for him. We all love and miss him."

He reached for her and they clung together, desperately needing each other.

"It will never happen again." Bill kissed her forehead as he whispered; "I'll be a better father and husband, I swear I'll never touch another drop.

Jennifer sighed. "Because we've both been through so much, I'll give you another chance."

He held her close and kissed her. "Thank you, you won't regret it." He looked at his watch. "I have to get to the office before your dad starts calling."

———————————

At 5 p.m., the table was set and Jennifer just took the roast chicken out of the oven when Bill walked in.

"Daddy," yelled his daughters as they rushed to him.

"Right on time," said Jennifer. "Come sit down and eat."

After dinner she cleared the table, while Bill read the children a story and got them in bed.

Jennifer curled up on the couch, reading a magazine, and when Bill came down she patted the seat beside her. "Thanks for putting the girls to bed."

Bill sat next to her and kissed her. He unbuttoned her dress and pulled it off, then laid her back on the couch.

Jennifer sat up. "The children might come down."

"No, they were asleep when I left the room."

The intoxicating musk of his body overwhelmed her and she unbuttoned his pants. "I need you so much."

"I love you." Bill's hands drifted over her delicate breast.

The blood coursed through her veins like an awakened river and she whispered, "Your hands feel so good on my body."

He explored her body, sending lightening jolts through her, and when he knew she was ready he entered her, with slow steady movements. The tempo of their love making became wild with passion. They held each other moving as one, until they climaxed. They lay side by side, content and peaceful.

She kissed his shoulder. "That felt like old times."

Bill kissed her gently. "Oh my, yes it did. Goodnight, my wonderful wife."

"I hope you meant it, when you said you'd stop drinking."

He reached for the bible on the night stand next to his bed and held up his right hand.

"I'll swear on the Bible."

---

Each night his daughters waited for him on the porch and he played with them before dinner. Later, he bathed and read them a story. Eight months passed and Bill had not touched alcohol. He came down the stairs after putting his daughters to bed and found Jennifer in the parlor, curled up on the couch, her face beamed with happiness.

"What are you so happy about?"

"I have a surprise for you, but I'm not going to tell you until we're in bed."

He grabbed her in his arms. "Is that right? Well I'll have to take you to bed right now."

Bill placed her on the bed and started to tickle her. "Okay, what's the surprise? Tell me or I'll keep tickling you."

She laughed. "Stop, I'll tell you." Jennifer hugged her knees to her chest and smiled at him. "We're going to have a baby. Hopefully, it will be a boy."

The color drained from Bill's face and his back stiffened as a picture of his dead son, lying in the casket, flashed in his mind."

"What's the matter? Aren't you happy about the baby?"

He smiled and whispered, "Yes, I'm very happy."

Jennifer knew something was wrong. "It's been over a year since Andrew died. I thought you'd be ready to have another child."

He lowered his head to avoid eye contact. "Of course. Of course I'm happy about the baby."

They heard the patter of little feet, and then the door burst open. Cassie and Margaret jumped on the bed.

"We heard you laughing; we want to have fun too."

Bill started to tickle them and Jennifer joined in. They laughed until they were out of breath, then cuddled together and went to sleep.

Bill slept for a while, but woke up, thinking about Jennifer pregnancy. He got up quietly and went down to the study and sat in his brown leather chair.

"I'm not ready for a baby."

He picked up a pencil and twirled it between his fingers, then threw it down on the desk. Pacing back and forth he thought about Andrew, and stared toward the liquor cabinet. Bill stopped, then went to his desk. As he started to work on a contract, his hands shook and he ran his hand through his hair. He walked to the liquor cabinet and stood in front of it. Drumming his fingers on the top he licked his lips, then turned away. He sat at his desk again staring, until his eyes burned. He couldn't stand it and ran to the cabinet, poured himself a shot of vodka, downing it in one gulp. Smacking his lips in satisfaction he placed the bottle back and sat in his leather chair.

"Ah! I just needed one to take this uneasy feeling away."

Bill closed his eyes and Andrew's face danced in front of him. He rushed to the cabinet and poured another drink, then another. When he realized what he was doing, he closed the bottle and slammed it back in the cabinet. He flopped on the couch, hiding his face in his arms and fell asleep.

# Chapter Three

During the first three months of pregnancy, Jennifer didn't feel well at all. When she felt better, she decorated the nursery and worked on the roses and begonias in her garden. She cut a bouquet of flowers and stared towards the house, when Nellie came over.

"I brought you two dozen eggs; the hens are laying them faster than we can eat them. My goodness those flowers smell wonderful."

"I love working in my garden." She handed Nellie the flowers. "I cut these for you."

"Thank you. I haven't seen much of Bill lately. How's he doing?"

Jennifer took her apron off. He's been working hard at the bank and seems to feel good. Want to come in for a cup of tea?"

"No thanks dear, I got plenty of work to keep two of me busy. Tell that son of mine to come see me."

Jennifer prepared dinner and waited for Bill on the front porch. When he came home, she put her arms around him. "I fed the children early and put them to bed. I thought we could have a romantic dinner together."

"Sounds like a good idea. It smells delicious, what are we having?"

"Your favorite, meat loaf and brown potatoes."

Bill kissed her. "I'm sorry I'm a little late, I had a lot of paper work to finish, but never mind that. How are you feeling?"

"Good. I'm so anxious for the baby to come, I spent most of the day decorating the nursery."

When they finished dinner, Jennifer yawned. "I feel tired."

Bill started to clear the table. "Why don't you go up to bed and I'll do the dishes."

Jennifer was sound asleep when Bill went upstairs. When he got in bed he tried to sleep but his mind kept thinking of the new baby. He went to his study and had a few drinks, then fell asleep on the couch.

---

Each night after work, he'd stopped at the speakeasy for just one drink. Nobody seemed to notice that he was drinking again.

He put his drink down and walked to the pay phone at the end of the bar. "Babe, I'll be a little late tonight. I have some work to finish up."

"Should I wait and have dinner with you?"

"No, don't do that. Just put my food in the oven, I'll eat it when I get home."

When he arrived home, Jennifer and his daughters were waiting for him in the parlor.

The girls ran to him "Will you read us a story? Please daddy."

Bill picked them both up in his arms. "Of course, I will. I look forward to my special moments with you."

Nellie and William walked in the door, "How are you feeling Jennifer?"

Jennifer held her stomach, "I'm uncomfortable, I can't wait till the baby comes?"

"It's bound to be any day now," said Nellie.

William was holding Cassie on his lap. "This Sunday is Easter; let's have an egg hunt for the kids and it will keep your mind off the baby."

Jennifer laughed. "Nothing can keep my mind off of this big belly. I feel like I'm carrying around a giant egg."

"I'll call Francis and Caroline and invite them over," said William.

"I'll invite my friend Maggie. She's married now and has a little daughter," said Jennifer.

———————————

Easter morning, Bill sat on the porch watching the children look for the eggs the Easter bunny had hidden. Francis sat next to him and said, "Those little ones are sure having fun, look how many eggs Margaret found." They watched the children for a while then Francis said, "How are you feeling? You look a little nervous, aren't you feeling well?"

Bill smiled and said, "Good, never better."

Francis lowered his voice. "Let's stop the small talk. Are you drinking again?"

"Of course not." Sweat covered his forehead and he wiped it dry with his handkerchief.

Bill stood up. "Would you like a cold glass of iced tea?" Without waiting for an answer he walked into the kitchen. His hands shook as he reached for the glasses. He walked in the study and stood in front of the liquor cabinet, and was about to open it, when he heard Francis behind him. Bill turned and smiled. "I was going to surprise you and make your favorite drink, a mint julep."

"That would go nice on this warm day. Are you having one?"

"No. I'm on the wagon, remember?" Trying to keep his hand from shaking, Bill fixed the drink and handed it to Francis,

"I remember. Don't you forget? Jennifer tells me you're working late at the office and I know that's not true."

Bill walked out of the room, pretending he didn't hear. "Let's see what's happening outside."

Cassie ran over to them with a live baby chick in her hands. "Look what the Easter Bunny left me." She kissed its little beak.

Margaret walked over with a bunny in her arms, her sweet face bright with excitement. "This is the best Easter I ever had."

Jennifer was talking to Maggie and her husband, when a sharp pain ripped through her. "Oh, that hurt."

Nellie looked at her watch. "I'll time the labor pains to see how close they are." Caroline rubbed Jennifer's back, and Nellie checked the time. "The pains are coming every ten minutes. Bill, get Jennifer's suitcase. We'll be leaving for the hospital soon."

"Maggie started putting the food in the ice box. Don't worry about the children. I'll take them home with me."

"Francis, call Doctor Forman and tell him Jennifer's on her way to the hospital," said Nellie. "Bill, William, get Jennifer in the car."

———————————

Doctor Forman whisked her to the labor room to examine her. "You're not quite ready. Rest for a while; I'll be back in a little while. The nurse will stay with you." He kept checking on her until she had dilated enough for him to feel the baby. "Nurse, take Jennifer to the delivery room."

Jennifer was struggling and was near exhaustion. "Push down one more time, harder, harder," said Doctor Forman. He pressed on her stomach. "That's it, that's it. Oh Jennifer; you have a beautiful baby boy."

They placed the baby on her chest and she held her son. Exhausted, she patted his little head as she whispered, "We'll name you Joseph Francis."

The doctor went out to talk to the family "Jennifer had a tough time, but the baby is perfect."

"Thank God, it's a healthy baby," said Nellie.

"When can we see her?" asked Francis.

"You can go in now. Just don't stay long; she needs to rest."

Bill leaned over to kiss her and Jennifer opened her eyes. He smiled and said, "How do you feel?"

"I'm tired. Did you see our new son? Isn't he wonderful?"

"Yes he is," said Bill. Jennifer closed her eyes and Bill took a seat across the room.

The nurse took the baby from Jennifer and handed him to Nellie. She held him close and noticed that Bill was not very excited about his new son.

"Bill, look how precious your son is. He looks just like you." He didn't answer. "Bill, look at your baby."

Bill glanced at his son and gave Nellie a thin-lipped smile. "Cute little thing, isn't he?"

Caroline took the baby and held him close. "You're lucky to have such beautiful children."

Jennifer drifted in and out of sleep, too exhausted to notice Bill's behavior.

Doctor Forman came in the room. "I suggest everyone go home and rest."

As they drove home Nellie said, "Bill, I don't understand your actions?"

"I'm just tired mom. I'll see you in the morning. I have to go to Maggie's house and pick up the girls."

William helped Nellie out of the car and smiled at Bill. "You have a healthy son, enjoy him."

Bill drove to Maggie's and his daughters asked, "How's Mama? Did she have the baby?

What is it?" they asked in unison.

"Whoa, hold on. Let me thank Maggie first." He gave Maggie a hug. "Thanks for taking them."

"That's what friends are for. What did Jennifer have, boy or girl?"

Bill sat on the couch and the girls climbed on his lap. "She had a baby boy."

His daughters squealed with delight, "We have a baby brother!"

"Okay kids lets go, I'll read you a story before I put you to bed."

After he tucked them in, he went down to his study and walked to the liquor cabinet. He opened it, then slammed the lid down and went outside. Bill ran down the road until he felt exhausted, then hiked back to the barn. He chopped wood until he craved nothing but sleep.

———————————

Jennifer asked Maggie and her husband to be the god parents. Father Donahue preformed the christening at the church, then everyone went back to the house. At the barbecue, Beer and wine flowed freely, while roast beef turned on the spit.

Jennifer was sitting in the living room trying to comfort her son and Caroline sat beside her. "Can I hold the baby?"

Jennifer handed the child to Caroline. "Sure, I need a break. He cried all night, Bill and I didn't get much sleep."

"You'd never know it, you look lovely. Is that a new dress?"

"Thanks, I bought it before the baby was born."

Joseph fell asleep in Caroline's arms and Jennifer called Bill. "Be a darling and put

Joseph in his crib."

"You look exhausted, we should have waited another month to have this party," said Bill."

His hands shook as he held the baby in his arms and the muscles tightened in his face.

Jennifer saw the expression and asked, "Are you all right?"

"Yes. Yes, I'm fine." He walked towards the stairs.

"I could have done that," said Caroline.

"I know but I wanted Bill to hold the baby. He hasn't held Joseph since he was born, I think the baby reminds him too much of Andrew."

Bill placed his son in the crib and looked down at him. "I do love you, but you'll never take Andrew's place." He tucked the blanket around the baby and went down to his study. He licked his lips, and then broke out in a sweat, as he paced the floor. His hands shook as he poured a shot of whiskey. "Ah! that's just what I needed."

He joined the party and no one noticed him sneak back for another. With each drink, Bill became more outgoing, telling jokes, making everyone laugh.

Jennifer walked out on the porch for a breath of fresh air and Maggie and her husband Tom were leaning against the railing. "Good gracious Maggie, you are smoking!"

Maggie took a puff and blew the smoke in the air. "It relaxes me and I think it makes me look sophisticated." Maggie struck a model pose with her hand on her hip and the other hand stretched out holding the cigarette in a long slim holder.

Jennifer laughed. "You're right, you do look like the girl in the Lucky Strike posters."

"Here take a puff and see how it feels." Jennifer inhaled the cigarette and Maggie said, "Now swallow it."

Jennifer started to cough and the smoke covered her face, stinging her eyes. She handed it to Maggie and she took a deep drag. "You have to try it a few times."

"I'm too busy with the children to worry about sophistication, I'll see you inside."

When she went back in the parlor, her father walked over and hugged her. "How are you feeling sweetheart?"

"I'm fine, Dad. Bill seems relaxed now and enjoying himself."

Francis watched Bill then walked away. "He's having a good time all right," then he thought, "I hope I'm wrong, but I think he just fell off the wagon."

# *Chapter Four*

Francis was impressed by the workload Bill handled. He was glad he had the Brandon account finished on time. He patted Bill on the back. "You are doing a terrific job. I think 1923 will be the best year the bank ever had." He smiled and felt happy that he was wrong about Bill drinking. "You've been on the wagon two years now, keep up the good work."

Margaret started kindergarten and Jennifer laid out a dress for her. "While you're getting dressed, I'll take Cassie and Joseph over to Grandma's house. I'll be right back"

Cassie went to her closet and pulled down a dress. "I want to go to kindergarten too."

Jennifer picked up Joseph and took Cassie's hand. "Honey, you're only three, you have to stay at Grandma's until I get back."

It was Margaret's special day, not only was she starting school but today was her birthday. After school Margaret sat at the table, in front of her birthday cake, waiting for her father to come home.

Bill was a few minutes late. He gave Margaret a big hug and said, "Happy birthday sweetheart. I'm sorry, I'm late."

"Did you get me a present?"

"I sure did." Bill reached in his pocket and took out a small box.

Margaret ripped off the paper. "Mama, look at the pretty gold bracelet daddy gave me." She hugged her father. "I love it."

Bill lit the five candles and said, "Make a wish before you blow them out."

She blew hard and only a few went, then Cassie reached over and blew the rest out.

Margaret pushed her away. "Hey, it's my birthday not yours! Now you can't have any cake."

Jennifer said, "Margaret, don't be mean to your sister."

"Yes, but it's not her birthday."

Bill laughed. "Here Margaret, you get the first slice with the flower on top. Cassie can have the second piece."

Baby Joseph, screamed with delight when they placed a piece on his highchair. Before they could stop him he had his face in it. When the party was over and the children were sound asleep, Bill went in the kitchen to help Jennifer clean up.

As he dried the dishes he said, "Francis gave me a compliment today. He thinks I'm doing a terrific job."

She kissed him. "I'm very proud of you. Would you like a cup of coffee?"

She poured a cup and set it in front of him at the table. Bill reached for the cream and knocked the coffee over. "Oops, I'm sorry."

"Darn! That's the new crochet table cloth, Nellie just gave us." Jennifer pulled it off the table and went to the sink. I'll soaked it in cold water. "I hope it doesn't stain."

"Never mind the table cloth. Let's go to bed and make love."

Jennifer put her arm around his waist and walked towards the steps. "Good idea. I'll let it soak and wash it in the morning."

Jennifer got up early and washed out the cloth, then sat by the kitchen window, watching the birds in the trees.

When Bill came down, he saw her staring out of the window. "Penny for your thoughts?"

"Why are you sleeping in your study, is something wrong?" She went over to the stove to start breakfast.

Bill patted her bottom affectionately. "After we made love, I couldn't sleep. I started thinking about the work I brought home, so I went to my study and finished it. I slept on the couch because I was afraid I'd wake you."

Jennifer placed a dish of scrambled eggs and toast in front of him and poured his coffee.

"How can you get a decent night sleep that way?"

"Don't worry I slept like a rock." Bill buttered his toast and finished his breakfast. "Time for me to I go, I don't want to be late for the morning meeting." He kissed her. "See you tonight."

It was 11 p.m. when Bill came home, Jennifer was already in bed.

"Babe, are you awake," he whispered. When she didn't answer, he went to his study.

Jennifer woke up in the middle of the night, "Bill, what's that noise?" She turned over, he wasn't there. She peeked into the children's rooms, they were sound asleep. Still hearing the noise, she went downstairs, the light was on in Bill's study. He was slumped over in his chair, mumbling to himself. At first, she thought he was talking in his sleep, but then she spied a bottle in one hand, and a glass in the other.

Jennifer grabbed the bottle. "Oh no! No, you're, you're drunk." She knocked the glass out his hand spilling the drink on his pants.

Bill looked at her with a sheepish grin. "I was just having a little nightcap to help me sleep."

"You promised you would never touch it." Jennifer's stomach churned with frustration. "You lied to me. You lied to everybody."

Bill tried to stand up, but lost his balance and fell out of the chair. He looked at her with bloodshot eyes as he pleaded, "It won't happen again. I just needed a little toddy."

"You're drunk; I don't want a drunkard for a husband." She ran upstairs and threw herself across the bed, beating the mattress in anger. "Damn you Bill, why did you start drinking again?" Jennifer sat up and held her stomach. "Dear God, what am I going to do, I'm pregnant?"

In the morning when she came down, Bill had breakfast ready. Cheerfully he said, "Good morning. I have your eggs just the way you like them."

Ignoring him, she poured a cup of coffee and went out on the porch. The children came down and she heard them laughing, as Bill fixed their breakfast. She sat in deep thought. Bill walked out on the porch and tried to put his arms around her, she pushed him away.

"Forgive me please, I'm sorry." When she didn't answer, he walked down the steps and drove away.

Jennifer watched him leave and whispered, "You promised me." Jennifer buried her face in her hands and her body shook as she sobbed.

The day dragged on like a heavy cloud, she didn't want to tell their parents. She stayed away from the farm and kept busy in her garden. When Bill didn't come home for dinner, she fed the children and put them to bed early. Jennifer sat on the couch trying to read, but couldn't concentrate.

She threw the book across the room. "Why is he so late?" It was after midnight when she heard his car and went out to meet him. "Where have you been? I've been worried."

Bill staggered into the study and poured a drink and then fell on the couch. Jennifer shook her head in disgust and went upstairs. He was not in his study when Jennifer got up in the morning, and the car was gone. She fixed breakfast for the children, and then sat drinking coffee.

Nellie walked in. "Good morning, any more coffee?" Jennifer poured her a cup and Nellie took her hand, "You look worried. What's the matter?"

"Bill's drinking again. He was so drunk last night he could hardly walk."

"Oh no, he promised you. Where is he now?"

"I don't know. He left before I woke up. I guess he went to work."

Nellie heard the children and went up to help Margaret get ready for school. When she came down she took Joseph and Cassie by the hand. "I'll take them home with me and you can use my car to drive Margaret to school."

"Thanks Nellie. Maybe you shouldn't tell William yet"

"He's got to know sooner or later. Oh, the keys are in the car."

Jennifer took Margaret to school, and went shopping. She thought about stopping at Bill's office, but was afraid he wouldn't be there. Instead she went home and worked in the garden.

At 5 p.m., Cassie sat looking out of the window. "When is daddy coming home? I want him to read me a story."

"Daddy has to work late. Sit down, your supper's ready." She put Joseph in the highchair, and gave him his dinner. "If you're a good girl, I'll read you a story."

"I want daddy to read us a story," said Margaret.

Jennifer's head was pounding and she had a headache that wouldn't quit. Margaret started to complain again. She had just taken two aspirins and slammed the glass down on the counter. "If you don't shut up and eat, I'll put you to bed now."

They quietly finished eating and Jennifer felt relieved when they were finally in bed. She paced the floor, as the clock struck 1 a.m., praying that nothing happened to him. Jennifer sat in the rocker staring out of the window, waiting for his car to come up the driveway. The phone rang and she jumped out of her chair to answer it.

"Jennifer, I got up to go to the bathroom and saw your lights, its 2 a.m. in the morning, is something wrong?"

"Bill is not home and I'm worried stiff."

"What's wrong with that son of mine? He doesn't have the sense he was born with. Do you want me to come over?"

"No. there's nothing you can do."

Nellie yawned. "Ok then, I'll talk to you in the morning."

Jennifer sat on the couch, forcing herself to stay awake. When she heard Bill's car, she went out on the porch and stood on the top step.

Bill staggered up the steps and almost walked into her. "What are you doing up?"

His breath burned her nostrils and she held her handkerchief to her face. "I want to talk to you."

"I don't want to talk." He tried to push passed her.

Jennifer placed her hand on his arm. "We can't go on this way. You need help."

Bill tried to focus his eyes. "Help, I don't need help. I need a drink."

Jennifer grabbed his arm. "Listen, please listen to me! You have to stop drinking, not only for me, but for yourself and the children."

"Let go of me." He pulled his arm free and shoved her backwards. "All I need is a drink." Bill staggered into the house mumbling, "I need a goddamn drink."

Jennifer screamed as she tumbled down the concrete steps, striking her head on the cast iron planter. Circles danced in her head and she fought the blackness closing in on her. She waited for her head to clear, and then tried to get up. Jennifer could feel blood flowing down her cheek, from a deep gash at the side of her head. She tried to stand up. "I've got to get help." Jennifer forced herself to stand and clung to the railing waiting for the dizziness to clear. When her head cleared she climbed the stairs, making her way to the kitchen. Cramps gripped her legs and another pain cut across her stomach like a knife. She bent over in agony. "Oh, my God, it hurts."

Jennifer reached the phone and called Doctor Forman, as blood gushed from her.

Doctor Forman found her unconscious on the floor and knelt beside her. The cut on her head had stopped bleeding, then he saw a puddle of blood between her legs. He carried her to the parlor couch, where he applied seven stitches, to close the gash on her head.

Jennifer moaned, and opened her eyes. "I really needed you."

He took a wet towel and washed her legs. "You had a miscarriage."

Jennifer started to cry. "I lost the baby?"

"Yes. I want to get you upstairs. Where's Bill?"

"He's in the study."

"Don't try to get up. I'll get him to help." Doctor Forman walked to the study and the air reeked with alcohol. He shook Bill. "Wake up! I need your help."

Bill turned sideways. "Leave me alone."

Doctor Forman went to the kitchen for a pitcher of water. He threw the water in Bill's face. "Wake up, you drunken bum."

Bill sat up coughing; his eyes seemed glued together as he tried to focus. "What! What's the matter?"

Doctor Forman yanked his arm. "Get up. I need you to help me get Jennifer upstairs."

Bill scratched his head and yawned. "Why? What is wrong with her?"

"You knocked her down the steps, and thanks to you she had a miscarriage. I'm sure you don't give a damn."

"What are you talking about? She's not pregnant."

"Get your ass off that couch and help me." When they reached the kitchen, Jennifer had walked up two steps. Doctor Forman grabbed her. "Don't do that, you'll start bleeding again."

"I'll carry her up." Bill tried to lift her, staggered and lost his balance.

"You're disgusting," said the doctor. Here grasp my hands. Now, Jennifer sit on our hands and we'll carry you up."

They eased her on the bed and Doctor Forman found a nightgown in her drawer. "You were only three months pregnant, it's not as bad as it could have been. Rest now and I'll let Nellie know what happened."

Bill was standing at the door watching. "Will she be all right?"

"Yes, if she rests and you don't push her down any more steps." He patted Jennifer's hand. "I'll check back this afternoon, and see how you are." He glanced sternly at Bill, "You better take care of her, or you'll hear from me."

Nellie ran over in her night gown, she was a little woman, half the size of Bill. When she saw him, she shook her finger at him. "You're turning into a no good drunken bum."

William walked in. "Now, now mother. Don't get your blood pressure up. Bill, come outside. I want to talk to you."

Bill walked back and forth on the porch. He ran his hand through his hair and sighed.

"Dad, I don't remember knocking her down the steps. I didn't even know she was pregnant."

William put his arm around Bill's shoulder. "Son, you've got to straighten out. You're ruining everyone's life."

He looked at his father with glassy eyes. His hands shook as he reached for his shoulder.

"I'll stop drinking, I really will." They stared at each other for a moment and Bill started for the door. "I, eh, have to get myself cleaned up." Bill went to his study and closed the door. He put his face in his hands and cried, "My God, what have I done?" He walked over to the liquor cabinet and poured a drink. "What did I do to my Babe?" The glass overflowed and the Vodka ran down the side of the cabinet and on the carpet. Bill gulped down the drink, then poured another one. He sat on the couch with the drink in his hand sobbing. "Babe, I'm so sorry. I hurt you."

William went into the kitchen. "Nellie, is there any coffee?"

"Yes. I just made a pot." She started to pour a cup when they heard the front door close. They looked out of the window and saw Bill getting into his car. "It's a little early for Bill to be leaving."

"The bank opens at 9 a.m.," said William, looking at his watch. It's just a little after 6 a.m."

Nellie poured the coffee as she watched her son drive away. "Good grief, what are we going to do with him?" She shook her head from side to side. "He'll drink himself to death if he doesn't stop."

Nellie took a breakfast tray to Jennifer. "How are you feeling dear?"

"My heads pounding, but other than that, I'm ok."

Nellie placed the tray across Jennifer's lap. "Doc. called and said he'll be over at 3 p.m. I'm surprised the kids slept through all this."

Jennifer sipped her coffee. "So am I. Where is Bill?"

Nellie took the tray from Jennifer. "Don't know really, he left early this morning. Do you want anything else?"

"No thanks Nellie. Oh, I hear the children now."

"I'll fix their breakfast, then William can take Margaret to school. I'll take Cassie and Joseph home with me." Nellie patted her hand. "Stay in bed and I'll be over later."

When the doctor came, he gave Jennifer some pills for her headache and examined her. "You better stay in bed for the rest of the day, but I think you'll feel better tomorrow. Call me if you need me."

Nellie brought her dinner. "I'll keep the children with me for the night. Has Bill called?"

"No, he hasn't, I hope he went to work."

Nellie kissed Jennifer's cheek. "I'll see you in the morning."

Jennifer tried to read, but the pills made her sleepy, she drifted off worried about Bill.

The grandfather's clock in the hallway struck twelve chimes and Bill walked into the coat rack in the hallway and it crashed to the floor. "Oops, got to be quiet, don't want to wake anyone." He bumped into the walls as he walked to his study, carrying a bottle of vodka. It fell out of his hand and broke. "Ooh, look what I did."

Jennifer found him sprawled half off the couch. His clothes were wrinkled and soiled and his lip was cut. She felt heartsick looking at him and closed his door.

William took Margaret to school and Nellie brought Cassie and Joseph home. "Do you want me to stay and help you with these little Indians?"

Jennifer gave the children a hug. "Did you miss mama?"

"Yes we did," said Cassie. "Grandpa was funny. He made faces at us."

"You're looking better, got color back in your cheeks," said Nellie.

"Thanks, I do feel better, you don't need to stay." Jennifer gave the children cookies and milk, and then sat them at the table. "Sit here while I talk to Grandma." They went out on the porch where the children couldn't hear. Jennifer lowered her voice as she said, "Bill came home drunk again last night."

"Where is he now?"

"He's in the study. Go talk to him. Maybe he'll listen to you."

"Sure, but I don't know if it will do any good."

They heard Bill go out the front door and Jennifer ran after him. "Bill! Wait. I want to talk to you." Bill got in his car and drove away.

Jennifer walked back to Nellie. "He's gone. God knows where." Jennifer let out a desperate sigh. "Father O'Brien said he wanted to talk with him, but Bill isn't home long enough to set up a time."

William walked in. "Where's Bill going?"

Jennifer sat down at the kitchen table. "Bill came home drunk again last night, and left this morning, before I had a chance to talk to him."

William poured a cup of coffee and sat at the kitchen table, drumming his fingers on the table.

"What's on your mind William," asked Nellie.

William hesitated for a moment then said, "I know Bill hasn't been to work because Francis called and wanted to know what was going on."

Jennifer got the pot and filled her cup as she said, "I told him about Bill. He said he'll pay Bill's salary for a while, but he won't be able to cover up for him much longer."

"I'd like to know where he hangs out all day," said William. "Drinking is illegal in bars. The speakeasy's are the only places you can buy booze and they're against the law."

"How could he go to a speakeasy? Aren't they hard to get into?" asked Nellie.

Jennifer gave a short laugh. "Are you kidding? You only have to knock on the door to get in. Where do you think he bought drinks before?" She shook her head in bewilderment. "Where is he getting the money to buy liquor?"

William gave Jennifer a hug. "I got to go milk the cows." He walked out on the porch and out of frustration pounded his fist on the porch railing. "He has no right to do this to us."

Jennifer waited that night hoping he would come home for dinner. Then a week past and Bill still hadn't come home. They searched everywhere and there was no sign of him.

Jennifer liked working in her garden each morning, it kept her mind off of Bill. Then, at noon, she would go over to the farm.

Nellie saw her coming and went out to meet her. "Is Bill home?"

"No. I don't know where he is. I'm a nervous wreck."

"Come inside dear. Where are the children?"

"They're playing out back."

William put his arms around Jennifer. "I'll try again to find him."

"Maybe I should go too."

"No, you stay here with the children."

William searched every speakeasy within a twenty-mile radius, before he gave up.

When he pulled into his driveway, Jennifer ran out. "Any luck?"

William shook his head. "I couldn't find him anywhere."

"Well, thanks for trying." Jennifer walked back to the house and sat on the porch, watching the children play.

Caroline drove up the driveway and Jennifer waved to her. "It's so good to see you."

"Is Bill home yet?"

"How did you find out?"

"Daddy told me."

"Does mother know?"

"No. Not yet, but it's a small town, news gets around."

"He hasn't been home for a week and I'm worried stiff."

"Where are those little darlings?" They came running when they heard Caroline's voice. "You're getting so big." Caroline played jump rope and tag with them for a while, then said, "Okay, I'm worn out, I've got to rest."

"They really love it when you play with them. Can you stay for dinner?" asked Jennifer.

"I'd love to but you know mother. She'll be waiting for all the news when I get home. I just stopped by to see how you're holding up. Is there anything I can do?"

"You can keep an eye out for Bill. I have no idea where he is." Jennifer started to prepare dinner. "I wish you could stay."

"Mother's waiting for me, and you remember how that is."

"Please don't tell her about Bill."

"I won't." Caroline kissed Jennifer. "I'll call you tomorrow."

After the children were bathed, Margaret asked, "Where's daddy?"

"Daddy had to go on a trip, he'll be back soon." Jennifer tucked them in bed and kissed them goodnight. "Go to sleep, I'll see you in the morning."

She went to her bedroom and sat in the rocking chair by the window, holding her rosary beads. She fingered each ivory bead as she prayed. "Please God, bring him home safely? Jennifer kept her endless vigil, staring out the window waiting for his car. She fell asleep until the first rays of sun woke her. Bill's car was not there.

After church, on Sunday, Nellie invited Jennifer and the children over for dinner. She fed the children then sat them on the floor, in the parlor, by the fireplace. She gave the children dolls and trucks to play with and cookies and milk for desert. "Stay here while we grownups eat and talk."

"These are new toys," said Margaret.

"Yes. Grandpa bought them as a surprise."

Nellie placed the roast chicken on the table and they sat down as William said, "We haven't heard a word from Bill."

"I know. It's been two weeks since he left," said Jennifer.

"It seems like he vanished from the face of the earth," said William picking up his fork. "Let's eat; we can't let this chicken go to waste."

After dinner Nellie said, "I'll go home with you and help put the children to bed."

"Thanks, they'll like that."

"Come on kiddies. Grandma's going to bathe you."

"You're not going to wash our hair, are you?" asked Margaret. "I don't like that."

"It's a deal, no hair washing," said Nellie.

# Chapter Five

Jennifer sat by the window, as she did every night, until she fell asleep. In the morning she made coffee and sat looking out of the kitchen window. Watching the birds in her rose garden.

The children came down for breakfast and Margaret said, "Daddy hasn't been home for a long time."

"I told you before, he's away on business. He'll be home soon." Jennifer handed her a brown bag.

"But you keep saying that and he doesn't come home."

"Put your lunch in your school bag and hurry, you don't want to be late." She hustled Margaret out the door. "Grandpa's waiting to take you to school."

The phone rang and Jennifer rushed for the phone. "Hello."

It's Nellie. "Have you heard anything?"

"No, not a word. No one has even seen his car. Could you watch Cassie and Joseph for me for a couple of hours?"

"Sure, honey. What's up?"

"I want to borrow your truck and look for Bill."

"If you wait till William comes back, you can have the car."

"No. He said he had a few errands to do and I want to go now."

"Sure, I'll take care of them, bring them over."

---

Jennifer drove up and down all the city streets, feeling depressed and heartsick. Out of desperation, she went to the police station and walked in the smoke filled room. She started down the hallway as a policeman, hand-cuffed to a scar faced man, passed her.

The man winked at Jennifer. "Hi, good looking."

The policeman yanked on the prisoners arm. "Keep your trap shut."

Jennifer went to the counter where a thin Irish cop was sitting. A cigarette dangled from his lips as he said, "I'm officer Mulligan, what can I do for you?"

Jennifer gripped her pocketbook tightly. "I want to report a missing person."

The cop scratched his bald head with the top of his pen. "Who is it?"

"It's my husband, he's been missing for weeks, and it's…"

Officer Mulligan handed her a paper. "Fill out this form and give me all the details. Make sure you give us an idea of what he looks like."

Jennifer started to fill out the form. "He has a car."

"There's a place on the form for the type car and license number."

She filled in both sides and handed him the paper. Officer Mulligan looked it over. "You forgot to put down how long he's been missing?"

"Err…two weeks."

Does he drink? Is he into the booze?"

"Yes, he drinks."

Officer Mulligan slapped the desk. "That accounts for him being missing. They get into the bottle and go off on a binge."

Tears filled Jennifer eyes. "How long will it take to find him?"

He laid the form on the table and at that moment the long gray ash hanging from his cigarette fell in the middle of the form. "Damn it." Officer Mulligan brushed away the ashes. "Can't tell how long it will take? We'll call you if we find him."

Jennifer gripped the side of his desk in desperation. "Can I call you tomorrow to see if you found out anything?"

"Lady…" He stopped and looked at the form. "Mrs. Rennie, I said we would call you." He got up from his desk and walked to his filing cabinet.

Her hands shook as she walked outside and leaned against the wall. She took several deep breaths, and then cranked the engine and climbed in the truck.

Jennifer started to cry. "Maybe I'll never see him again."

She drove home and kept busy outside, weeding and pruning the flowers. After dinner, she helped Margaret with her homework, and put the children to bed. She read for a while, then went to bed. She couldn't stop thinking of Bill. Jennifer got up and sat in her rocking chair, by the window, holding her rosary beads.

———————

The phone rang as Jennifer came in from hanging the wash. She answered the phone. "Hello."

"This is Officer Mulligan. Is Mrs. Rennie there?"

"This is Mrs. Rennie. Did you find my husband?"

"No, but we found his car down by the mines. It has two flat tires, and a dented fender. Whoever had it ran it out of gas. It's at the station garage, you can pick it up anytime, but you'll have to sign for it."

"Thank you so much, Officer Mulligan." Jennifer called the farmhouse and Nellie answered. "They found Bill's car down by the coal mines."

"Did they find any sign of him?"

"No…The car has two flat tires and it's out of gas. Can William go with me to get it?"

"Let me put him on."

William took the phone. "Nellie just filled me in. Sure, I'll go with you. I'll take my jack and a couple of old tires that still have some tread, and a jug of gasoline. I'll be right over."

As they were driving home, William said, "I got a neighbor that can pound out those dents. I'll give him a call."

"Thanks for going with me; I don't know what I'd do without you and Nellie."

Caroline called as they walked in the house, "Did Bill come home?"

"No, but the police found his car."

"How are you holding up?"

"He's been gone three weeks and I haven't been sleeping. I hope you didn't tell mother."

"No, but she knows. The police went around town asking if anyone saw him and a neighbor told her. Then she asked Father Donahue and he told her to ask you." Caroline laughed.

"I acted like I didn't know anything."

"Thanks. I'll let you know if I hear anything."

# Chapter Six

It was 2 a.m. in the morning when Jennifer was startled awake by a rattling noise. "What in the world is that?" She looked out of the window and saw a cloud of dust. An old black ford was coming up the driveway. Jennifer ran down the stairs and peeked out of the window. It was a moonless night and hard to see. The man looked like a shadow in the dark and it frightened her when he banged on the door.

He continued to knock as he yelled, "Anybody home?"

Jennifer opened the door a crack. "What do you want?"

He was dressed in a long black coat and the wide rim on his black hat, shaded his features.

His beady eyes scrutinized her as he adjusted his narrow wire glasses.

"Are you Mrs. Rennie?"

Jennifer kept a tight hand on the door, ready to shut it, "Yes, I am. What do you want?"

He raked his fingers through his gray beard that hung down to his chest. He extended his bony hand. "I'm Pastor Markus." Jennifer hesitated before taking it. A faint smile crossed his face. "Is this the home of Bill Rennie?"

Jennifer folded her arms in front of her "Yes. I'm his wife. Do you know where he is?" When he didn't answer her voice became shrill. "Do you know where he is?"

The pastor placed his hands together. "Yes. He's safe. Praise the lord and hallelujah. May I come in?"

Jennifer hesitated, trying to decide if it was safe to let him in. She opened the door further. "Yes, come in." She led him to the parlor. "Please sit down. I want to call our parents."

Nellie answered the phone. "Whose car is that in your driveway?"

"It's a man who knows where Bill is. Call my father, then come over. He frightens me."

When she returned to the living room, Pastor Markus was sitting on the couch. He pointed to the statue of the Blessed Mary over the fireplace and the crucifix on the wall. "I see you're a Catholic family."

The door burst open and William and Nellie stood in front of the man, both talking at the same time. "Who are you? Where is our son?"

Pastor Markus stood up, towering over them. "If you calm down, I'll answer your questions."

Francis came in the front door and joined the group. "Just who are you and how do you know my son in-law?"

Jennifer raised her voice to be heard. "Why don't we sit down and let him talk."

Pastor Markus sat on the couch and clasped his hands on his lap. He cleared his voice before saying, "A month ago I found him in an alley down by the mines. He was unconscious, robbed of everything, including his clothes."

"Oh my poor son," said Nellie.

Jennifer started to cry as William patted her shoulder. "Hold on now. Let him finish."

"He was a bloody mess. Head cracked wide open, had a concussion."

Francis leaned forward. "What hospital is he in?"

"Bill isn't in a hospital, he's at my house. My wife and I cleaned him, fed him hot soup and took good care of him. We got down on our knees and prayed for him every day, and the Lord healed him."

Francis jumped to his feet. "Are you crazy? You should have taken him to the hospital, he could have died."

Pastor Markus smiled. "In our religion we don't believe in doctors. We let the Lord heal us. He choose to keep Bill on this earth to be a better person."

William's face was red with frustration and he stood over Pastor Markus. "What kind of religion lets a man suffer?"

"William, sit down," ordered Nellie. "Let him finish the story. Maybe he'll finally tell us when we can fetch Bill."

"Thank you, madam," said Pastor Markus. "We are a church of self-ordained ministers who believe in faith healing."

"I don't give a damn what you believe, that's your business," said William. "Just tell us where our son is."

"He's at my house. Three weeks ago he regained consciousness, but couldn't remember a thing. It was just this evening he remembered, who he was."

"Take us to him right now," said William getting up from the chair.

"Can't do that." The pastor stood up and snapped his hat against his leg. "I gotta go. I just came to let you know he's well and will be home in a week." The pastor started toward the door, and then stopped. "Bill is a changed man. He wants to come home when he's ready." He put his hat on and walked out the door.

"I'm coming with you," said William "I want my son."

"Can't let you do that, sir."

"Yeah and how are you going to stop me?"

"I don't mean to be rude, but I need to abide by my word. I convinced him to let me come because I knew you would be worried. I gave my word, you wouldn't follow me back."

After he left, William headed for the door, "Come on let's follow him."

Nellie grabbed William's hand. "I want our son home as much as you do, but I think we should do what the preacher says."

"Maybe he's lying," said Francis.

William sat down. "The preacher might be a little loco, but I don't think he's a liar." He leaned over and hugged Nellie, "We'll just have to wait."

Each day, they expected to see Bill coming up the driveway, but there was no sign of him. Jennifer tried not to think about him and baked a chocolate cake in case he came home.

Nellie and William came in the kitchen. "Something smells mighty good."

"I was just having a cup of tea; do you want some?" asked Jennifer.

"We sure do, and a piece of that cake too," said Nellie.

Jennifer poured the tea and William set a basket on the table, "I brought you some eggs. Oh! Can I have a piece of that chocolate cake too?"

Jennifer cut him a large piece. "Why do you suppose Bill doesn't want to come home yet?"

"We'll just have to be patient. Find out when he comes home," said William. He took the last bite of his cake and gulped down his tea. "I can't hang around here any longer. I have work to do."

William hoed through rows of corn, until he felt a pain in his back. As he stretched his arms and body, he looked toward the hill. He thought he saw someone coming, but the sun reflected off his glasses. He took his glasses off and squinted then ran toward the house shouting, "Nellie, Jennifer, come quick, Bill's home."

Jennifer looked in the distance and screamed, "It is Bill, I can tell by his walk."

He looked thinner as he strolled down the hill, wearing the same black pants and coat that Pastor Markus wore. The wide brimmed hat shaded his face, but Jennifer knew it was him. She ran to him and fell in his arms.

Her voice quivered. "I'm so glad you're home. I thought I'd never see you again."

Bill's face had a peaceful glow as he whispered, "Hi, Babe. I missed you."

She tried to hold back the tears, as she hugged him. "Why didn't you come home sooner? We were so worried."

"I had things to straighten out in my mind." He put his arm around her as they walked home.

Nellie gave him a big hug. "We're so happy you're home. Then, she hit his arm. You had no right to worry us."

Bill laughed and with a faint tremor in his voice said, "I had a lot of healing to do, but the Lord made me whole again."

"What the hell is he talking about?" asked William.

Bill shook his father's hand. "Good to see you Dad." He let out a sigh and sat on the steps. "It was a long walk, but it's good to be home." He put his head in his hands and was silent for a moment, then spoke in a whisper. "The Lord found me and saved me from the depths of hell. He told me to cast away my worldly sins." Bill stood up and raised his hands to the sky.

"Hallelujah, I have been brought into the kingdom of God."

William stared at him and scratched his head. "I think my son's off his rocker. We better get Doc. Forman to give him a once over."

Nellie touched Bill's shoulder. "Maybe you should go in and lie down."

"No, Mother. I'm fine. The Lord has healed me and I'm a new man. I was doomed forever, and God saved me."

Jennifer took his hand. "Come inside, dear. The children will be home soon, they'll be happy to see you."

Bill sat at the table and Jennifer put her arms around his neck. "I missed you so much. I thought you were dead."

"Thanks to the Lord, I'm not." He pulled her on his lap and took a Bible from his coat pocket and began to read it to her.

Jennifer took the Bible and placed it on the table. "Talk to me. I'm dying to find out what happened to you."

"It was a long walk and I want to relax. Let's talk about it later."

Jennifer went to the window. "I hear the children outside. Nellie must have told them you are home."

The door opened and they rushed into his arms, covering him with kisses. "Daddy, we're so glad you're home."

"Grandpa said you saw God. Is that true?" asked Margaret.

Bill hugged them and put his hand to his chest. "I didn't see God, but I felt him inside."

"I want to feel him too," said Cassie. She put her little hand on his chest and felt around.

"I don't feel him. Where is he?"

Bill laughed and the glow of his smile was exhilarating. "Come on, let's go outside and play on the swings."

Jennifer watched him with the children. He looked so peaceful and serene, like the Bill she married, but something was different.

---

Jennifer propped her pillow on the bed and waited for Bill to get in bed. When he lay beside her, she turned on her side. "I'm dying to know what happened."

Bill closed his eyes and his lips moved in a faint whisper as he prayed. Jennifer studied him. He looked older, more serious. He opened his dark brown eyes and they softened at the sight of her. "It's good to be home."

Jennifer touched his shoulder. "Tell me what happened?"

Bill stroked her hair lovingly. "I vaguely remember. I was drinking in a speakeasy, on the north side of town, by the coal mines." Bill turned on his side to face her. "I met two coal miners, one was a big bruiser, the other short and thin. They offered to buy me a drink and then we got in my car and the big guy was driving. "Then everything went black. When I woke up I was lying in a dark cold place. It smelled like urine and I felt sick. I tried to get up, but couldn't."

"The pastor said, they beat you up in the alley and he found you in your underwear."

Bill's brows drew together. "My head was pounding and my body ached. I thought I was going to die. Then high above me, I saw this golden glow, shining down from the sky. I reached up, trying to touch it." Bill made grabbing motions with his hands. "I tried to bring it closer and thought if I could get inside the light, I would be safe and warm. Then everything went black."

He stared into space then looked at the concern on Jennifer's face. He pulled her closer and their lips met in a soft tender kiss. Bill's desire illuminated his eyes and he searched for a sign of rejection. "I love you and need you."

She gave him a sensuous smile as she kissed him passionately and a delightful shiver ran through her. "It's been so long since we made love," said Jennifer.

Heat rippled through her as she recognized the flush of sexual desire that she hadn't felt for months. He kissed the nape of her neck and Jennifer reached down and unbuttoned his pajamas, gently massaging him.

He moaned, and then grabbed her hand. "Stop, I'll come too quickly if you keep that up."

Jennifer quivered beneath him as she felt waves of ecstasy, flowing through her. "Make love to me now." She gasped as her body arched toward him.

It seemed like forever since they had made love and they cuddled together exhausted. He kissed her gently. "Good night my sweet Babe."

Jennifer pulled the covers over them. "I'm so glad you're home."

# Chapter Seven

Francis stopped by the next morning and Jennifer was cooking breakfast. She greeted him with a huge smile. "Bill's home?"

"Yes William called me. I came over and see him and have some of your great pancakes and eggs."

"Glad you did. Would you like some coffee?" She filled a cup and set it in front of him.

Bill walked in the kitchen and sat down at the table and Francis said, "I'm glad you're home son. You're looking fit as a fiddle."

Bill sipped his coffee and never answered.

Francis gave Jennifer a confused look and she shrugged her shoulders.

"Something smells good," said Francis. "Are those fresh rolls in the oven?"

The children came down and raced to Francis. "I want to sit next to Grandpa," cried Cassie."

"No, I do," said Margaret pushing her away.

"Whoa! Take it easy. I'll sit between you two and I'll hold Joseph on my lap."

Jennifer gave Bill a cup of coffee. "Margaret could you pass me the sugar."

Francis finished his pancakes and patted his belly. "What a delicious breakfast. Bill, can I talk to you in private?"

"Sure, we can go in my study."

When they entered his office, Bill shut the door and Francis sat on the couch and said, "I don't know how to tell you this. We had to give your job to someone else."

Bill stood against the wall with his hands in his pocket. "So…"

"When you disappeared, the boards of directors got mad as a hornet's nest."

Bill walked over and sat next to Francis. "Are you trying to say I don't have a job anymore?"

Francis wiped his forehead with his handkerchief. "Not exactly. Jennifer doesn't realize that you really haven't been working for the bank for the past five weeks. She thinks I pulled strings and put you on sick leave."

"Look, Francis. I don't want you to go out on a limb for me. Don't worry about my job, the Lord will look after us."

A puzzled look came on Francis's face. "Bill, listen to me. I'll get you a job at the bank. It will be in a different department, but I guarantee you'll have a job with a good income."

"Don't bother." Bill put an arm on his father-in-law's shoulder and led him to the door. "I'm going to work for the Savior's Church."

Francis turned swiftly, almost knocking Bill over. "You're what? You can't work for the

Savior's Church, you're a Roman Catholic. The priest would never allow it."

Bill's voice rose in anger. "The priest didn't help me when I was blind drunk. What did they do for me when I was half dead in an alley? Do you think I care what they're going to say now?" He threw his hands in the air. "The Lord wants me to go forth and teach his way of life."

Francis stood in a daze, wondering what he was talking about. "You have your family to take care of. What kind of money can the church pay you? Think it over. I'll find you a position in the bank paying your old salary."

"The Lord will take care of us."

Francis walked out of the room and Jennifer saw the expression on his face. "You look upset. What were you two talking about?"

"He doesn't want to work at the bank anymore."

"Why?"

"I'll let him tell you." He kissed her cheek. "Goodbye, call me later."

Jennifer walked in the study and Bill had two bottles of vodka in his hands and she ran toward him. "Oh no, not again."

Bill laughed. "Don't worry; I'm not going to drink it." He walked to the kitchen and poured the liquor down the drain. "I will never drink this devil's brew again."

"I was sure you were going to." She put her arms around his waist. "I don't want to lose you again."

Bill saw the love in her eyes, and looked at her sadly. "I'm not going to work at the bank."

"Why?" Jennifer walked over to the table, waiting for him to continue. She couldn't stand the silence and blurted out, "That's what you've done all your life."

Bill put his hands on her shoulders. "Sit down, I want to talk to you."

She sat on the edge of the chair twisting her hands. "If you had a fight with my father, I'll make him take you back."

He knelt before her. "Try to understand what I'm going to say. I've been called by the Lord, to save the sinners and guide them into a better life."

A look of confusion crossed Jennifer's face. "I don't understand what you're talking about? You can't preach in church. Priests can't be married."

Bill looked at her sternly. "I'm no longer a Catholic."

Jennifer jumped to her feet. "What are you talking about? Of course, you're Catholic. We've been Catholic all our lives."

"Not anymore." Bill put his hands on her shoulders and looked deep in her eyes. "We, as a family are now faith healers. We believe God will take care of us. Our family will worship God in the Savior's Church, and worship in the love and light of Jesus Christ."

Jennifer felt confused, and then she became angry. "I think your concussion has affected your brain. How can you ask me to give up a religion I believe in? I won't do it!"

"You saw how God cured me and brought me from the streets of hell. You must understand how important this to me."

Jennifer stood up and placed her hands on her hips. "If you had talked with Father

Donahue, like I asked you, he would have saved you." They stood staring at each other. Jennifer walked to sink and rinsed the dishes. "You're asking too much. I won't do it."

Bill's voice pleaded, "If you truly love me, you will join the Savior's Church."

"If I truly love you! That works both ways. I can't and I won't join that church. I'm a Roman Catholic and I love my church. I know nothing of this strange thing you're involved with."

Jennifer stamped out of the room and went upstairs. She stayed in her room for hours mulling over their conversation. There was no solution. Twilight reflected in the window and made her realize how late it was.

When she went down to prepare dinner, Bill was sitting on the couch with the children reading the bible.

"Daddy's reading us a story about baby Jesus," said Cassie. She patted her little hand on the couch. "Want to sit down and listen?"

Jennifer smiled at her innocent daughter. "No honey. I have to cook dinner. You can tell me about it later."

After they ate, Bill put the children to bed, then sat next to Jennifer on the sofa. "Please do what I asked. I feel so peaceful and blessed and I know what I'm doing is right for our family."

He reached out to embrace her, but she turned her back to him. "I'm tired and confused. I need time to think. Good night."

She went upstairs and Bill followed her. When they were in bed, he cuddled close to her. She moved away. "Good night."

Bill got down on his knees and Jennifer heard him pray. When he finished, he leaned toward her. "The Lord will show you the way. His light will guide you. Goodnight my sweet Babe."

Jennifer tried to go to sleep, but kept thinking about the changes in her husband. How was she going to deal with this?

––––––––––––––––

When Jennifer came down the next morning the children were dressed and Margaret ready for school. Bill greeted her with a bright smile. "Good morning Babe. How did you sleep?"

"I didn't sleep well; I was awake most of the night."

"I'll take Margaret and enroll her in public school this morning."

"What! You're taking her out of Catholic school. You can't do that."

"Yes I can, Margret go out to the car."

"I don't want to change school. My friends are all there and I love Sister Mary."

"I said get in the car. I'll be right out."

Margaret left crying and Jennifer pleaded, "It's the middle of the school year, can't you wait."

Bill put his hand up. End of discussion. After I enroll her, I'm going over to the Savior's Church. "I want to find out when I can start working."

Jennifer's face was tight with anger. "Why do we have to change our lives to please you? What makes you think your way is right?"

He looked at her as if he was in a trance. "I know it's the right thing to do and I want this more than anything in life."

After he left, Jennifer took the children to the farm and Nellie greeted them at the door.

"How are my little grandchildren this morning?" She took Joseph in her arms and saw the look on Jennifer's face. "What's wrong, you look upset?"

Jennifer sat at the brown oak table in the kitchen and her lips quivered. "Bill has converted to this new religion and wants me to change too."

"What, I never heard of such a thing. What are you going to do?"

Jennifer paced the floor. "He's even taking Margaret out of Catholic school."

"What! That's not right, I'll get William to talk to him tonight; maybe he can talk some sense into him."

"This is so upsetting; Margaret's supposed to make her First Holy Communion next week. That will be another fight."

"Maybe he'll change his mind."

"I don't think he will, he's so determined. I don't know what to do. Oh well, I better go home. I have a load of wash waiting"

When she went back to her house, Caroline was at the door. "I hear Bill's back. Where is he?"

"He just left."

"You don't look happy, what's the matter?"

"He's become a religious freak and wants me to change my religion."

"Good Grief! What are you going to do?"

"I want to talk to Father Donahue. Will you take care of the children?"

"Sure, I'd love it. Take my car."

When Jennifer returned, Caroline had the children outside on the swings.

"How'd it go?" asked Caroline.

"I had a long talk with Father Donahue and he's coming to the house tonight. I hope he can change Bill's mind."

"Either the concussion or that preacher did something to make Bill change. I hope the priest can help."

"Were the children any trouble?"

"Heavens no, it was fun taking care of these little darlings. Let me know what happened. I have a few errands to do"

Jennifer grabbed her arm. "Please don't tell mother."

Caroline crossed her heart. "I promise."

At 5 p.m., Father Donahue sat in the parlor waiting for Bill to come home. He patted Jennifer's hand. "Have faith my child, I'm sure I can make him realize he should not give up the Catholic religion."

Bill walked in and saw the priest and slammed the door. "What are you doing in my house?"

"I invited him. He wants to talk to you."

Bill's eyes blazed. "I don't need to listen to a priest. Get out of my house. I have nothing to say to you."

"My son, you're confused. I've come to give you guidance and help you."

Bill opened the front door. "I am not your son, nor am I confused. I want you to leave now."

Father Donahue put his hand out to Bill. "My son, we all get confused sometimes."

"Shut up and get out!"

"Don't talk to Father Donahue like that; he's here at my request." She took Bill's hand. "Listen to him, at least for my sake."

Bill stood by the open door. "I said, get out Donahue, I don't need your help."

William walked in at that moment. "What in holy name is going on here? Why are you ordering Father Donahue out of your house?"

A muscle flickered in Bill's jaw as he stared at his father. "Stay out of this Dad."

Father Donahue put his hand on Jennifer's arm. "I'm sorry, I couldn't help him." He made the sign of the cross. "Bless you my child. I'll pray that God will help you with your troubles." He stared at Bill. "I've known you since the day you were born. I baptized you. I'm extremely surprised at your actions."

William watched Father Donahue leave. "What's happening, son, why are you acting like this?"

"Dad, I'm a big boy. I'll do what I feel is best for my family. We are joining the Savior's Church."

"Wait a minute, son. You…"

"Bill put his hand up and stopped him. "Don't say a word Dad. Either accept my decision or never speak to me again."

William put his arm around Jennifer and whispered, "I'm sorry. I thought I could help, but I can't." He walked toward the door. "I'll always be here to help you."

At first Jennifer tried to reason with him, then she argued for weeks. Bill was determined to do as he planned. Each morning, he fixed the children's breakfast and read them the Bible, while they ate. He took Margaret to school, and spent the day at the Savior's Church.

Pastor Markus was pleased with Bill's progress. "I'd like you to give the service, two nights a week and on Sunday mornings?"

"I would be honored and I'll continue to print pamphlets for the sinners and distribute them in the afternoon, along the streets."

"I have something else you can help me with. Sometime this week, you could visit the sick parishioners. Spend some time and pray with them."

"That would be very rewarding," said Bill.

When Bill went home and tried to huge Jennifer, but she pulled away as he said, "Pastor Markus asked me to preach before the congregation. I am so happy."

Jennifer pushed him away. "You spend every day and some nights there. How much money is he paying you?"

"Well, he's giving me what he can now, but the nights I give the service he'll split the collection with me." Bill handed her five dollars.

Jennifer looked at the money and threw it on the table. "You've been home a month and this is all the pastor gave you?"

"I told you I'll get more when I give the sermon."

"Since daddy stopped your salary, I've been going crazy trying to make ends meet. We can't live on five dollars."

He sat down at the dinner table and smiled. "Don't worry. God will take care of us."

---

Jennifer had been taking the children to mass, each Sunday, after Bill left for his church. Then the following Sunday, Jennifer woke up and heard the children talking in their bedroom and wondered why they were up so early.

Then she heard Cassie say, "Where are we going daddy?"

Jennifer threw a robe on and went to their bedroom. Cassie and Margaret were dressed and Bill had Joseph's shoes in his hands.

She braced her arms across the doorway. "You are not taking the children to that church."

Bill pushed the children in front of him and walked toward her. "Get out of my way." Bill pressed against her arms. "From now on they're going to church with me."

Bill forced Jennifer's arms down and she swung them back on the door jam. "You're not taking them. Margaret has her First Communion today."

Bill forced her arms down and held them there. "She's not making her Communion and that's final. She's going with me."

Jennifer blocked him with her body, but his strength won out, he pushed the children past her.

Margaret looked at her parents with pleading eyes. "Why can't I make my Communion? Sister Agnes is going to be mad at me."

"You can't take them. I won't let you!" Jennifer, tried to block the stairway.

The children's eyes watered as they cried out, "Why are you and daddy fighting?"

"They are not part of your freaky religion," shouted Jennifer.

Bill pushed her aside and hustled the children down the steps. "Come children, we are leaving."

They lagged behind their father and called out, "We'll be back, Mama." Then they looked at their father. "Won't we, Daddy?"

Jennifer sat on the steps feeling lost and beaten, but determined. She dressed and went to church.

After mass, she went to the rectory and talked to Father Donahue. "He's taking the children to his church and I don't know what to do. Margaret was supposed to make her Holy

Communion today, but he wouldn't let her."

Father Donahue patted her hand. "With Bill's attitude there's not much we can do. Bring

Margaret over tomorrow around noon; I'll give her the communion rights."

"Oh thank you father. Is there anything else we can do?"

"We must pray that he'll realize the mistake he's making and come back to us." He sighed, "It's a hard cross for you to bear, but we must pray for the strength to help you through this."

Jennifer walked home confused and depressed; her home had turned into a battle field. She prayed that Bill would stay at his church all day tomorrow. "Oh God, I hate to ask my child to lie."

The next day Jennifer took a chance and called Caroline; she was ready to hang up if her mother answered.

Then she heard her sister's voice. "Oh I'm so glad you answered, can you come over now? I need you."

"Of course, what's the matter?"

"I'm taking Margaret to church. Father Donahue is going to let her make her confirmation; I need you to stand for her."

"Did Bill say it was okay?"

"If he finds out, he'll be raving mad. Please don't tell anyone."

"All right, I'll be right over." When Caroline got there, Jennifer's eyes were all red. "You've been crying, what's the matter?"

"Bill takes the children to church with him each Sunday and is insisting I go with him. We're fighting all the time."

"What happened when Father Donahue came over?"

"Bill threw him out of the house," Jennifer blew her nose and dried her tears. "Come on we're late. Nellie's taking care of Cassie and Joseph; she thinks we're going shopping."

Sister Agnes and the priest were waiting for them at the altar. Margaret was dressed in a white lace dress and looked like an angel. After the ceremony, Jennifer sat in the pew with her and they prayed.

She took Margaret's hand. "Honey, you know what a secret is?"

"Yes. If someone tells you something and asks you not to tell anyone, you promise you never will."

"That's right. Now, I don't want you to tell your daddy about your communion."

"Daddy didn't want me to have communion. Why doesn't he like Father Donahue anymore?"

"I don't know honey, but let's pray he'll change his mind. In the meantime, it's our secret."

"I promise mommy."

Caroline put her arm around Jennifer. "I know you feel guilty going behind his back, but I would have done the same thing."

"Thank you so much for doing this for me. It's our secret."

The struggle between Bill and Jennifer went on for weeks, and each time he won and took the children to church.

She watched them leave, as they pleaded with her. "Please come with us, Mama. We don't like sitting alone; it scares us."

"Maybe someday, but right now I can't."

Jennifer hated the constant battling. She got dressed for the Sunday morning mass and was a little early. She sat on the couch in the parlor trying to relax. Her eyes wandered around the room and stopped at the empty wall over the fireplace. She stood up quickly. "The crucifix is missing and where's the Blessed Virgin Mary? How dare he take them down." She ran to the farmhouse. "Nellie, Bill took my crucifix and…"

"Calm down honey. I watched him throw them in the trash barrel yesterday and I took them out as soon as he left."

"Oh, thank you. Where are they?"

"I have them in the spare bedroom, for safe keeping. Are you ready for church?"

When they returned home, Caroline was waiting in the driveway. "I saw you at mass, but the church was so crowded I couldn't sit with you."

"I'm glad you stopped over. I have something to tell you. I'm pregnant."

Bill walked in with the children. "Hey, Caroline good to see you."

"Good to see you. How are you feeling?"

"I never felt better in my life. Did Jennifer tell you that I'm a pastor in the Saviors church?"

"I can't see how you can do that. You're catholic."

"I'm no longer catholic and neither is my family. I don't want you to interfere."

"Don't talk to my sister like that. I told you I'm not changing my religion."

Caroline started to leave then turned and said, "You're driving my sister crazy. Maybe my mother was right after all." She slammed the door as she left.

Bill shrugged his shoulders. "As far as I'm concerned, she's no longer family."

"She's my sister, and she'll always be welcome here. I need to talk with you about another problem."

"What's the matter?"

"I'm pregnant."

"Praise the Lord," Bill got down on his knees, "Thank you, dear Lord, for giving us a child to bring up in your light." He turned to Jennifer and pleaded, "Please come to church with us. We can rejoice with the people of the parish, for the blessing of a new child."

Tears filled Jennifer's eyes. "No. I can't do it. I don't want to bring a child into a house full of hatred." She walked out of the room and called to the children, "It's time for dinner."

The following Sunday, Margaret woke her mother. "Please come to church with us Mama. We don't like sitting in those seats by ourselves. Daddy screams and hollers and it scares us. Please, Mommy. We want you to come."

Cassie and Joseph climbed on the bed and hugged her. "Please Mama. We don't want to go without you, but daddy will make us."

Jennifer's heart felt heavy, as she listened to them. She wondered if Bill was putting the children up to this. "I don't want to do this," she thought. I'm giving in against my will, but I will for the sake of my children. She got dressed and went with them. Anger knotted her mind and she didn't want him to have the satisfaction of wining. Every part of her fought giving in. As they drove closer, the old dilapidated building stood out in the distance. She could see the white paint peeling from the clapboard. The trees and bushes were spindly and neglected to the point of despair. Dark clouds hung over the church and an eerie mist hung close to the earth. Bill opened the dark pine door and it squeaked on its rusty hinges. Twelve brown pews, worn and sagging, stood on each side of the room.

Bill proudly led his family to the front pew and he pointed to a pale thin woman sitting at the piano. "That's Mrs. Markus, I'll introduce you later." They sat down and Jennifer held Joseph on her lap. Margaret and Cassie sat on each side of her. "I'll join you after the service," said Bill.

"This is where we always sit," said Margaret.

Jennifer looked around and stopped at Mrs. Markus and thought, she looks so shy and timid. She could understand why, living with that weird man. She must be kind because she took care of Bill when they found him. She saw Bill walk up three steps to a green pulpit and look down at the twenty people chatting in the pews.

He held his hands up. "Let's all turn to page 332, Nearer My God to Thee."

A hush came over the church as Mrs. Rebecca Markus started to play. The people stood up and their harmonious voices filled the church. Jennifer and the children got up and the woman behind her handed her a hymnal.

When the song ended, Bill smiled and his loud voice echoed through the church. "Welcome to the Lords house."

Jennifer stared at him and couldn't believe that he was going to preach to these strangers.

"Let's all pray," said Bill.

Jennifer bowed her head and as Bill prayed she said, "to Our Fathers."

Bill waved his hands in the air shouting, "Sinners are headed for damnation. Are you a sinner?" He pointed at a woman in the third row and with a sweep of his arm included the whole congregation. "Search your soul. If you are, get down on your knees and ask for forgiveness."

Jennifer was horrified at the contorted expression on his face and the ferocity of his voice made her shudder. The children moved closer to her and she put her arms around them.

"Praise the Lord, Hallelujah!" the congregation shouted.

Jennifer couldn't help comparing the quietness of the Catholic service to this cacophony of voices. Struggling with her feelings, she gripped her rosary beads that were tucked in the folds of her skirt. "I shouldn't be here," she thought.

White specks caught her eye where the green paint had chipped from the pulpit. It glistened in the harsh light, from the uncovered bulbs, that swayed back and forth on frayed wires. Halfway through the sermon, thunder roared and streaks of lightning flashed across the sky. Heavy rain poured down on the little wooden building, making the tin roof rattle, like pans beaten with a spoon.

Jennifer blessed herself as she recited, "Hail Mary, full of grace, the Lord is with thee." She gripped her rosary tighter and kept praying. She was sure God was angry with her for coming to this church.

"Hallelujah!" the congregation shouted, as their hands lifted up toward the ceiling. "The Lord is washing away our sins."

When the service ended, Jennifer was shaking. She had to get out of there; she wanted to go home. She took the children's hands and started up the aisle.

Bill stopped her. "I want to introduce you to the congregation." He told the children to stay in the pew and led Jennifer to the front of the church. The people gathered around, eager to meet the new pastor's wife. Bill beamed with pride as he introduced her. "This is my lovely wife Jennifer."

She smiled. "It's a pleasure to meet everyone." She started to walk away, but Pastor Markus placed his large bony hand on hers. His touch felt cold and rough, she pulled away.

His lips twisted into a strained smile that made Jennifer cringe. His shrewd eyes narrowed as he studied her intently. "How are you, Mrs. Rennie?"

Jennifer glanced nervously toward her husband. She wanted to yell to him, make him stop talking and take her home. He was engrossed in conversation with a group of people.

When she didn't answer, Pastor Markus moved closer and placed his hand on her shoulder. "I'm glad you decided to become one of us."

She felt intimidated by him and took a step back, letting his hand slide off her shoulder. She forced a smile. "I'm only here to accompany my children."

"Oh! Is that right. Well, I'm glad to see you."

Bill finally came over and took Jennifer's hand. "Are you ready to go home?"

Pastor Markus slapped Bills shoulder. "Great sermon. Goodbye Mrs. Rennie, see you next Sunday."

# Chapter Eight

Jennifer dressed the children early for church and prepared breakfast. She had been going to this church for three weeks and only went for the children's sake. She was able to go to mass during the week without Bill knowing. Jennifer prayed she would be able to hold up under this pressure. While she dressed, she tried to convince herself that as long as she worshiped the same god, it didn't matter what church she went to.

Bill walked in the room. "I want to leave for church as soon as you're dressed."

"Why, what's the hurry? It's only 7:30 a.m.; church begins at 9 a.m."

"I have something important to do when I get there."

Margaret and Cassie lagged behind as they walked to the car. Bill grabbed Cassie's hand. "Stop dragging your feet and keep up with us."

"Why are you so grouchy?" asked Jennifer.

"I have a lot on my mind."

When they entered the church, Pastor Markus was waiting for them by the front pew. "Glad you got here early." He handed Jennifer four white robes. "Take the children to the restroom and put these over your undergarments."

Jennifer took them. "Why, what are they for?"

"Today, you and the children will be baptized by the Holy Spirit."

She threw the robes down on the pew. "No! I never agreed to this."

Pastor Markus picked up the robes and shoved them at her. "Your husband is a minister of this church and you and the children must be baptized."

Jennifer spoke through clenched teeth, "We are already baptized. We're Catholic."

Bill grabbed her arm and squeezed it. Red marks stood out on her skin where his fingernails dug in and she cried out in pain. His six-foot frame towered over and for the first time in their marriage she felt threatened. "Take the children into the bathroom and put on the robes."

She twisted from his grip; her eyes blazing. "No, I won't do it." Bill put Joseph in her arms and with hands firmly on her shoulders and pushed her into the bathroom.

Their daughters followed crying. "Daddy, don't hurt mommy. Why do we have to put on these white things?"

Bill threw the robes on the counter. "Get changed."

The children cried and held on to each other. "Why is daddy doing this?"

"Jennifer kneeled in front of them and put her arms around them. "Please stop crying, everything will be all right." When they calmed down, she sat on the toilet seat fighting back the tears. I never saw Bill angry, she thought. She had to figure a way out. Maybe we can sneak out the back door. Maybe he's busy with Markus? She peeked out the door and no one was in the hall. "Children be quiet and follow me." They started down the hall and when they turned the corner, Bill was leaning against the wall.

He grabbed Jennifer's arm. "Why don't you have the robes on?" He pulled her back to the bathroom and pushed her in. "Put them on now."

Jennifer kicked at him. "No, I won't."

He grabbed her and stared in her eyes. "Put them on now, or I'll do it." He undressed

Joseph and said, "Margaret, Cassie, get your clothes off and put on your robes." The children started to cry and Bill hollered, "Stop crying or I'll give you something to cry about."

Jennifer was in tears as she put the robe on and without Bill noticing tucked her rosary beads into her brassiere. Calmly Jennifer said, "Go join the pastor while I help the children?"

Bill stared at her then said, "I don't trust you."

She helped her daughters finish dressing and tried to stall for some time by slowly folding their clothes and placing them neatly on the counter.

Bill led them to the front pew. "Sit here and don't move."

After the opening song, two men went up on the platform and lifted a section of the floor, revealing a large square tank full of water.

Pastor Markus stood at the top of the steps that led to the water. "Let us pray and ask forgiveness for our sins." He bowed his head. "Lord, we have lost souls who have come to be baptized in your name. Wash away their sins forever. Amen"

As the pastor prayed, Bill escorted a man and two women, dressed in white robes, up to the pool. "Take your shoes off."

Pastor Markus helped the women into the water and whispered, "Get down on your knees and hold your breath as you go under."

He placed his hand on her forehead. "Dear Lord, we have brought this sinner to you. We ask that you wipe away her sins, so she may enter your kingdom." His one hand covered her nose, while his other hand pushed her forward. When the water covered her, he pulled her up and shouted, "Hallelujah! You have entered into the light and love of our Lord. Go and sin no more."

After the other two were baptized, Bill picked up his son and led the family up to the platform. Jennifer was shaking as she held her daughter's hands. She kept thinking over and over again, "He might put me under the water, but I'll always be Catholic."

"What are we going to do Daddy?" asked Cassie.

"You and Margaret are going to become lambs of God." He knelt by her. "Don't be afraid, nothing will hurt you."

Margaret pulled back. "I don't want to get all wet!"

Tears flowed down Jennifer's cheeks as Pastor Markus helped her into the water. "Look, tears of joy. Praise the Lord, hallelujah," shouted the congregation. Pastor Markus whispered, "Kneel down," as he pushed Jennifer down on her knees. Her back stiffened when he gripped her shoulders. "Don't fight it, it will be over quickly." He placed his left hand over her nose and pushed hard against her back, with his right. When the water covered her he slid his hand off her nose and cupped her breast, squeezing it firmly. Jennifer grabbed his hand and struggled to get away. The water rushed up her nose and she coughed and gagged.

When she surfaced he grinned and offered his hand. "Let me help you up the stairs."

She pushed him away and whispered, "You hypocrite."

He took her by the arm and helped her out of the water. "Hallelujah, you have been brought into the light and love of our Lord. Go and sin no more." Pastor Markus then knelt down by the little girls. "There's nothing to worry about. God will take care of you."

Margaret looked at her mother. "I don't want to do this."

Jennifer grabbed Bill's arm. "Bill stop this, the children are too young to go through this."

"Be quiet," said Bill as he reached for Cassie.

The pastor firmly placed his hand over Margaret's nose. "Remember to hold your breath." He quickly lowered her into the water and when it was over, Margaret ran to her mother, shivering and whimpering, "I'm cold and wet mommy. I want to go home."

Cassie tried to run off the platform, but Bill grabbed her by the waist and handed her to Pastor Markus. "Hold your breath little one," he said as he placed his hand over her nose and lowered her into the water. Cassie became hysterical and twisted and squirmed, she pulled his hand away and screamed.

Jennifer grabbed her daughters and thought, "damn you Bill for doing this to us." She hugged her children. "Momma's got you. You're going to be all right."

Bill handed Pastor Markus his son and Joseph's legs flailed in the air, kicking the pastor in the stomach.

"I don't want to go in the water," screamed Joseph.

Pastor Markus laughed. "Frisky little thing, aren't you? Hold your breath now." He quickly submersed Joseph and he came out of the water screaming and kicking.

Bill grabbed him and held him close. "You are fine son; you should be proud. You've just been baptized."

Jennifer led her shivering children to the restroom. She seethed with anger and dreaded sitting through the service. They drove home in total silence and she held her temper until the children were in bed.

Bill came in the kitchen and Jennifer was sitting at the table drinking a cup of tea. "Can I have a cup?"

She slammed down her cup and stood up. "How dare you do that to me? I said I'd go to that that church, but I didn't say I would change my religion!"

Bill took her hand. "Don't get excited. It was for your own good."

She yanked her hand away. "I know it was for you." She stuck her face close to his, her hands clenched stiffly by her side. "Pastor Markus wouldn't let you preach at church if we weren't baptized. Would he?"

Bill rubbed his hand nervously across his face. "I knew if I asked you ahead of time, you wouldn't do it."

Her eyes blazed. "That's why you were so nervous this morning. You had it all planned. Is that what your new religion is about? Making people do what they don't want to?"

"No, not at all." Bill looked at her lovingly and pushed the stray tendrils of auburn hair from her face. "I love you and I want my family to be together in our church. Once you learn more about the religion, you'll change your mind." Cupping her chin, he searched her face for understanding.

Jennifer stiffened and pulled away. "You tell that filthy Markus to keep his hands off of me."

"What are you talking about?"

"He squeezed my breast when he had me under the water. Your high and mighty Markus is the biggest sinner of them all."

"Oh, no, you're mistaken." Bill shook his head in disbelief. "His hand must have slipped when he was bringing you out of the water."

"Yes sure it just slipped, right off my nose and onto my left breast. Ha!" With fast strides, she walked out of the room and went up to their bedroom.

She was in bed when Bill came up and he sat on the bed next to her. "I'm sure the pastor didn't mean that." When she didn't respond he added. "The church is our family now and things will be different in many ways."

Disgusted with his weird ways, she rolled her eyes. "Now what are you talking about?"

"Our friends will be past friends. We are going to involve our lives completely in the congregation of the church."

"You don't mean we're giving up our friends do you? Why I've known Maggie and my nursing chums since grammar school."

"They would never see things the way we do. We are one with Christ." Bill took off his pants and put on his pajamas, as he continued, "They are still steeped in their mundane life. We have gone beyond that."

"We!" Jennifer gave a mocked laugh. "You mean you. I'm trying to stay in my life."

Jennifer turned her back on him. "I'll never give up my friends, no matter what you say." He started to say something and she interrupted. "I'm going to sleep. I have an early appointment with Doctor Forman."

"You what! Cancel it?"

"I can't; I'm in my third month."

"I'll have one of the midwives from the church examine you." He looked at her sternly.

"We no longer believe in doctors. The Lord will heal and take care of us."

Jennifer looked at him like he was out of his mind. "Yeah sure." She turned away from him.

Bill pulled her back. "I mean it Jennifer. Cancel the appointment or I will." Her nightgown pulled up passed her stomach when he pulled her over. It aroused him. She squirmed to get away from him, but he kissed her. His features softened as he ran his hands through her hair and kissed her again.

"Stop it, let me alone," she said trying to get away from him

He held her down with his arm and legs and with his free hand pulled her nightgown up. "Stop squirming."

He tried to enter her but she squirmed sideways, kicking him in the side. "Leave me alone."

Bill rolled over and held his side. "You hurt me!"

Jennifer jumped out of bed. "Is this what your church teaches you? Do they tell you to force yourself on your wife, make her submit? Even if she doesn't want to? You're acting like a dog in heat."

Bill raised his hand to strike her, but stopped. Instead his voice softened. "I'm sorry

Babe, I didn't mean to do that. Forgive me."

Jennifer crawled in bed and turned away from him, as tears ran down her cheeks. She wiped them away and fell asleep, wondering what happened to her gentle husband?

———————

Bill was leaving when Jennifer came down to prepare breakfast. She stood at the window watching him drive away with Margaret. After the other children ate she sent them outside to play. She was in deep thought, when Nellie walked in.

"What's been going on? I haven't seen or talked to you for a while."

"I'm okay." Jennifer sipped her coffee. "There's a fresh pot on the stove, if you'd like some?"

Nellie poured a cup. "Is Bill still going to that newfangled church?"

Jennifer sighed. "Yes, he's become a preacher for the church."

Nellie's voice rose in surprise, "Oh no! What is wrong with him?" She filled Jennifer's cup and splashed some cream in it. "Did Margaret make her First Holy Communion?"

Jennifer didn't answer.

"Well, did she?"

She didn't want to say yes and put Nellie in the middle, so she lied. "No. Bill wouldn't let her. He takes the children to his church and I can't stop him. Finally, I had to go with him for the children's sake. Honestly, Nellie, I'm not sure I can handle this. He had us baptized into the faith healing religion."

Nellie almost spilled her coffee. "Into what?"

"Do you remember Pastor Markus, that weird man who found him? Well, he converted Bill to this religion and now Bill has become a preacher in his church."

"Goodness gracious, sake's alive." Nellie shook her head in dismay. "How can he do that?"

"I don't know, he's acting so strange." She sat quietly for a few moments. "I don't want to convert to that religion, but I don't want to leave him. The disgrace of being divorced would be too much for me to handle."

Nellie studied Jennifer's face before she asked, "Do you still love him?"

"Right now I'm not sure and Mother's words keep echoing in my mind."

"What did she say?"

Jennifer repeated her mother's words slowly. "Mark my words. You'll regret the day you married him. I don't want her words to be true."

"Did she really say that?" Nellie's face was grim, as she walked to the door. "I'll call Father Murphy and have him talk to Bill."

Jennifer jumped to her feet. "Don't do that. Remember he threw Father Donahue out. You don't know how angry he gets."

"You poor dear, you have it rough. What else can happen?"

"I'm pregnant."

Nellie fell against the back of the chair. "Oh no! How far along are you?"

"Three months, I wish to God I wasn't pregnant. I don't want to have a baby when my life is such a mess."

"You'll feel better about the baby when it comes. Right now things seem complicated and they could change. Have you been to see Doctor Forman?"

Jennifer carried the dishes to the sink. "That's another issue. Bill refuses to let me see him." Her lips trembled as she added, "He's going to have one of the midwives from the church deliver the baby."

Nellie shook her head from side to side, "Now, I know my son's lost his mind."

Jennifer dropped the cup and it crashed to the floor and the pieces flew across the room. "Now, look what I've done." She burst out crying as she got the dust pan and broom. "I'm so upset, I can't think straight." She started to sweep up the pieces. "I don't know what to do. Bill says we don't need doctors, the Lord will take care of us."

Nellie hugged her. "Holy mackerel child, you have a burden to carry on these shoulders." She held her for a while then patted Jennifer's back. "Do you want me to take the children for a while?

"No, they help keep my mind off my troubles. It's Saturday, I'm going shopping if I can borrow your car."

"Of course, you can. Try not to worry; maybe he'll change his mind."

"Nellie, the most important job in my life is to protect my children, and keep them happy. I'll deal with things, one day at a time." She walked outside with Nellie and called to her children, "Come on. Let's go shopping."

# Chapter Nine

Sunday morning Pastor Markus went over to talk to Patty Schultz, a young woman in his congregation. Her mother had recently died and she had taken over her job as midwife. Patty was shy and always wore drab dresses with her hair pulled back in a knot. Patty at twenty-one was still unmarried and this upset the pastor.

Patty had just walked into church and Pastor Markus approached her. He took her hand as he said, "You are a lovely young woman. You should be married."

"I'm much too busy to even think about it."

"Nonsense, I'm going to introduce you to Arthur Bradford. He's a good man and he's looking for a wife."

Patty shivered. She knew Arthur and couldn't stand looking at his big nose and buckteeth. "Maybe some time, but right now I'm too busy. Excuse me, I have to go to the restroom."

She stopped to talk to a lady in the back of the church and Arthur walked up. "I would be honored Patty, if you would have dinner with me tomorrow night."

Pastor Markus had put him up to it and was standing nearby and said, "Why, of course she will."

"I'm busy tomorrow night," said Patty

"Cancel whatever plans you have," said Pastor Markus. "It will do you good to get out and have fun." Patty stared at him and started to object, but the pastor gave her a stern look. "Patty I don't want to hear any excuses."

She gave Arthur, a weak smile, he thought it was a smile of approval. "I'll pick you up at your house at 7 p.m.?" Patty didn't answer.

When Arthur walked away, Pastor Markus took Patty's hand. "He is a perfect gentleman and he will make a good husband."

"I don't want to go out with him."

"Now, now Patty, you should never be too busy to find a husband. You'll like him once you get to know him."

After their first date, Patty found they had very little in common. Then, he asked her out again and she refused.

On Sunday, Arthur asked Patty to go to dinner with him. Pastor Markus stood nearby and made sure she accepted.

Pastor Markus made sure he was close by every time Arthur asked her out. After several months, Arthur made a point to sit next to Patty at church.

When it was over, he said, "Patty, stay a minute I want to talk to you."

Pastor Markus walked over and stood behind them. Whenever the pastor was near she felt nervous and even more so now. "Oh my," she thought, "the pastors behind me, Arthur's up to something."

"What does this moron want now," she thought. I can't stand to even look at him.

"Patty, we have been going out for two months and I would like you to become my wife."

"No Arthur. I can't marry you." She got up and started walking towards the door.

Pastor Markus took her by the arm. "I'd like you to come to my office; I want to talk to you."

"What's the matter?" When he didn't answer she followed him to his office.

Pastor Markus shut the door and sat at his desk and stared at her for a moment. He placed his hands flat on the desk as he said, "I understand Arthur has asked you to marry him."

"Yes, he did, but I can't marry him."

"Why not? He's a God fearing honest man."

"Because I don't love him."

Pastor Markus slapped the desk with his palm. "You will learn to love him." He drummed his fingers on the desk and stared at her. "God put us on this earth to marry and multiply and you will marry him."

Patty started to cry. "Please Pastor Markus, don't make me marry him."

"Now, now don't cry. You're twenty-one; this may be your last chance to get married. Now tell me you'll do it."

"I don't want to marry him. How can you make me marry someone I don't love?"

He stared at her and shook his head. "That's not the right answer."

Patty hung her head. "But I don't." The pastor banged the desk with his fist. "I am your pastor and you'll do as I say."

Patty jumped when he banged the desk and started to cry. "All right I'll marry him, but only because you're forcing me too."

"Good, good. At Tuesday night service I'll make the announcement that you and Arthur will be married in two weeks."

Patty jumped up from her chair. "Two weeks, that's too soon."

Pastor Markus held her by her shoulders and stared into her eyes. "I said, two weeks from today."

---

The congregation attended the wedding and Patty cried as the pastor said, "I now pronounce you man and wife."

Married to a man she disliked, she refused to sleep with him on their wedding night. The next morning she put her black medical bag in her car and went off to work.

Jennifer had just swept the front porch when Patty pulled into her driveway. She recognized her from church, but didn't know her very well. "Hello Patty, what a pleasant surprise."

"Pastor Markus asked me to stop by. I understand you're three months pregnant."

"You're the midwife? You're so young!"

"I may look young, but I've had many years of experience." Patty reached in the car for her bag. "Can we go inside; I'd like to ask you a few questions before I examine you."

"Yes, come in." They sat in the parlor talking, and then went up to the bedroom. She felt uncomfortable with such a young woman and took her time undressing.

"Was your last delivery normal?" asked Patty

"The last birth was breech; I hope this one is a normal."

When the examination was over, Patty said, "You're in fine shape, I don't see any problem so far."

"You're very gentle. I felt uncomfortable with you at first, but I feel better now."

Patty closed her bag. "I've been doing this for a long time." They started walking down the steps. "I'll be back in a month. Here's my telephone number if you need me."

Jennifer still felt uneasy with having a midwife and decided to make an appointment with Doctor Forman.

"My husband has forbidden me to see you and has engaged a midwife for me."

"I'm sorry to hear that. I've delivered all your children, but there's not much I can do under the circumstance."

"I'm worried I'll have another difficult birth. How can I be sure Patty knows how to handle the situation, if it becomes critical?"

"There isn't any way of knowing ahead of time. You could ask around at the congregation and see if anyone had a breech delivery with her help."

"I really want you to deliver the baby."

"Jennifer, I can't go against your husband's wishes. If there is the least bit of concern, have Nellie call me."

The months dragged on and the children were excited about the new baby. Her life was like a nightmare. Going to church two nights a week and twice on Sunday's. Jennifer felt over powered by the heavy burden. She had given up fighting over religion. In body only she went to the services, her mind and soul was still catholic. Each Wednesday, she snuck off to mass and talked to Father Donahue, then felt some peace.

Jennifer was in her ninth month, her stomach was so big, it was hard to lie flat. She fluffed her pillows and sat up against them. She couldn't sleep and as soon as it was daylight she went downstairs to get something to eat. The aroma of the coffee spread through the house and Bill came down yawning.

"What are you doing up so early?"

"I couldn't sleep. Would you like some eggs?"

"Sure, make me two."

Jennifer placed the eggs on the table and took a few bites of her breakfast. "Nothing tastes good to me anymore."

She began clearing the table and Bill said, "Why don't you sit down and relax. Have a cup of coffee with me?"

"I feel better standing." Jennifer walked to the sink and started to wash the dishes. A sharp pain made her cry out.

Bill jumped up. "What's the matter?"

Jennifer hobbled to a chair. "The baby's coming, call Patty and Nellie now." Another sharp pain went through her body and she cried out, "Please get Patty."

Nellie and William came over right away. "Let me help you upstairs so you can lie down."

Margaret came running from her room. "What's happening? Is the baby coming?"

William huddled the children together. "Yes, your mama's ready to have the baby. Come with me, I'll take you to my house."

Patty went directly to Jennifer's room. Nellie was undressing Jennifer. "I'll do that while you get the towels and hot water."

Jennifer screamed. "I can't stand the pain."

Bill held her hand. "Put your pain in God's hands. He will help you through this."

With each pain she squeezed his hand as she pleaded, "Please call Doctor Forman."

"Calm down, Patty and God will handle everything." Bill walked to the other side of the room and watched Patty's every move.

Nellie wiped Jennifer's forehead and held her hand. "Breathe deeply, dear."

With each pain, she screamed and her fingernails dug into Nellie's hand. "It hurts too much, I can't take it anymore."

Nellie saw how Jennifer was suffering. "Bill, you have to call Doctor Forman." She grabbed his arm. Remember the agony she went through with the last breech birth? Well this is worse. Call him now."

"No. Stay out of this, Mother. God will take care of her." Bill got down on his knees and prayed.

Patty checked the dilation after each pain and whispered to Nellie, "The baby is coming out bottom first. I'm going to try and turn it." After several hours Patty said. "The baby won't budge and the vagina wall is tearing."

Jennifer let out a scream, her body arched upward. "Please get Doctor Forman, please."

Nellie felt helpless as she wiped the sweat from Jennifer's face, "It will soon be over"

After twelve agonizing hours, they heard Patty say, "Here he comes, it's a beautiful baby boy." Jennifer passed out from exhaustion and Patty smacked the infant's tiny bottom, waiting for his first cry.

The baby lay limp in her arms. "The baby is not breathing."

"Oh no," cried Nellie. She took the baby and felt for a heartbeat. "Dam you Bill, it's your fault, this child is dead. You should have called Doctor Forman; he would have saved the baby."

Bill put his head in his hands and sobbed, "Mother, God took our child because it wasn't time for him to leave the Lord's care." Then he got down on his knees and prayed.

Patty looked up to the heavens. "Amen, the Lord wasn't ready to let him go. He's up there sitting alongside of God."

Nellie felt numb as she said, "I hope you can live with yourself. You'll have your dead son on your conscious for the rest of your life." She walked out of the room.

Jennifer slept all day and woke up feeling groggy; her lips were parched and dry. When she tried to get up, Patty rushed over. "Don't get out of bed, you're too weak."

"I have to go to the bathroom."

Patty reached under the bed and brought out a flat pan. "Use this today, tomorrow you'll feel stronger."

Jennifer's lips stuck together as she asked, "Did I have a boy?"

Patty poured a glass of water. "Drink this; it will moisten your mouth."

Jennifer took a sip. "Let me hold my baby." Patty didn't answer and Jennifer said, "Will you please bring me my baby."

Patty fixed the sheets on her bed. "You need to rest."

"I want to see my baby now!"

Bill heard Jennifer and rushed up the steps. "Hi, Babe, how are you feeling?" He sat on the side of the bed and put his arm around her.

"Why won't Patty bring me my baby?"

Bill hesitated, then tightened his grip on her shoulder. "Our baby went back to heaven with God. The Lord wanted him to stay in heaven a little longer."

Jennifer stared at him. "What are you saying?" Bill rubbed her back, but didn't answer.

Her mouth quivered, "You're saying my baby is dead?" Heavy sobs retched through her body and Bill leaned over to comfort her. "Don't touch me. You let my baby die. You should have called Doctor Forman."

"Here's some hot tea, it will make you feel better," said Patty.

Jennifer pushed it away. "My baby is dead because you wouldn't let me have my doctor."

Bill looked at Patty and said, "I'm worn out and need some sleep."

Patty sat on the side of Jennifer's bed and said, "Sometimes the Lord does things that are hard to understand."

Jennifer pushed her away. "I don't want to hear it."

"Listen to me, he has good reasons for what he does, please have faith."

"What kind of God gives a mother a child, then takes it away?" Jennifer's sorrow felt like a huge painful knot.

"The Lord giveth and taketh away. Just have faith in him. Let's pray." She knelt down by Jennifer's bed and reached for her hand. "Dear Lord, have mercy on this mother."

Jennifer yanked her hand away and screamed drowning out Patty's voice. "Get out, get out, I don't want you here."

Patty left as she continued to pray, "Guide and help her find, through this sadness."

———————————

Jennifer stayed in her bedroom, refusing to eat. "I lost my baby. Maybe it's because I said I didn't want it. Maybe that's why God took him." She clutched the rosary beads and rocked back and forth in her chair.

Nellie knocked on her door. "I need to talk to you about your children."

"My children, I completely forgot them!" whispered Jennifer. "Come in."

Nellie opened the door. "It's so dark in here, let me open the shades." The sunshine brightened the room and Nellie gasped. "You're so pale and thin." She rushed over and hugged her. "You've got to eat and get your strength back."

Jennifer rocked harder in the chair. "I feel horrible!"

"I know you do, honey, you had a tough delivery. Patty did everything possible to save the baby. The struggle was just too much for him."

"If Doctor Forman had been with me, he would have saved my baby."

"Maybe. Maybe not. I talked to Doctor and he said breech births are very hard on the baby." Nellie stroked Jennifer's hand. "I described the way Patty handled the delivery and he said she did everything right. The only thing he could have done was give you something for the pain."

"Yes, that would have helped a lot. He also would have cut me to help the baby." She stopped rocking. "I would have named him Francis after my father."

"I'm sorry for the agony you've been through, but you have to snap out of it. Your children miss you."

Jennifer wiped her nose; her voice was husk. "I miss them and love them so much."

"Caroline and Maggie have been stopping by to see you. Maybe you should call them."

"I can't call Caroline, Mother might answer the phone. I'll call Maggie."

---

A week later Bill sat next to Jennifer and said, "I think you're well enough to start going to church with the family."

"I don't want to go."

"You need to get out of the house. The fresh air will do you good."

"I'll take walks."

Margaret and Cassie sat on the bed. "Please Mom, we want you with us."

---

Sunday night Jennifer and the children waited for Bill at the back of the church. Pastor Markus stood at a distance watching her, then walked over. Glad to see you, Mrs. Rennie. You have your slender figure back."

"Thank you Pastor Markus," she said turning away from him.

"I'd like to talk to you. Could you come to my office?"

Jennifer pointed towards Bill. "I'm waiting for my husband,"

Pastor Markus gripped her arm. "Come with me. Bill's busy right now. The children can sit in the back pew and wait for you." She tried to pull away, but he led her to his office and shut the door. Jennifer sat in the chair by his desk. He sat across from her and adjusted his tie as his eyes stared at her modestly low neckline.

Jennifer placed her hand across the top of her dress. "Why did you bring me in here?"

Pastor Markus sat back in his chair and cleared his throat. "I'm glad you're feeling better."

"Thank you. I believe you wanted to talk?" He didn't answer. "Why did you pull me in here?"

"Well," Pastor Markus cleared his throat again. "When you come to church you..." He leaned forward placing his hands on his desk. "You stand out from the other woman of the congregation."

Jennifer leaned toward the desk. "Stand out! I don't know what you mean?"

He cleared his throat again. "The dresses you wear are flamboyant, sometimes a bit low at the neckline." His eyes gaped at her bosom. "It would be more lady-like if you wore plainer dresses in muted colors." He picked up a pencil and tapped it on his desk.

Jennifer deliberately leaned over his desk. Pastor Markus's eyes bulged as he saw the swell of Jennifer's breast so close.

She stared straight into his eyes and poked her finger at his chest. "Don't you ever tell me how to dress. I come to your church for the sake of my marriage. I will never allow you to tell me what I can wear." She stomped to the door, then turned. "I want you to stop staring at me with your evil eyes. If you have something to say to me, tell it to the Lord." She slammed the door and went to join her children.

As she walked to the back of the church she looked at the other woman in black and gray shapeless dresses, with white collars. The fabric had tiny obscure flowers of muted colors. Every woman wore black stockings with flat, black shoes. She couldn't picture herself dressed like that. But with the little money Bill made, she couldn't afford nice clothes.

Bill walked up to her. "What did Pastor Markus want?"

"He wanted to know how I was feeling. Jennifer smiled, she was not going to discuss it. Bill picked Joseph up and said, "He's such a caring man."

# Chapter Ten

Jennifer wasn't happy with her new life, but for the children's sake she abided by her husband's wishes. She kept her peace of mind by going to mass during the week. She felt better when she discussed her feelings with Father Donahue. She always picked a day when she knew Bill would be busy at church. Nellie stood by as an alibi if needed. Nellie and William kept them fresh vegetables, milk and eggs, and Bill brought home just enough money to get by.

The next day she was ironing the children's clothes and thought back at a time when money was not an issue. Growing up her family was wealthy and she had everything. Now, she thought, we barely make ends meet. She longed for the good days. Bill was reading his Bible by the fireplace, making notes for Sunday's service.

Jennifer looked at the shirt she was ironing and said, "This is too small for Joseph."

Bill looked up. "Did you say something?"

"I said Joseph's shirt is too small for him. The children are growing out of their clothes, and we don't have the money to buy new ones."

"Maybe my mother could teach you to sew."

"It still would cost money for materials and patterns."

"But a lot less. Go ask her."

When Jennifer went into Nellie's kitchen, she could smell the apple pie in the oven. The sweet aroma filled the air. "Hmm, that smells good."

Nellie wiped her floury hands on her apron. "Thanks. What's up?"

"The children are growing out of their clothes and I'd like you to teach me to sew."

"Do you want to go to town now and get some patterns and material?"

"I don't have the money right now. Can you show me on some old things you have?"

"Sure, come into the living room, I'll set up the machine."

Before I was married the seamstress was teaching me, until mother found out. She said, "Young ladies of means didn't do that kind of work."

Nellie showed her how to peddle the machine, thread the needle and wind the bobbin.

Jennifer was good at sewing straight lines. She practiced every day and was making progress.

Two weeks later a church member, Mr. Frazer, stopped by the house. Jennifer answered the door. "What a pleasant surprise, won't you come in?"

"Only got a minute. Pastor Rennie said you were looking for a sewing machine? I want to offer you my late wife's machine."

"How kind of you, how much do you want for it?"

"Not a cent. It's been sitting in our garage since Myrtle died, two years ago. I'm sure it still works, might need a little oiling."

"Thank you so much. Are you sure you won't come in?"

"No, I have an errand to do." Mr. Frazier pointed to his car. "It's right in the trunk; can your husband help me?"

"He's not home, but I can help you."

When the machine was inside, Jennifer thanked him again and when he left she danced with joy. Quickly, she dusted the mahogany stand and polished the shiny steel wheel. "Now, I'll see if it works." Jennifer placed a dress that had a rip seam, under the needle and put her feet on the wide iron peddle. As she worked her feet up and down, the needle moved. "It works! It really works." Jennifer sewed the seam shut and felt happy. "Now, if I could afford some material."

When Nellie came over she was surprised. "The machines almost new. Where did you get it?"

Jennifer told her, then said, "Look, I repaired some of the children's clothes."

Nellie inspected them. "You've only been at this for two weeks and you're sewing like a professional. It's time to buy some patterns and material."

"We have to wait until Bill gets paid, maybe I can buy it then."

Francis stopped by the next day at lunch. He didn't like to come when Bill was home. Jennifer fixed him something to eat and they sat talking.

"How are things going for you?"

"I'm holding up, but it's hard. I sneak to mass whenever I can for peace of mind."

"I know, Father Donahue told me. You know you and the children could come live with me."

"Thanks Dad, but I hate to separate the children from him. They do love him."

"I know, but look what you're going through. I don't know how you make it on his salary."

"The children have adjusted; I'm the one that can't. I'm trying to keep the family together"

"Well, if I can help let me know. Time for me to get back to the old grind." He took her hand and placed a fifty dollar bill in it. "I love you daughter."

"Daddy, you don't have to do this."

"I want to. Go buy yourself something nice," he said, as he left.

Nellie and Jennifer went shopping the next day and bought patterns and material. Bill never inquired where she got the money; his mind was on the church.

Nellie taught her how to cut out a dress with the pattern and how to sew the dress together.

Jennifer caught on quickly and soon was able to make clothes for the children. A few days later, Nellie came to see how Jennifer was doing.

"Look at the children's clothes I made."

Nellie examined them. "These are well made; your work is beautiful."

When I finish making the children clothes, I'm going to make something for myself."

We didn't buy a dress pattern for you?"

"I'm going to copy one of my dresses and make a few adjustments, to stay fashionable. I don't care if Pastor Markus likes it or not."

Nellie patted Jennifer on the back. "That's the spirit. Don't let the old buzzard get to you."

Jennifer closed the sewing machine. "It's time to make dinner, want to stay? I'm making welsh rarebit. It's a quick meal and the children love it."

"No, I already have dinner simmering. See you tomorrow."

After supper she cleared the table. "Margaret, you and Cassie do the dishes. I want to finish the dress I'm making for you."

Bill heard a car pull into the driveway and looked out of the window. He scratched his head. "I don't recognize the car; I wonder who it could be?" They walked out on the porch.

A strange man and woman got out of the car, then the back door opened. Pastor Markus climbed out.

"Pastor Markus is something the matter?" asked Bill.

"Not at all, I just wanted you to meet Reverend Austin Carter and his wife. They're with an organization called Missionaries of Christ."

Bill reached out and shook the reverend's thick callused hand. "I'm pleased to meet you."

Jennifer led them into the parlor. "Please have a seat."

Pastor Markus sat in the overstuffed chair and put his feet on the footstool. "I'll let Reverend Carter do the talking."

Reverend Carter sat on the couch, his back ram rod straight and his head tilted up. "I understand you have been with the Saviors Church for three years."

"That's right," said Bill.

"I've heard good things about you and your wife."

"Thank you." Bill was not sure where he was heading.

Reverend Carter crossed his legs. "We're looking for a couple to go to Colombia, South America. To replace the missionaries that are there now."

Bill's brows wrinkled with interest. "Where in Columbia?"

"The area is called Cartagena. Pastor and Mrs. Ryan are there now. He has made great progress befriending the tribe. You see, the Kogi Indians live in the jungle outside of Cartagena, they were hostile and rejected outsiders."

Jennifer interrupted Reverend Carter. "Excuse me, Reverend Carter. Would you and your wife like a cup of tea?"

Pastor Markus spoke up, "I'm sure they would and I'll take a cup too."

Jennifer stared at him and thought, "I wasn't talking to you."

Nellie walked in and interrupted her thoughts. "I'll make the tea."

Reverend Carter continued, "The Ryan's have taught the natives to read, write and speak English and of course their main objective is to turn the heathens into Christians."

Nellie served the tea in Jennifer's finest porcelain cups, along with homemade cookies. She whispered to Jennifer, "I'll tuck the children in bed and let them know you're busy."

Jennifer looked over at Reverend Carter. "Why are they leaving?"

Pastor Markus leaned forward. "They've been there for five years and it's time for them to come home."

Bill's face lit up like a bright candle. "It sounds like a wonderful opportunity."

Jennifer was startled by Bill's remark and the blood drained from her face. She nudged Bill. "Let's not make any quick decisions."

Reverend Carter continued, "The Kogi tribe live in Cartagena, Columbia, in the jungle. Far away from civilization. They were poor and completely illiterate. They knew nothing about Christianity until the Ryan's arrived. Now they are educated in the word of God."

Pastor Markus stood up and held his hands out. "We need to continue to save those souls, baptize them into the light of God!"

Reverend Carter gave him a stern look, then smiled at Bill and Jennifer. "We'd like you and your family to go to Colombia. Take over where the Ryan's left off." Reverend Carter sipped his tea. "How old are your children?"

"Margaret's seven, Cassie's five and Joseph's three," answered Jennifer.

"Good ages, they'll be able to adapt quickly to the new way of life."

Bill smiled. "As I said before, it sounds like a great opportunity."

"It is. Take advantage of it my friend," said Pastor Markus.

"Of course, if you decide to go, we would expect you to stay for five years," said Reverend Carter.

"Five years!" Jennifer glanced at Bill.

"Of course, we would train you. Pay all your expenses."

Jennifer smiled at Mrs. Carter. "What do you think? Would you go to Columbia?"

She started to answer, but Reverend Carter interrupted. "It's never been offered to us."

Mrs. Carter bit her lip and said, "Our job is to recruit people." She sat quietly, staring at the pictures on the wall. Crossing and uncrossing her ankles.

Jennifer wanted some input from her. "Would you take your children to Colombia?"

Mr. Carter touched his wife's hand. "We are not blessed with children, so we can't say."

Jennifer watched Mrs. Carter squirm in her seat and thought, "What's the matter with her? Isn't she allowed to speak for herself? I can see she's upset." As she listened to the men, she became increasingly uneasy with Bill's excitement.

"Where would we live?" asked Bill.

"You would live in the small cabin that Pastor Ryan and his wife lived in. It has the basic needs."

Pastor Markus stood up again and waved his hands in the air like a Shakespearean actor.

"What a wondrous feeling it must be to be able to help such ignorant people."

Jennifer stifled a laugh. "There goes Markus showing off," she thought. Then she asked,

"Pastor Markus, if you think it's so wonderful why don't you go?"

Bill looked at her then said, "Jennifer, please be quite and listen."

Pastor Markus cleared his throat. "I'm needed here to build the faith of my congregation."

Jennifer smiled. "I see." She wished he would go. She'd love to get rid of him.

Reverend Carter looked over at Jennifer. "I understand you were a nurse."

"I am a nurse, but I haven't worked for years."

"Think of the help you could give the Kogis." He stared at her so long she had to look away. "With your knowledge of healing and God's blessings, you would be a miracle to the people."

Jennifer sat quietly keeping her eyes away from Reverend Carter's. She wasn't going to commit to anything. Bill on the other hand felt so fascinated by the idea. He couldn't sit still and paced the floor.

"How would we get food and personal things we need?" asked Bill.

"A freighter comes into Cartagena once a month and would bring any supplies you requested. A man named Pedro works at the shipyard and will deliver everything to the mission."

"Well, what do you think?" asked Pastor Markus as he focused on Jennifer. His cold eyes stared at her and she glared back defiantly, as he continued, "Bill, it would be a great opportunity for you to preach the word of God. To see the world. Think of the education your children would get."

Bill looked at Jennifer and saw the deep concern in her eyes. "Thank you Reverend Carter for enlightening us. We'll talk it over. It entails a lot of changes and not an easy decision."

"Of course." He stood up and shook Bill's hand. "Here is my card. Talk it over and get back to me."

Bill walked them to the door and when he came back he said, "What do you think?"

She closed her eyes and put her hands over her ears. "I don't want to discuss it now, I've heard enough for tonight." She walked wearily to the steps. "I'm going to check on the children, then go to bed."

---

Jennifer woke up at 5 a.m. in the morning and couldn't go back to sleep. She tossed and turned thinking about the conversation with Reverend Carter. We'd have to live in the jungle for five years. In a small wooden house with bugs and animals all around. What diseases would the children pick up? She turned on her side and tried to sleep. The thought of the poor Kogis and the good she could do for them ran through her mind. I wouldn't have to have crazy Markus, staring down the front of my dress. She laughed and kicked back the covers and propped up her pillow. It would be a challenge, but she could practice her nursing skills. She sat on the edge of the bed as another idea came to her. It would be a great learning experience for the children. She could tutor them along with the native children.

Bill woke up from all the movement. "What's got you up so early?"

"I've been thinking about Colombia. Maybe we could go, but what would we do with our house?"

He sat up. "The house, you mean all you're worried about is the house?"

"I love our house and don't want to sell it."

"You mean you really want to go?"

"I've never been outside of Pittsburgh. It would be a great adventure."

"If you really want to go, mom and dad could rent it until we returned. I can't believe you're willing to do this."

Wrinkling her nose, she said, "I'd like it better than going to the Savior's Church four times a week. I wouldn't have to see Markus either."

"I wasn't going to pressure you into this. Are you sure?"

Jennifer said firmly, "Yes, I'd like to try it."

"Hey, there's no trying. Once we make a commitment, we're stuck for five years."

She mulled the decision over in her mind before replying, "I still want to do it."

Bill clapped his hands. "That's great. I'll call Reverend Carter and give him the good news."

Reverend Carter was pleased with their decision and scheduled their training. He gave them a list of things they should take. Now, it was time to tell their parents. They went over to the farmhouse and Bill said, "Mom, Dad, sit down, we have something to tell you."

"Jennifer, you're not pregnant again, are you?" asked Nellie.

"No, but it's important. We're going to Colombia, South America, to do missionary work."

William gasped. "What are you crazy? I hear people are killing each other over there."

"Don't do this," pleaded Nellie. "It's so far away from home. You don't know what it's like."

"Don't try to talk us out of it," said Bill.

"At least leave the children with us," said Nellie. "You don't know what diseases they'll get."

"No, they're coming with us. We will be doing the Lords work and he will take care of us," said Bill.

Nellie grabbed Jennifer's arm. "I know you don't want to go. Stay here with the children."

"Actually it was my idea. Bill isn't forcing me to go."

---

Jennifer was sure this is what she wanted, but there was still something nagging at the back of her mind. After she attended mass on Wednesday she met Father Donahue in the rectory. "Are you sure this is what you really want to do. Are you sure?"

"Father, my whole life has changed in these past few years. I am so tired of being force to go to the Savors church against my will. I'm tired of sneaking the children to catechism each week; I can't see my old friends. Nothings the same. I feel like a prisoner. I need a change."

"But you'll be living in a strange country in the jungle for five years. You know nothing about the living conditions. Doesn't that frighten you?"

"It does in some ways, but I also look at it as an adventure. I know it will be a different way of life, but I'll be helping the poor Indians. I can use my nursing skills to heal them and I'll feel free again."

"Then you must go. God will guide you and I'll pray for your safety. Maybe this will change Bill's way of thinking."

Jennifer went home feeling peaceful; she knew it was the right thing to do. As she looked at the list of items that they needed to take, the door-bell rang. Jennifer opened the door and gasped. "Mother, what are you doing here?"

Freda pushed past her and looked around the parlor. "Nice house your father bought you. That good for nothing husband of yours couldn't scrape two nickels together. I told you not to marry him, but you wouldn't listen. He's cast away his religion, and forced you to change yours. Now he's taking you away to be killed by the wild Indians."

"How did you find out so fast?"

"It's a small town, Jennifer. Everyone knows. I won't allow you to take my grandchildren into such a wild area. You will leave them with me."

"I would never let you raise my children with your hateful ways."

"Jennifer, I'll not let you take my grandchildren out of the country."

"Save your breath, Mother. You haven't talked to me in years and now you want to take my children? It will never happen."

"I forbid you to take them. I won't allow it."

"You should have come years ago and enjoyed the children. But no! You had to be stubborn. Jennifer pushed her toward the door, "Get out of my house."

Freda shouted, "I'll be back with the police. I'll have you arrested for child cruelty."

Jennifer slammed the door and stood against the wall; her body trembled. "How did she find out? I haven't even had a chance to tell Caroline and daddy?"

# Chapter Eleven

Jennifer closed the suitcase. "We've spent three months preparing for this adventure and now we are ready to go."

Bill sealed the box he was packing and put his arms around her. "Are you excited about going?"

"Yes I am. I'm nervous too. The children know we are moving, but they don't know where."

"We'll tell them this afternoon," said Bill.

When Margaret and Cassie came home from school, Bill sat the three of them on the sofa. "Children, you know we are moving, but we haven't told you where."

Margaret said, "We were afraid to ask. We thought you would get mad at us."

"I'm sorry I've made you feel that way. From now on you can ask me anything you want," said Bill. We are going to a place far away where there are monkeys and many different animal. We'll live in a beautiful wooded area where there are waterfalls and ponds to swim in."

"That sounds like fun," said Cassie.

"Can I play with the monkeys?" asked Joseph.

"It will be fun. A whole new way of living," said Jennifer.

"But what about school and my friends," asked Margaret?

"Your mother will teach you and all the other children there," said Bill.

Cassie and Joseph liked the idea. Margaret was a little unsure. "Suppose we don't like it?"

"Margaret, don't you worry about a thing. You will like it, I promise," said Bill. "Why don't you go out and play now?"

Jennifer started packing; she knew it would be warm there, so she took only their summer clothes. As she folded one of her dresses, she said, "I'm glad we took the Spanish course. It wasn't as hard as I thought it would be."

Bill laughed, "*Usted exacto Senorita.*"

"Senior, *usted habla* Spanish."

"I hope we said it right. Oh well, it's good to practice. I do feel better since I talked to other missionaries. They seemed to enjoy the experience." Bill patted his pocket. "I've got our documents and customs regulations. I think we have everything?"

Reverend Carter and his wife came over and checked the list of things they should take. The reverend looked over the page. "Did you pack light clothing? The jungle is hot and humid.

"Yes we have plenty of light loose clothes," said Jennifer.

"How about mosquito netting? The long rainy seasons bring lots of insects."

Mrs. Carter spoke up, "Pack plenty of toilet articles. I hear they are hard to find."

Bill checked each thing off the list. "Yep, we have plenty. I'll send you a list of what we need when we start running out."

"I have your one way tickets. They gave us a discount. You will be giving church services to the crew."     "Why only one way?" asked Bill.

"When you're staying that long, they only book one way on these tramp freighters. When your time is up, we'll pay for your return ticket and notify you of the date of return. We never know what freighter we can get. A lot of them don't take passengers."

"Oh I see, hmm, I guess you know what you're doing," said Bill.

"Oh, we do. I'll send enough supplies with you to last six months. You can give me your personal list and the freighter will deliver it every three months," said Reverend Carter. "There are no telephones, so you'll have to telegraph us for anything special."

---

On March 15, 1925, they were ready to travel. Caroline and Francis came to house to say goodbye. "You're leaving and we have no idea when we'll see you again," said Caroline.

"I'm going to miss you both," said Jennifer.

"I heard about Freda coming over," said Francis. "She has a lot of guts thinking she could take the children."

"When I saw her, I was shocked. I was hoping we could make up before I left."

William walked in. "Hi Francis. I guess you're as upset with these two as we are."

"Don't start," said Bill. "We're leaving on the freighter today and that's it."

The children were dressed and ready to go. Margaret ran up to Caroline. "We're getting on a big ship and sailing across the ocean."

Nellie came in with a package, and gave it to Margaret. "I brought you some goodies to eat on the ship."

"Thanks, grandma. Do you know we're going to live in the jungle?"

"Yes. You be careful. Nellie tried to hold back the tears as she hugged Joseph. "I'm going to miss you so much." She put her arms around Jennifer. "I don't want you to go."

William picked up a piece of their luggage and said, "The rest of the luggage is in my truck. Cassie, you and Joseph can ride with me."

Nellie took Margaret's hand. "You and your mom and dad will come in my car."

"We'll meet you there," said Francis. "I have to pick up Maggie. She wants to say goodbye."

———————————

They stood on the dock at the port in Philadelphia, looking for their ship. "It's a freighter called the Everex," said Bill.

There's your ship on dock four," said William. "It looks like a rusty bucket of bolts to me."

"It does need a paint job," said Jennifer.

William and Bill unloaded the truck, and then looked for Reverend Carter. "I see his car coming, and there's a truck following him," said Bill.

"I'm a nervous wreck thinking about you and the children in the jungles," said Nellie.

"We'll be fine. It's so exciting," said Jennifer.

When the reverend arrived, they shook hands. "I see you're ready to go. My men will load your supplies at the edge of the gangplank. The crew will carry them on."

Francis's car drove up and Maggie jumped out. "Jennifer, we were afraid we'd miss you. Maybe I should go with you. I could use a good vacation."

Jennifer laughed. "I'm not sure what we're getting into, but I'll let you know. Maybe you can visit."

"Yeah sure. I couldn't afford it. Take good care of yourself and write to me."

Caroline wiped her tears. "Take care of those little ones." She blew her nose and grabbed Jennifer. "I'll miss you."

Francis couldn't look at Bill. He pulled Jennifer away from the group. "I love you daughter. I'll never forgive Bill for what he did to you. Now, he's dragging you off on a fool's mission."

"Daddy, he's not making me do this, I wanted to go. With my nursing skills, I can help the poor natives." She put her arms around his neck and kissed his cheek. "I love you daddy and I will miss you so much."

"I'll miss you too sweetheart, please be careful."

Once on board, tears and kisses filled the air. Bill and Jennifer waved from the railing and the children jumped up and down, shouting goodbyes.

"This is frightening," said Jennifer. "Leaving our family and sailing across the ocean. I hope the weather is good?"

"Look at the sky, Babe. There isn't a cloud anywhere and the seas are calm."

The ship sailed out of the harbor and Jennifer looked out over the vast expanse and thought, "I wonder what my future holds? Will I really be able to handle this?"

She took Bill's hand and said, "We're not used to the sea, we've lived inland all our lives."

"Don't worry, you'll be safe. Let's go look at our staterooms."

Bill held the heavy door open and the family walked to the deck below. "I asked the captain to put the children in a room next to us."

Jennifer laughed when she saw their stateroom. "It's rather small and dark, if I stretch my arms out I can touch both sides of the room. Look how skinny the single beds are."

"I want to see my room," said Cassie.

They went next door to the children's quarters; the room was the same size but had a single bed and a bunk bed.

"Wow look at the bunk bed," said Joseph. He climbed to the top bunk. "This is mine."

Margaret sat on the single bed. "I don't want to be in the same room with them. I want my own room."

"Stop complaining and unpack," said Bill.

They had just finished putting all their things away, when the dinner bell rang and a crewman was waiting outside their doors. "You'll be eating with the captain and officers. I'll escort you."

When they walked into the dining room, Captain Morrison said, "Welcome aboard. Hope you're hungry? The food's good and there's plenty of it."

The Captain introduced himself and the officers to the family, then passed a large crock of beef stew. Bill served Jennifer and the children, then passed it to the officers. The men finished the dish and ordered more, eating like it was their last meal.

The family ate slow, as Jennifer whispered to Bill, "I wonder what kind of meat this is. It has a funny taste."

"I can assure you that it is beef," said the captain. "We have to salt and season our meat to keep it fresh on the long voyage."

"I'm very sorry," said Jennifer.

Captain Morrison smiled. "As you can see my men love it."

The children ate half of their meal and Margaret said, "Can we please be excused?"

"Don't you want desert?" asked one of the officers.

The galley door opened. The cook came in with vanilla cake with chocolate syrup on top.

"Wow. That looks good. Yeah, we want some," said Joseph.

After dinner Bill thanked the Captain. "We really enjoyed the meal."

The Captain smiled and shook Bills hand. "Tomorrow morning at 9 a.m. bells, I'd like to show you where the chapel is."

"Okay. I'll meet you here."

"Come children, we're going to take a walk on the deck," said Jennifer.

They walked along the deck, their path brightened by the moon gleaming down. Jennifer sighed, "My, it's a beautiful night. The stars stand out like diamonds in the sky. If the weather stays this calm, the trip will be a pleasure."

The waves splashed against the ship, sending a mist of salt water in the air. Bill breathed deeply, then sneezed. "It's so fresh and clean; it tickles my nose."

They sat in the deck chairs with light blankets over them, listening to the waves, while the children ran around the deck, playing hide and seek.

Bill yawned. "This salt air is getting me sleepy. I think I'll head to bed."

"Good idea," said Jennifer. "Help me round the children up and we'll all go down."

---

In the morning, the captain showed Bill a small room with fifteen seats. "This is where you'll hold church services on Sunday's. Also, this is where you can talk to the men if they are troubled."

"Is there a light switch? It seems dark in here."

"This use to be a storage room, there's no electricity in here. We light lanterns."

"What time do you want me to start on Sunday?"

"Well, the crew has chores early morning, so 11 a.m. would be good. Now, I have to get back to the helm. I'll see you later, if you have any questions."

Bill walked the deck, talking to the crew until Jennifer and the children came out.

"Are you ready for breakfast?" asked Jennifer.

When they entered the dining room, two large platters were brought in.

"Scrambled eggs, I love them," said Joseph digging in.

"Margaret, pass the sausage and potatoes," said Bill.

When they finished eating, they went on deck and sat in lounge chairs while the children played. Good weather continued through the week and the sun and salt air refreshed their spirits.

Jennifer stretched out on the lounge chair. "It's so relaxing, but it makes me feel sleepy"

"Don't get too relaxed. Remember the children have school work to do."

"I want them to get used to the ship first. I'll start on their studies this afternoon."

After lunch, she gathered the children together for their lessons.

"Do we have to? We wanted to play checkers with monk," said Margaret.

"Monk, who's Monk," asked Jennifer?

"He's one of the crew, he swabs the decks," said Joseph.

Jennifer laughed, "Swab the deck! You're talking like a sailor already." She handed out the books. "This will educate you better than checkers."

Dark clouds hovered over the ship and the wind became stronger, whipping the pages of the books. "Looks like a storm is coming," said Jennifer. "Let's go inside and study." Before they reached the door, the rain poured down and thunder rolled through the sky. "We'll study in your stateroom." Jennifer guided them down the hall. "The ship is bouncing around, so hold on to the rails. I don't want you to fall."

They studied all afternoon until the dinner bell rang. Holding on for dear life, they made it to the dining-room. Captain Morrison helped them to their seats.

"Please don't go out on the deck. We're expecting sixty knots winds," said the captain.

"I don't feel good," said Joseph holding his stomach.

The galley boy rushed over with a bucket. "Here lad, use this if you up-chuck."

The color drained from Jennifer's face. "Let's go back to our stateroom."

Bill helped them to their rooms and made sure they had water and buckets, then went back to the dining room. The weather didn't bother him. When he finished eating, he took tea and crackers back to his family. "Are you feeling any better?"

"No, the jarring motion is terrible." She pushed the tea away. "I can't hold anything down. Neither can the children."

He handed her a pill. "The ship's doctor said that this will make you feel better."

Surprised he was giving her a medication; she drank it down quickly. "Did you give the children some?"

"Yes, and I tucked them in."

Jennifer and the children stayed in their cabins, waiting for the weather to change. Bill came in the room every few hours to see how they were feeling.

Not wanting to use the word medicine, she said, "The pill helped a lot, but it makes me sleepy. How much longer can this weather go on? It's been five days."

"Captain Morrison said it should break by tomorrow." Jennifer was lying on the bed and Bill crawled in beside her. He rubbed her back as he said, "My poor Babe. I love you."

In the middle of the night, the seas calmed and the sun rose in a clear sky. The birds squawked loudly, circling the ship.

Bill woke Jennifer. "Look out the port hole, the sun is shining."

"Oh, it's so good to see the sun again." Jennifer dressed and went out on the deck. "It feels wonderful to be in the calm weather, feeling the warm sunshine." She sat in the lounge chair letting the gentle breeze fan her. After lunch, she held class for the children and two hours later she said, "Okay kids, you're done for the day."

"Good," said Cassie. "We want to play checkers with Monk."

Jennifer stood by the railing, looking out at the horizon, while Bill read his Bible.

"In the distance the ocean looks like it meets the sky," said Jennifer. "It's beautiful, but I'm tired of seeing nothing but water. We've been on board for three weeks and I feel bored and confined." She let out a deep breath and sat next to Bill. "Will we ever see land again?"

He smiled and took her hand. "We should see it soon."

Jennifer got up. "I'm going to walk around the deck for some exercise." She walked around twice, and then stood by the railing staring at the vast ocean. Her eyes spotted something dark. Jennifer held up her hand to shade her eyes. "I think I see something…I see land!" Jennifer ran back to Bill and the children and pointed her finger, "I see land over there."

Bill grabbed the binoculars from Monk. "Show me, I want to see it." He moved the binoculars around until he spied a small brown spot in the distance.

"Let me see," said Margaret trying to grab the binoculars.

They watched the land grow bigger as the ship sailed closer and Jennifer yelled, "Look there's a huge mountain."

"Is that snow on the top of it?" asked Bill.

Captain Morrison stood on the upper deck and called out, "Those are the Sierra Nevada Mountains." He joined them at the railing. "You'll always find snow on the top."

Margaret and Cassie felt excited and danced around the deck chanting, "We're getting off the boat. Yippee!"

"It will take three days before we reach land," said the captain.

"Will we really see monkeys and all kinds of pretty birds?" asked Joseph.

"Oh yes." The captain ruffled Joseph's hair. "There are lots of birds and animals for you to see."

"I can't wait to get on solid ground," said Jennifer. "I wonder who's going to pick us up."

Bill put his arm around her. "Don't worry, Reverend Carter said someone would be there."

As Colombia grew closer, the fragrance of flowers mingled in the salty air. "Everything is so green and vibrant," said Jennifer. She saw Bill staring into space. "Penny for your thoughts."

"I'm just wondering if I'll be able to communicate with the poor souls. I can't imagine what the church will look like." He hesitated before adding, "God will show me the way."

# Chapter Twelve

It was 5 a.m. in the morning when the ship docked in Cartagena. One of the largest ports in Colombia. It was already hot and muggy as they stood on the crowded dock watching hordes of people go by.

"This is complete chaos. I've never seen anything like it," said Bill.

Monk placed their luggage in front of them. "It's always like this in Cartagena."

When Bill was counting the luggage, a dark-skinned man grabbed one of the bags. Bill tried to pull it back and shouted, "Don't touch it. Someone's coming to meet us." The man couldn't understand what Bill said, but the tone of his voice made the man drop it. They stood guarding their luggage, as they scanned the crowd. "This is so frustrating," said Jennifer. "We have no idea who we're looking for."

The crew stacked the boxes of supplies next to them and Monk said, "Keep an eye on your things. Sometimes people want to borrow them."

"Borrow them?" Jennifer, raised her voice. "You mean steal them."

Monk laughed. "No, they feel they are borrowing them. They just forget to give them back."

The sun was brutal and they were hot and thirsty. Jennifer put her hat on to shade her face. "We've been waiting in this heat for two hours, what if no one comes?"

Sweat ran down Bill's face as he said, "Someone will be here." The children started to argue and he yelled, "Stop arguing over that piece of luggage. There's enough suitcases for each of you to sit on." Bill paced back and forth scanning the crowd. "This might be him." He pointed to a dark skinned man walking toward him.

The man's long, black hair was blowing in his face. He walked up to them brushing it aside and offered his hand. "*Buenos dias*, I am Eduardo. Are you Pastor and Mrs. Rennie?"

"That's right," said Bill, shaking the man's hand. "Boy, are we glad to see you."

He put his hand out to Jennifer and she brushed her hand against his. "We were beginning to think you forgot us." She could see large dirty sweat marks under the arms of his flowery shirt. The smell of body odor made was overpowering.

"I'm sorry I'm late, but my wagon broke down." He signaled to four men sitting nearby. "*Puede usted ayudarme lleve este mi equipaje mi carritos.*"

"What did he say, Mama?" asked Cassie.

"He asked those men to help with our luggage."

"Si," smiled Eduardo patting Cassie on the head. "You speak Spanish?"

"The children don't speak the language yet, but my wife and I do," said Bill.

Jennifer laughed. "We still have a lot to learn."

Eduardo picked up two suitcases and said, "Follow me."

A line of men also followed, each carrying two bags; others carried a box on their head.

"How far is the village?" asked Bill, trailing behind Eduardo.

"We are going to the Sierra Nevada de Santa Mari's area, it's a rough ride and takes mucho time."

Jennifer groaned, "Mucho time! How long is mucho time?"

"Maybe five hours."

He led them to a large wooden wagon with a tired old horse rigged to it. The animal whined as its tail swatted the black flies that buzzed around his rump. The men piled the luggage on the wagon, barely leaving room for the family.

"Children, sit up front with Eduardo, you'll be safer there," said Bill.

Bill pushed the boxes aside and helped Jennifer find a seat, then climbed in next to her. The dirty roads had large pot holes, and the wagon bounced hard, as the wooden wheels ran into each hole.

Jennifer wiggled around. "I can't get comfortable and my back side is hurting."

"This is taking too long," said Bill wiping the sweat from his brow. "I thought you said it would be five hours! It's almost seven."

Eduardo didn't answer. Ten minutes later the horse stopped in front of a dilapidated house on stilts. Trash was strewn everywhere.

"We're here," said Eduardo.

Bill's mouth dropped open. "This can't be it! Are you sure this is the right place?"

"Si, Senior. This is where Pastor Ryan lived."

Boxes were piled in front of Jennifer and she couldn't see the house. "Let me off this wagon." She let out a moan, "My bones ache from that dreadful ride." She looked at the house, and cringed. "This is nothing, but a shack!"

They walked closer and Bill said, "It doesn't look safe, the tree trunks are barely nailed together. I can see spaces between each log."

"What's that stuff on the roof?" asked Jennifer.

"It's dried palm leaves," said Eduardo. "Maybe a few missing, but I'll fix it."

Eight, five-foot narrow stilts held the house off the ground. Seven wooden, rickety steps lead to the porch.

Jennifer glanced up. "Good Gracious, there's holes in the porch floor!"

Cassie spotted two pigs sleeping underneath the house and ran toward them laughing. "I see pigs!" The animals scampered out squealing and heading right for her.

Jennifer screamed, "Bill, do something."

Eduardo pulled Cassie out of their way. "You're scared of pigs?"

"Cassie be careful" Bill said, as he stood back and examined the house. "The windows are only cuts in the walls. There's no glass or screens to keep the bugs out." He pointed at the door.

"It's nothing but a five-foot, oblong opening." A faded, flowered cloth hung across doorway, hanging in the breeze. They stood silently looking at the house, until a rustling sound diverted their attention.

"Look out! Pigs are coming back and there's a goat with them," said Eduardo. He pushed the children out of the way.

The animals stampeded toward them, chased by two mangy dogs. The children screamed as the animals ran under the house and out the other side.

Eduardo looked at the families expressions and laughed. "Hey, they won't hurt you."

Jennifer pulled the children close to her. "Not only is the house a wreck, but we have to contend with wild animals."

Eduardo looked disappointed. "It's a nice casa. Maybe needs a little work, but I'll fix it."

"You're right. It needs a little work to make it feel like home," said Bill in an unconvincing voice.

Jennifer wrinkled her forehead. "Are you kidding?" She walked to the back of the house and surveyed the grounds. "It looks like they had a flower and vegetable garden, but the weeds have taken over. We might as well go inside. Maybe it's not as bad as it looks."

The steps creaked and wobbled as they walked up to the porch. "Walk slowly and be careful where you step," said Bill.

Jennifer went inside and birds flew out the open windows. She screamed and ducked. "Look at this mess, broken dishes everywhere and it's dusty and dirty." She shivered when she saw a large black spider weaving a web in the corner of the ceiling.

Bill rubbed his hand over the dusty wooden table, "Looks like the furniture is a bit worn." There were four wooden chairs around the table and he picked up the one with a broken leg. "I can't believe anyone would live in this dump."

"I wonder how the other two rooms are." Jennifer walked into the largest one. "Bill, come look at the mattress. I can't sleep on this!"

"Why! What's wrong with it?" Bill walked towards her.

"The center is sunken in and it's covered with urine stains. This is disgusting." Jennifer walked back to the main room. "Where's the stove and sink, isn't there any water?"

Margaret started to laugh and pointed to the hole in the roof. "Look, there's a monkey. I want to play with him."

The monkey chattered away as he stared down at them. Eduardo clapped his hands. "Come Fife. Meet your new family."

"He was Pastor Ryan's pet."

"How long has it been since the missionaries left?" asked Bill.

Eduardo touched each finger as he counted, "Uno, dos, tres - three months," he said as the monkey jumped on his shoulder.

"Three months! Was it in this condition when they left?" asked Jennifer.

Eduardo shrugged his shoulders. "I think Fife's been living here. She is a funny monkey; she likes to throw things."

Jennifer threw her hands in the air. "I can't stay here tonight. Not in this mess. Take us to a hotel. We'll clean it up tomorrow, when we're not so tired."

"Senora, the hotel is maybe five to six hours away," said Eduardo sadly.

"Five or six hours! My back would never take it," said Bill. He put his arm around Jennifer. "We have to stay and make the best of it." He walked in one of the bedrooms and picked up the mattress. Bill heaved it over his shoulder and took it outside. "I'll come back for the other ones later." He found a clothesline, hanging between the house and a tree. He swung the mattress over it and picked up a thick stick, gave it a hard smack. Dust flew out, making a thick gray cloud that smelled of urine.

Jennifer pulled up her skirt and ripped the bottom of her Petticoat off. She tore it in pieces and handed them to the children. "You can start dusting. Now, what am I going to sweep the floor with?"

"I'll show you," said Eduardo. He handed Jennifer a pole with palm fronds tied to the bottom. "You sweep with this."

She groaned, as she examined the make-shift broom. "Well, it's better than nothing."

Eduardo brought in the last of the supplies as he said, "Tomorrow I'll take you to meet Mana of the village."

Bill had come back for another mattress and asked, "Did you say mama?"

"Ma-na," answered Eduardo. "He is our chief and makes all decisions for the tribe. When a new baby is born, he sometimes takes the child as his own. It is a high honor."

"Wait a minute," said Jennifer. "Are you saying he can take any child that's born and make it his son or daughter?"

Eduardo grabbed the monkey that climbed on his head. "Si! It's big honor for Madre to give up baby to Mana."

Margaret went over to Eduardo. "Please, let me hold the monkey."

"Be quiet, Margaret. I'm trying to understand something," said Jennifer. "What happens if the Madre doesn't want to give up the baby?"

"Madre must." Eduardo placed the monkey on Margaret's shoulder. "Don't touch Fife. Let him get use to you." Then he turned to Jennifer, "Chief takes it anyway. He has twenty children. Only five come from his wives."

"Wives! Bill, what have we got ourselves into?" said Jennifer.

"Babe, for heaven sakes calm down. Eduardo, how far away is the village?"

"Maybe fifteen minutes." He walked to the door. "I must tell the chief you are here. I see you man 'ana."

As Eduardo climbed into the wagon, Jennifer called out, "Wait a minute. Where's the toilet?" Eduardo's gave her a blank stare.

"You know the bathroom."

Eduardo shrugged his shoulders.

Bill yelled over her shoulder, "The servicios."

"Oh si, si." Eduardo laughed and pointed to the woods. "In there."

Jennifer and Bill ran down the steps and followed him up the path. They could smell the toilet before they saw it.

Eduardo stopped in front of three walls made of bamboo trunks. The fourth wall was a braided straw flap. "Here it is."

Jennifer rolled up the flap and the stench took her breath away. A mass of black flies flew out.

She held her nose as she peered inside. "This is it?"

A big hole had been dug in the ground and a wooden chair sat over it. The legs were cut short and a hole cut out of the seat.

"Good heavens! This is where we go to the bathroom?" said Bill.

"No, no," said Eduardo as he squatted. "Make poops and pee, pee here."

Jennifer walked away holding her nose. "This is disgusting. The whole place is disgusting."

"God has provided us with a house and it's up to us to make it livable." Bill took her hand. "Come, let's go back and finish cleaning up that mess."

After they worked for a few hours they could see the sun was setting. "We better look for some candles or we're going to be cleaning in the dark," said Jennifer. "There's a kerosene lamp hanging in each room. Uh-oh, the glass covers are broken."

"I found three candles," said Margaret. "We'll light one in each room."

"Okay kids, get your rags and start dusting," said Bill as he carried out another mattress.

After working for three hours, Jennifer sat down on one of the rickety chairs and yawned. "I'm exhausted, but at least it's clean enough to sleep here."

"I'm hungry," said Joseph throwing down his rag.

"Eduardo said he'd leave some food for our dinner," Bill walked out on the porch. "Here it is. Looks like we eat chicken and potatoes, and there's also a pail of water."

"I'm so hungry, I could eat this whole thing myself," said Jennifer.

When they finished eating, Jennifer dug through the boxes for sheets and pillow cases. "I'm glad I remembered to bring pillows."

Bill yawned. "I'm too tired to work any longer."

Jennifer took a cloth drenched in bleach water and wiped each mattress, then picked up the bed linens. "Children, I'll help you make your beds. Bill, you can make ours. Then we're all going to bed."

She blew out the candles and tried not to think about the stains under the sheets. She kissed Bill goodnight and said, "Something doesn't seem right."

Bill yawned. "Why do you say that?"

"Reverend Carter said the missionaries would be here when we arrived. Eduardo said they left three months ago."

"So what?"

"Why did they leave three months ago?"

"Will you go to sleep? Tomorrow we'll get the full story."

# Chapter Thirteen

Jennifer woke to the pleasant sound of chirping birds. She smiled when the monkeys started to chatter in the nearby trees. Things seem brighter after a good night's sleep. Jennifer stretched, then she let a scream.

Bill sat up. "What in the world is the matter?"

"My…my…" She couldn't get the words out and pointed to her legs.

Bill yanked the covers off. "Holy mackerel. Where'd that black snake come from?" He got out of bed trying not to frighten the snake. "Don't move. Just stay still."

"Get it off of me!"

"Don't move." Bill grabbed the five-foot snake behind the head and ran toward the porch. The snake twisted wildly in his hands.

At that moment Eduardo came up the steps. "Oh, you found Jogo."

"Jogo, you mean it has a name?" Bill handed him the snake.

"Si, Pastor Ryan, loved Jogo, he wore him around his neck. Jogo's a good mouse catcher."

Eduardo took the snake from Bill as Jennifer came out on the porch. "Mice, what are you talking about?" She let out a squeal and jumped back. "Will you get rid of that snake?"

The children heard the noise and Margaret asked, "What's the matter?" The girls started to scream when they saw the snake, but Joseph reached for it. "Let me hold it."

Eduardo pushed his hand down. "Let me show you how you hold Jogo." He put the snake around Joseph's neck and placed the child's hand behind its neck. "This is how you hold him."

"He's too heavy," said Joseph.

Eduardo held the snake while Joseph sat on the floor. Margaret and Cassie sat at a distance. They slowly moved closer when they saw the snake was harmless.

"Let me pet him," said Margaret.

"I get to pet him first," said Cassie reaching her hand out.

"Jogo likes all this attention," said Eduardo.

Bill smiled. "Seems like we have more pets than we bargained for."

Jennifer went in the bedroom to get dressed as she said, "I don't mind as long as they're friendly." After she dressed, Jennifer searched through the boxes looking for the food they packed. "It will probably be in the last box."

"I have some good food." Eduardo ran out to the wagon and brought back two baskets.

They were filled with papayas, mangos, bananas and fresh eggs.

"This is a real treat." She hugged Eduardo. "Thank you very much. You've been very helpful to us."

"Where's the frying pan? I'll cook breakfast." said Bill.

"What will we cook it on?" asked Jennifer. "There's no stove or running water."

"Come. I'll show you," said Eduardo.

They followed him to the back of the house where a three sided, stone wall stood. An old icebox rack lay across the top.

"That looks like a barbecue pit," said Bill.

Eduardo gathered wood. "Fire will be a ready in no time."

Jennifer looked in at an old wooden box sitting by the pit. "Here's the pots and pans!"

Bill cooked the eggs and they ate outside on a huge plank of wood that sat on four logs. Their chairs were fat tree stumps.

"This is like a barbecue back home," said Margaret.

"Not quite," said Jennifer, pushing the monkey off the table.

After breakfast, they unpacked the boxes and suitcases. By mid-afternoon Jennifer had washed the old flowered curtains on the door and windows. She placed a lace cloth on the table to hide the digs and scratches.

"There, the place looks much better," sighed Jennifer

Margaret and Cassie carried in some wild flowers. "Here Mama. We picked these for you."

"Thank you, that was very thoughtful." Jennifer found a glass jar and placed the flowers on the table. "That brightens up the place?"

Jennifer sat at the table looking around. She ran her finger on one of the knotholes showing through the lace cloth. "I do feel better, now that the place is clean. But it still lacks a lot of the creature comforts."

"We knew it wasn't going to be like home," said Bill.

"You've got to admit, it was a horrendous beginning. I hope there are no more surprises."

Bill pulled Jennifer to her feet. "Our next surprise is meeting the chief."

---

Eduardo led them down the road and thick foliage bordered the pathway. There were wild flowers clustered around each tree, adding multicolor to the lush green forest.

"This is lovely and peaceful," said Jennifer, breathing in the fragrant filled air.

Eduardo stopped by a rippling stream and splashed water on his face. "*Bano*," he said rubbing his wet hands up and down his arms.

"I guess this is where we bathe," said Bill.

Jennifer dipped her hand in the water. "It's so blue and clear."

They continued walking upstream and then Bill stopped. "Look at that magnificent waterfall."

Eduardo cupped his hands, filled them with water and drank it. "*Aqua potable.*"

Bill scooped up the clear clean water in his hands and drank it. "Ah, that tastes good. I guess we found our drinking water."

They each took a drink then followed the stream to where it branched off. Eduardo said, "*Bibada.*"

"This place is surrounded by trees," said Bill. "It must be the village swimming hole. What a pretty spot."

"It's so beautiful, and all these bushes and trees provide a lot of privacy," said Jennifer.

"I want to take a swim," said Joseph.

"Me too," said Cassie as she started to take off her dress.

"Don't do that," said Jennifer. We'll come back later and swim."

They walked a mile through the thick forest, listening to the chatter of the monkeys. Eduardo stopped and put his hand to his ear. "Listen to howler monkeys, they make mucho noise."

"Look, there's a big black and red bird in the tree," said Margaret.

Eduardo patted her head. "You have good eyes. That's a trogon bird. We eat them."

The bird flew away and Eduardo said, "There's a nest in the tree, I'll lift you up and let you see." After each child looked at the eggs, he pointed at another tree. "Over here is a big iguana. Maybe five-feet long."

Joseph backed away. "Will he bite?"

"No. He won't bite, but you have to watch out for his sharp tail."

Women and children greeted them as they approached the entrance of the village, and they all started to talk at the same time.

"Welcome, we are happy to see you."

The ladies and young girls had black straight hair that hung down to their waist. On their tan bodies they wore colorful sack-like dresses and belts made of brightly colored, woven fibers.

The native boys walked close to Joseph bumping him with each step. He pulled away. "Why do they have to walk so close to me?"

The boys had bare chests and dusty, black pants, cut off at the knees. They each wore a leather pouch around their waist that held a knife.

"Why are they carrying knifes?" asked Joseph

"They are learning to be hunters," said Eduardo.

The native girls stared at Margaret and Cassie's golden blonde hair. One of them pulled

Margaret's braids.

"Ouch! Don't pull my hair," yelled Margaret.

Eduardo clapped his hands. "*Basta. No esta bien. Estncia.*" The children stopped chattering and quickly lined up behind him.

Jennifer and Bill walked under the village archway and looked around. "It's much larger than I expected," said Bill.

Twenty, small thatched, huts stretched out in a circled shaded by palm trees. The chief's house stood in the middle and it was three times larger than the others. It was made out of bamboo trunks tied together with tough vines. A plaque carved with iguanas and snakes hung over the doorway. A frame of braided leaves decorated the four window openings, and on the roof stood a cone shaped dome. It was a log, carved with monkeys and birds.

The women threw bougainvillea flowers on the path and smiled as they greeted the family.

"Look at the adorable babies." Jennifer touched the honey colored skin of one of the baby and his dark brown eyes sparkled.

"Hmm, something smells delicious," said Bill

"Come see." Eduardo led them to a pit where a whole pig was roasting on an open fire.

Jennifer watched as the woman turned the animal. The skin crackled in the fire, sending sparks in the air. Jennifer jumped back and the women giggled at her reaction.

The flowering curtain on the large hut opened and a tall majestic man stepped out. He was carrying a carved wooden staff. He held his head high; he walked towards them wearing a multi-colored wrap draped across his tan shoulders. It barely covered his strong muscular chest. Thick black curls surrounded his beaming face and his dark brown eyes twinkled with friendliness.

"I am Chief Melardo. Welcome to our village."

Jennifer whispered to Bill. "His teeth look like big white pearls."

"Please visit with me." Chief Melardo beckoned them to his hut. Then, he said to a young boy standing nearby, "Take care of the pastor's children until we come out." The chief pointed to large square woven mats on the floor. "Sit, sit."

Bill spoke slowly. "*Gracias*, we are glad to be here. We've come to help your people."

"We have been waiting for you," said Chief Melardo.

Jennifer's curiosity was eating at her. "Why did Pastor Ryan and his wife leave early?"

The chief scratched his stomach. "A message came about Pastor Ryan's *hija*. How do you say in English? daugter."

"You mean daughter?" asked Jennifer.

"*Si*, his *hija* was sick; they needed to leave."

"We understand," said Bill slowly.

"Why do you talk so slow?" asked the chief.

"I'm not sure how good your English is."

"My English is good, don't you think?"

"Yes it is." Bill's bottom was getting uncomfortable on the hard dirt floor and he changed positions. "Your village is much larger than I expected. Could someone show us around?"

"Yes, number one wife will help you." The chief went to the door and shouted, "Missia, come here."

A girl about sixteen-years-old came running into the hut and seemed annoyed. "Mana, what do you want?"

Bill and Jennifer stared at her. "She's lovely," said Jennifer.

Missia wore a long cotton dress with a colorful overskirt. She was fully developed and her lovely young breasts pressed tightly against the top of the dress. A flower tucked over her ear stood out against her long, black hair.

Bill stared at Missia's taunt nipples, and then looked away as he thought, "Get thee behind me, Satan."

Jennifer looked puzzled. "You have more than one wife?"

"*Si.*" A broad grin filled the chief's face. "I have three other wives, but Missia is the best."

Bill's mouth dropped open. "Four wives, that's sinful."

The chief waved his hand. "I know. Pastor Ryan said it was not right to have four wives, but I fixed everything. I call the other three good friends." He giggled and rubbed his sweaty stomach. Bill looked bewildered and shook his head as Chief Melardo continued, "Missia was Mrs. Ryan's helper, she knows everything." His chest stood out proudly, "My wife speaks good English and Mrs. Ryan taught her to read and write."

Jennifer took Missia's' hand. "I'm very glad to meet you. I would like you to help me too."

Missia smiled. "I would like that. I promise I will work hard." Missia started walking out of the door. "If you follow me, I will show you our village."

They walked through an abundant garden of abacas, gardenias and other tropical flowers. Monkey's jumped from tree to tree, following them.

"The church is just ahead," said Missia.

The white wooden church stood out among the flowering vines. Bougainvillea grew across the top of the doorway and windows. Palm trees circled the building, like tall guards with feathery fronds for hats.

"The church is built better than our house." said Jennifer.

Bill touched the wood on the side of the building. "They did a great job. Even stripped the bark from the tree trunks and painted them white."

Two three-by-four openings were on each side of the building. A six-foot doorway had been cut at the front of the church. Inside long, split logs were set in four rows. Each could hold ten people. Bill noticed a makeshift wooden platform at the front of the room. He walked up to where a huge, four-feet-high log stood. It served as a podium. The bark had been stripped and angels were carved in the wood. Two rows of flowers in clay pots stood in front of the podium, and a delightful fragrance filled the room.

Bill stood on the platform staring around the room taking in the serene atmosphere.

Jennifer said, "You look pleasantly surprised."

"I never expected anything this nice."

"Do you want to go see the infirmary now?" asked Missia.

"I'd love to," said Jennifer. "How far is it?"

"It's just up the path, a short way."

"Bill, are you coming with us?" asked Jennifer.

"You go. I'm going to stay here for a while."

They walked up a hill to a connecting path that brought them closer to the chief's hut. At the top of the hill, the natives had built a small lean-to. Woven mats were tacked to poles to form three walls and palm fronds were draped across the top for a roof.

"This is the infirmary. Do you like it?" said Missia.

"Are you sure this is it?" Jennifer walked inside. "At least it's clean."

Narrow slabs of wood held up by wooden pegs lined the only wall. Coconut bowls and brown, woven, cloth bags sat sparsely on the shelves. A long narrow table stood in the center, covered with a clean white cloth. Jennifer walked over to an old wooden desk, warped and scarred. She sat on one of the two stumps that served as chairs.

Jennifer laughed and said, "Talk about bare necessities." She walked over to the shelves and started to open the brown bags. "Let's see what kind of supplies they left us."

Jennifer heard a sound and turned to find an old woman standing by the entrance. Her shoulders were humped and she adjusted the faded wrap that hung around her body.

She limped towards Jennifer. "*Buenas tardes.*"

Jennifer said, "*Buenas tardes.*"

The woman lifted her skirt and showed her ankle. Jennifer helped her sit down. Puss oozed from the gash and Jennifer could smell the putrid odor. "Let me see what I can find to clean the cut." She searched bags and bowls, and then found two jars in the desk drawer, one marked sterile water, and the other peroxide. After she washed the wound, she doused it with peroxide. "Now, I need something to draw the infection out." Jennifer found a bar of yellow laundry soap and remembered a remedy the midwife had taught her. She scraped chips from the soap with an old scalpel, then mashed it, mixing sterile water, to make a paste.

"Missia, do we have any sugar?" Missa went to a table that held a small jar and handed it to her. Jennifer mixed a pinch of sugar into the soap. "Missia, apply this paste to the cut, while I find something to bandage it." She found a roll of bandage in the bottom desk drawer and wrapped the woman's foot. Jennifer patted the woman's shoulder. "I'd like to examine it again in two days."

The woman stared at Jennifer and muttered, "*No, comprendo.*"

"She doesn't speak English," said Missia.

"I'm sorry I should have known. Touching the woman's hand, she said, "*Venir dose dia.*"

The old woman smiled and said, "*Si, gracias,*" and hobbled out of the infirmary.

"Whew," said Jennifer, "How's that for quick thinking?"

Missia smiled. "You'll do very well."

"I'm going back to my house to gather the supplies I brought," said Jennifer.

"Thank you for your help and I'll see you tomorrow."

# Chapter Fourteen

Rosa was only twelve-years-old, but loved to help in the infirmary. When she heard the new nurse had arrived, she wanted to surprise her. Rosa got two baskets and went over to her brother who was sitting under the banyan tree.

"Ramos," she said scratching his back. "Will you please go in the woods with me? I want to collect herbs for the new nurse."

"Don't bother me. Can't you see I'm making new arrows for the hunt tomorrow?"

"Please, Ramos. Come with me. I don't want to go alone"

"No, I have to finish the arrows today."

Rosa looked at him with her large brown eyes. "Please. I can't do it alone."

Ramos looked at his sister's sweet face and put down his arrow. "Okay. Let's go."

They walked a long way into the thick jungle until Rosa spotted a bush of lemon verbena. "I want to pick some of these flowers, they make you sleep." Then she found some Quebracho. "I need these, they take away stomach aches."

When the baskets were full, Ramos said, "Okay, let's go back now?"

"Wait, I see some passion flowers and Guarana leaves. I have to pick some. They're hard to find."

"We'll get them next time."

"No. I want to get them now. Take these baskets back and bring me two more."

Ramos stamped his foot. "No, it's time to go back."

"Please, I need these for the new nurse. Please, Ramos."

He took the basket from her. "I'll go, if you promise to stay right here."

"I promise." Rosa gave him a kiss on the cheek. "I'll cut the passion flowers, and then start on the Guarana tree. You can help me when you get back."

He pointed his finger at her. "Don't forget; stay right here, I don't want to hunt for you."

Ramos ran three miles to the village and grabbed two baskets from his hut, then started to run back.

Missia called to him, "Ramos, come here."

"I can't. I have to get my sister."

"Come over here now."

"Okay." he walked over to her.

"I want you to meet the pastor's daughter Margaret."

"Welcome to our village," said Ramos, and then turned to go.

"Ramos, I want you to show Margaret around. Take good care of her."

He handed Margaret a basket. "I have to meet my sister, follow me."

"Where are we going?"

Ramos grabbed her arm. "Just follow me."

They ran through the forest and Margaret gasped for breath. "Will you slow down? I can't keep up with you."

"Keep running, we're almost there."

Romos stopped. "This is where she was. Right by the passion flowers." Ramos called out, "Rosa where are you? Come on, stop being funny." He spotted her basket of herbs and cut branches and knelt down to examine the ground. "Look, Margaret, others have been here. There are many footprints where she was kneeling." He looked around. "Come, we'll follow the footprints and see where they go." The tracks led deep into the jungle.

"You're getting too far ahead of me," yelled Margaret. "Wait. I don't want to get lost." She heard Ramos scream in the distance and ran towards the sound.

Ramos screamed again, "Hurry, I need you."

When she got close, she could see Ramos's sister hanging from a banyan tree. "Oh no," she cried.

A noose was around Rosa's neck and her head hung forward, resting on her naked chest.

Margaret screamed. "Who did this to her?"

Ramos's eyes overflowed with tears as he pulled his knife from its sheath and gave it to Margaret. "Help me get her down!"

Tears filled Margaret eyes and her hand trembled as she took the knife. Her lips quivered as she said, "What should I do?"

"When I lift her up you cut the rope." He held his sister in his arms sobbing, "Please Rosa, don't be dead."

Margaret cut the robe and helped Ramos lay Rosa on the ground. She covered her naked body with the ripped dress lying nearby.

"Margaret, run back to the village and bring help," said Ramos.

"I don't know my way, I'll get lost."

"No, you won't." He walked her past the banyan tree. "Follow this path; it will take you to the village, hurry."

Margaret ran, praying she wouldn't get lost and when she reached the village she screamed, "Dad, Mama, help, help."

Bill and Jennifer were talking to Chief Melardo and ran to her. "What's the matter?"

Margaret gasped for air. "Something bad happened to Rosa. Ramos sent me for help."

"Show us where they are, girl," said Chief Melardo. He signaled his two best hunters, "Uno, Weyno, follow me."

"We better go too," said Jennifer. "She might need our help."

When they arrived, Ramos was cradling Rosa's head in his lap crying ,"Rosa, wake up."

Jennifer felt Rosa's head. "She's still alive; we better get her back to the infirmary."

"Why would someone want to kill her?" asked the Chief.

Jennifer examined Rosa. "She's been raped. They didn't want her to identify them."

The chief looked at the rope made from the fiber of the agave plant. Several small pieces of wood stuck out from the braids. He showed the noose to his hunters. "Do you see why noose didn't kill Rosa."

They both nodded. "Yes, the wood stopped the rope from tightening."

The chief motioned with his hand, "Go, find them."

The hunters ran off, disappearing into the jungle like magic.

Bill got down on his knees and placed his hands on Rosa's head and prayed, "Thank you, God, for sparing this child's life. Amen."

"Let's get her back to the infirmary," said Jennifer brushing Rosa's hair from her face.

Bill carried Rosa to the infirmary and placed her on the table. She was still unconscious when Jennifer washed and examined her.

When she finished, she whispered to Bill, "They brutally raped her, she's torn and bruised."

Maria wept silently by the table as she asked, "Will my daughter die?"

"No, no," Jennifer said as she hugged Maria. "She'll live; she will be alright."

Maria's eyes opened wide as she stuttered over the word, "*Unconsa?*"

"Don't be frightened. It just means she's sleeping."

As the day darkened, the villagers lit torches, staying by the infirmary. The moon rose high in the sky, casting a light into the infirmary.

Rosa woke up, screaming, "Madre, Madre."

Maria put her arms around her daughter. "*Shush mi bebe. Madre's aqui. Mamas here.*"

Jennifer had fallen asleep at her desk, and woke up when she heard Rosa cry out and went over to her. "Everything is all right now, honey."

Rosa covered her face with her hands. "Oh Madre, those men did nasty things to me. Why did God let them do it?"

Maria wrapped her arms around her daughter and kissed her gently. Then Maria's face twisted in a hateful grin. "We will find them and make them pay for hurting you."

Bill heard Maria's angry remark and put his hands on her shoulders. "Do not seek revenge. Vengeance is mine, sayeth the Lord."

Jennifer helped her off the table and said to Maria, "Take Rosa down to the lagoon and let her sit in the cool water for a while. It will wash away the seed of those horrible men."

———————————

In the morning the hunters returned to the village and went to the Chief's hut. He was sitting on the floor, smoking his pipe. "Sit with me and rest. You look tired."

Bill saw the hunters go in and stuck his head in the doorway. "May I join you?"

Chief Melardo nodded, then asked his hunters, "Did you find them?"

Uno's shoulders went back proudly. "We followed the tracks to their camp and two hombres were loco drunk talking about the emeralds they would find in the mountains."

"How did you know they were the right men?" asked Bill.

Uno's face turned red and his fists clenched. "They were bragging about what they did to Rosa. The short man laughed and said she had nice *seno's*."

Bill looked puzzled. "What is that?"

Uno put his hands on his chest. "Tities. Then the mucho big man bragged how he made her moan with his big *puka*."

The chief slammed his pipe on the log next to him. "They are evil men."

Uno continued, "He said it was too bad they had to kill such a nice piece of ass."

Weyno's face twitched as he added, "The short one said she would never squeal because the rope shut her up."

Bill sat with his fist clenched, grinding his teeth as he prayed. "Let the wrath of God come down on these evil men."

"Did you punish these terrible men?" asked the chief.

"*Si*, we found a mucho grandee fire ant hill," said Weyno. "We waited for them to go to sleep. Then dragged them by their hair to the ant hill and staked them across it."

"I found a beehive in a nearby tree and poured honey on their stomachs," said Uno.

Bill jumped to his feet shouting, "You shouldn't have done that. You should have left it to the lord. He would have punished them."

Chief Melardo put his hands on Bill's shoulder to quieten him. "Weyno, tell me the rest."

Weyno laughed. "We scooped the fire ants up with coconut shells and poured them over the dirty pigs. We left them screaming for mercy."

The Chief slammed his hand down on the log next to him. "The evil pigs deserved to die a horrible death." He stood up and slapped his men on the back. "Well done, now go eat. You must be hungry."

Bill trembled as he spoke, "Your men should have left them alone. You must have faith in God. He would have made sure they were punished."

"We have faith," said Chief Melardo. With a smile of satisfaction added, "We just help him a little."

Bill gave the chief a bewildered look and walked down the road. He sat under a palm tree and closed his eyes. "How can I make them understand?"

Jennifer was in the infirmary and saw him sitting there, she went out to him. "What's the matter? You look down in the dumps."

"I'm confused, and I'm not sure how to handle what just happened."

Jennifer sat beside him and stroked his head. "Tell me about it."

"Weyno and Uno killed the men who raped Rosa. I tried to tell the chief that God would have punished them, but he wouldn't listen." Bill shook his head and sighed. "This is all new to me, and I'm not sure how to get through to them?"

Jennifer kissed him on the cheek. "It was a horrible thing those men did to one of their children, and they wanted revenge. They have their customs and it takes time to change."

Bill sat thinking, and then asked, "Where are our children?"

Jennifer got up and took his hand and pulled him to his feet. "Let's go home." As they walked down the path Jennifer said, "Missia's teaching the girls to weave and Joseph went hunting with Ramos and his friends. They're teaching him how to use a bow and arrow."

They held hands as they walked along, cooled by a refreshing breeze and the fragrant

bougainvillea's scented the air. When they came to the lagoon, Jennifer sat on a boulder by the water's edge, looking at the tranquil surroundings.

"The water looks so refreshing. Let's go swimming. It will help you relax." Jennifer stripped off her clothes and jumped in.

"Babe, get out of there. Suppose someone comes by?"

"You're such a stuff shirt," laughed Jennifer. "The lagoon's protected by large bushes. We'll hear anyone who comes up the path." Jennifer floated on her back. "Ah! this feels so good."

"It does look refreshing." Bill quickly took off his clothes and ran in the water. "Oh boy, this is great." He floated on his back, letting the water flow over him.

"We're not doing anything the natives don't do," said Jennifer giggling like a school girl.

The sun reflected on Bills tan, muscular body as he floated peacefully. Jennifer swam closer and her eyes settled on his pale soft penis bobbing up and down. She felt a ripple of desire and placed her hand on it. Her touch startled Bill, and he sunk under the water. Jennifer laughed and kissed him as she reached under the water to caress him.

Bill pushed her hand away. "What if someone comes?" A knot formed in his throat as his eyes roved over her slender naked body and suddenly he didn't care. Bill took her in his arms, and kissed her as they slowly sank beneath the water. Her long legs wrapped around him and they bobbed like a top in the peaceful lagoon. Bill maneuvered her to waist deep water and his erection searched for her warm spot. Jennifer felt his heart pounding against her breast and a delightful shiver of passion ran through her. She put her hand under the water and gently guided him as their bodies connected. They climaxed together as they drifted beneath the water. Feeling content they floated on the water, letting the soft breeze fan their bodies.

Bill reached for her hand. "I feel so relaxed."

Jennifer smiled. "See. I know what's good for you."

Bill laughed. "What's good for us now is to get dressed, before someone catches us."

# Chapter Fifteen

When they walked into the house, Jennifer stopped suddenly and gasped. "The place is a total mess."

Broken dishes lay everywhere and their books had been ripped apart. The curtains at the windows were torn, hanging by a thread.

"Why would anyone do this?" said Jennifer. They heard a chattering noise and looked up. Jogo was sitting on a rafter eating a banana.

"Jogo get down here!" hollered Bill.

The monkey jumped up and down squealing, then threw the banana peel on Bill's head.

Jennifer laughed as she started to clean up. "He sure knows how to trash a place. I think we'll have to put a leash on him when we're not home." She picked up her hand mirror and waved it. "Come down Jogo and see the pretty monkey."

He climbed down and Bill tried to grab him, but he jumped on Jennifer's shoulder. She sat at the table and looked in the mirror, while the monkey watched.

She turned the mirror towards him. "See the pretty monkey."

Jogo looked into the mirror, primped his hair and smiled. Jennifer turned the mirror away and looked into it. Jogo squealed and climbed on her head, then peered into the mirror, smiling, showing his teeth.

She laughed and hugged the monkey. "You didn't mean to make a mess, did you? You were just having fun."

"Yeah, he has fun and we clean it up," complained Bill, getting out the broom.

"Well, at least we know how to capture him when we need to. He loves to look at himself."

"Vanity is a sin," said Bill sweeping the broken glass on to a piece of cardboard.

Jennifer looked at Bill with a sly grin. "Don't tell me monkeys sin too?"

Bill kept sweeping and never answered.

---

They woke up the next morning hearing a pounding noise. Eduardo was replacing the roof and repairing the holes in the porch. After breakfast Jennifer unpacked her sewing machine and fabrics, then spent the rest of the day making curtains and mattress covers. Bill repaired the furniture and cleaned up the makeshift toilet area. Two women from the village brought braided mats for the floors, and pillows for the chairs. The bright pillows and rugs went perfect in the house. The children weeded the old vegetable area and when they were done started walking down the road.

"Wait a minute," said Jennifer. "You haven't made your beds, or cleaned your rooms."

"Our friends are taking us fishing," they said in unison.

"Not until you clean your rooms. That's your daily chore and you know it."

Dragging their feet and mumbling, they wandered back to their room. Jennifer prepared lunch. She served melons, papayas and hard biscuits.

After lunch, Bill put on his shirt and said, "I'm going to church to get things organized."

"We'll walk with you," said the children.

Eduardo had just finished repairing the loose boards at the side of the house and he walked inside just as Jennifer found the box of medical supplies.

"Eduardo could you help me carry this box to the infirmary."

Eduardo picked up the box. "It's not heavy; I can carry it by myself."

They walked to the village and when they entered the infirmary, Missia and Rosa was there.

"What do you have in the box?" asked Missia.

"These are the medical supplies. Here's the list of everything in the box. I'll teach you how to use them."

Jennifer opened the box and handed Rosa fifty rolls of bandages and tape. She then gave Missia twelve boxes of herbs. "These are horse chestnuts. They're good for bruises and pain." She placed them in a palm basket. "Two bottles of horse chestnut oil for cramps, eucalyptus leaves for coughs and bronchitis. I'm glad I brought the mint leaves for indigestion and oh yes, mint seeds. I can grow all we need." Near the bottom of the box were several bottles of vinegar that she'd use as an antibiotic. Tucked between everything were bottles of peroxide and Epson salts.

"Oh good here's the boxes of black pepper, it stops bleeding." She picked up three boxes of dried centaury flowers. "This is good for dyspepsia, worm infestation, fever, loss of appetite and many other ailments. Thank goodness I didn't forget the carline thistle for washing wounds and for colds."

"You brought a lot of medicine. I never heard of any of these things," said Rosa.

She started to place the supplies on the shelves and Rosa said, "Let me do that."

As they placed the last package on the shelf, Jennifer said, "Now we are fully equipped and can handle almost any ailment."

"The villagers like you," said Missia. "They say you are very caring."

Jennifer saw her first patient, the old lady with the sore ankle come in. She was carrying a live chicken by the feet.

"*Gracias*," she said handing Jennifer the chicken. She pulled up her skirt to show Jennifer her ankle.

Jennifer handed the chicken to Rosa and washed her hands. As she cleaned the dirt from the woman's leg, she said, "It's completely healed!"

The old woman grabbed Jennifer's hand and kissed it. "*Gracias*," she said as she walked away.

Jennifer looked puzzled. "Missia, why did she give me this chicken?"

"That's payment for healing her foot. Our people are proud and like to reward someone who helps them."

"That's thoughtful." Jennifer sat at her desk and started to read, but stopped when she heard a whimper. A chubby little toddler was standing in the doorway.

She went over to the little girl. "What's the matter?"

Tears ran down the child's honey-toned cheeks as she said, "Missy nurse, I hurt."

Jennifer held her on her lap and hugged her. "Where does it hurt, honey?"

The child pointed to a tiny scratch on her arm.

Jennifer dried the little girl's tears. "Let me make it better." She cleaned the scratch with peroxide and put a bandage on it. "Does that make it feel better?"

The little girl nodded. "Yes."

"Good. Would you like me to tell you a story?" The child's smile made Jennifer tingle. She put the child on her lap and told the story of the Three Bears.

When the little girl left, Jennifer stood up and stretched. "Missia, I need a breath of air.

I'm going to take a walk."

She walked down the path and saw Bill was sitting under the banyan tree. "Hi. Looks like you need a break too." Jennifer sat next to him and leaned back against the huge trunk. She stretched her arms up, touching the banyan leaves as she sighed. "Our lives are so peaceful; I don't miss our old life at all. I only wear loose dresses with panties underneath," said Jennifer laughing. "Our daughters wear flowered wraps. We've all gone native but you."

"I feel better dressing more conventionally. After all, I am the pastor."

"Aren't you hot wearing black pants and white shirts with long sleeves? Why don't you dress like Joseph in cut off pants?"

"The people respect the way I dress and I'm getting them to attend church again."

"You are getting a larger crowd. The first few Sunday's only five people came, and last Sunday ten showed up."

"We'll see how many come to service tomorrow." Bill stood up. "I've got to go work on my sermon."

Sunday morning Bill stood at the podium as twenty-five villagers entered the church. The women were dressed in long tan, sack dresses. Big straw hats with flowers tucked in their brim, sat proudly on their head. Their yellow, straw sandals slapped up and down against the floor as they walked down the aisle. The men strutted in wearing knee length tunics of blue and tan over black pants. Black sombrero were cocked to the left side of their heads. Their barreled chests stood out as they moved stiffly to the pews in lizard sandals. The women talked and giggled, while the men chewed cocoa beans and spat in the aisles.

Chief Melardo entered wearing a multi-colored robe and a majestic straw hat, covered with feathers and beads. The people stood and bowed, as he walked to his carved chair on the platform.

Bill smiled down from the pulpit at everyone and lifted his hands. "Welcome to the Lord's house. I'm glad to see so many people here today. Praise the Lord."

Everyone repeated softly, "Praise the Lord."

Bill kept his hands in the air as he continued, "The lord loves you and watches over you. He wants you to live by His ten commandments. The Lord says, Thou shall not covet thy neighbor's wife."

The congregation looked at each other, shrugged their shoulders. They did not understand.

Bill saw their puzzled look. "The Lord says thou shall not sleep…" He stopped and repeated the word in Spanish, "The Lord says thou shall not *dormir* with another man's wife."

The men looked at each other and grinned, showing their stained teeth. "*Si, Si.*"

The women giggled and hid their faces.

Bill raised his voice. "Thou shall not steal, or take what does not belong to you. Hallelujah. Praise the Lord."

Two men in the front pew jumped up from their seats and yelled, "Praise the Lord," then proudly pushed out their chests.

"Very good," said Bill. "Praise the Lord and hallelujah. God loves you one and all."

Two people sitting in the back stood up and shouted, "Hallelujah! Praise the Lord."

Then, the whole congregation got into the act and screamed, "Hallelujah! Praise the Lord."

The church shook from their roaring voices, as they tried to out shout each other. The chief grinned at the exuberance of his people and the congregation began to dance.

Joseph and Ramos started to laugh and shout, "Hallelujah!"

Jennifer reached over and pinched their arms, "Behave yourselves."

"Quiet! Be quiet please," shouted Bill.

A man in the front row beat the side of the pew, making the sound of a bongo drum.

Bill hammered on the podium with his fist. "Shut up."

The dancing and singing continued until Bill slapped his Bible against the podium. "*Cerrado arriba*," he screamed.

A hush went over the congregation and they looked at Bill like naughty children.

"The service is over. Bambus," said Bill.

He was flustered and tried to compose himself. He stepped down from the podium and walked to the doorway.

Bill shook their hands. "Thank you for coming."

After everyone left, Jennifer kissed his cheek and couldn't help from laughing. "It looks like they enjoyed the service."

Sweat dripped down Bill's face; he wiped his forehead. "From now on, I'll watch how often I say praise the Lord and hallelujah. I'm going home to take a nap."

"Okay, I'm going to take a walk; it's a beautiful day."

Jennifer walked into the woods enjoying the fragrance of the flowers. She took her rosary beads from her pocket and prayed. She was deep in thought as she walked along the trail, thinking how much she missed her sister. Also Nellie who was always so pleasant. She almost walked into a pile of boulders that was at the edge of the road. Jennifer noticed an opening between the huge rocks. This would be a perfect spot to put the statue of the Blessed Virgin Mary. She sat on a rock and thought; this could be my little secret sanctuary.

The next day she got up early and left a note for her family saying she was at the infirmary. She took the statue to her secret place and prayed. "Dear God and Blessed Mary help us on this adventure and protect us from all harm. Please help Bill be more understanding, both with his family and the villagers."

---

Bill and the children walked to the village, he went to church and the children joined their friends. Joseph was learning to make arrows and the girls were making baskets. Later, Bill took a break and went to the infirmary to see Jennifer.

She was working at her desk. When she saw Bill's expression, she asked, "What's the matter? You look down in the dumps?"

"I can't seem to get through to the people. Only half of them show up for afternoon classes. When I talk to them, they stare at me with blank faces."

"Don't worry; I think you're doing a great job." Jennifer continued to check the records of her patients.

"I want everyone to attend class."

Jennifer put her pen down and said, "During the day, they have their chores. Not everyone has time to come." She patted his hand. "Besides, they learn about Christ when we teach them to read and write on Fridays."

Bill smiled at her. "You look at things differently than I do. I guess I expect too much."

Missia ran in the infirmary shouting, "Come, Jennifer, Salina's ready to have her baby."

Jennifer grabbed her medical bag. "I'm sorry Bill, I have to go. This will be the first time they asked me to deliver one of their babies."

When they arrived Salina's legs were spread apart and she was crouched over a soft bed of grass. Two women stood on each side, holding her arms for support.

Jennifer took Salina's arm. "Come, lie on your bed."

Salina shook her head and the women shouted, "No, No."

Jennifer tried to pull Salina. "You must let me help you."

"No, No, she's in position to have the baby," said Missia, pulling Jennifer away.

With each pain Salina groaned and bore down, while holding on to the women for support. After a short time, with the help of gravity, the baby slid out of the womb and dropped on the soft mound of grass, unharmed.

Missia picked up the infant, "It's a beautiful baby boy." She bathed him in warm water then handed the baby to Jennifer.

She took the child and examined him. "He's perfect; his skin is so soft and golden. Look at all the hair he has!" Then Jennifer gave the baby to Salina. "You have a healthy, wonderful baby."

On the way back to the infirmary, Jennifer said, "I never saw anyone give birth that way. It looks awkward."

Missa smiled, "The mother has less pain that way."

Jennifer felt the experience was overwhelming. Everyone was in bed when she arrived home.

She crawled in bed next to Bill and said, "They have an odd way of delivering babies."

"They have their way of doing things," said Bill. "They have a free spirit life. Everyone gets along. They work when they feel like it and the children are given a lot of attention."

"The women treat our children like their own. Margaret and Cassie can climb trees as well as the boys and Rosa keeps them busy making nets and hammocks."

Bill fluffed his pillow. "Joseph is really good with his bow and arrows. Ramos says he can kill a boar as well as he can. This really is a stress free life." Bill turned and blew out the candle.

"I wonder why my mother and father haven't written lately. We always get our mail with the supplies."

"You know, I was thinking the same thing. It's been a couple of months since we've heard from my dad and Caroline. I hope nothing's wrong."

"Maybe they're just busy. I'm sure everything's fine." Bill reached over and kissed Jennifer goodnight.

# Chapter Sixteen

It was the day before Christmas of their third year. Jennifer and the children looked for a small tree they could decorate. They found a small palm tree and wrapped flowering vines around it. Margaret and Cassie took crayons and drew pictures of Santa and candy canes. Then hung them on the tree. The villagers loved the tradition and helped them decorate. On Christmas day, they roasted a pig, sang songs and exchanged gifts. The family was happy in their new world. No demands were made of them. Jennifer loved working as a nurse, caring for the natives medical and educational needs. Bill loved teaching the gospel and did his best to save their souls. Their children adapted to the free life; it was like an extended vacation.

Now, it was April and the start of another rainy season. The rivers overflowed, flooding the grounds. Jennifer placed wooden bowls under the leaking roof of the infirmary.

"I'll be glad when this monsoon is over," said Jennifer. "Everything is drenched."

"You should be used to it by now," said Missia. "One more month and the rain will stop."

Jennifer could see the women working under tarps of palm fronds. They were rendering the fat from Trogon birds, which the men had killed that morning. When the women finished, they drained the oil into large wooden jugs. They used it for cooking and filling the lanterns. She could smell the mouth-watering aroma of the trogon birds roasting on the spit.

She took a stick to scrape a lob of meat from the searing bird. "This is delicious!"

Bill walked over. "Hmm, it smells great. Cut me a piece too. Where are the children?"

"Ramos took them with him. They are trapping lizards. Missia says they're good to eat,"

Jennifer handed Bill a piece of meat. "Uno's going to use the skins for shoes and bags."

"I love it here, even the rainy weather doesn't bother me," said Bill.

"We only have a year-and-a-half left of our five years," said Jennifer as she pulled another piece of meat from the bird. "Maybe we should think about extending our stay."

"I love it here, but let's think about it," said Bill. "You look a little pale, do you feel okay?"

Jennifer burped, then said. "My stomach is upset, but I'm trying to ignore it. I ate some strange fish yesterday that Missia was cooking. I don't think it agreed with me."

Bill laughed, "You must have an herb for that."

That's funny, laughed Jennifer. I'm going back to the infirmary. I'll take something then. I have to empty the bowls, they're probably overflowing. Want to come help me?"

"No. It sounds like a losing battle to me. I have a few things to do at the church."

When Jennifer arrived at the infirmary, Missia was taking care of a little girl. She had a cut on her knee. Missia looked at Jennifer. "You don't look so good."

Jennifer smiled, "My stomach is upset from that fish you cooked yesterday?"

"The pariah fish? It will eat you if you don't eat it first," laughed Missia. "Oh! I emptied the bowls and they're half full already. She stared at Jennifer and said, "Why don't you go home and lay down?"

"No. I'll be fine. I think I'll sit at my desk and have a cup of mint tea."

Jennifer could see the community hut where the natives were weaving. She watched as their busy hands moved like lightening, making mats, hats and shoes.

When Bill came in, he saw Jennifer staring into space. "Penny for your thoughts."

"I was just watching the people work. They laugh at everything."

"I know they do, it's contagious. Are you ready to go home?"

"When I get there, I am going straight to bed. I'll never eat that fish again."

"Get some sleep. You'll feel better in the morning."

"Don't worry about the children. They're eating in the village," said Jennifer as she climbed into bed.

She slept through the night and woke up in the morning feeling sick. She ran to the porch and threw up over the railing.

"I must be pregnant." She paced back and forth on the porch, waiting for Bill to wake up.

Bill came out and looked at Jennifer. "Do you feel any better?"

"No. I don't."

Eduardo ran up the stairs and smiled. "I'll bring Joseph's good present." He pulled a baby iguana out of his pant pocket.

"Go wake him up. He's still asleep in his room," said Jennifer. She turned to Bill. "I want to tell you something."

"You looked worried. Is everything okay?"

"I'm pregnant."

Bill was taken back for a moment, then he started pacing the floor. He walked over and knelt in front of her. His voice was strained as he said, "Babe, I'm always happy when you're carrying our child."

Tears streamed down her cheeks. "I didn't think too much about it when I didn't get my period the last two months. Missia told me the monsoon weather can throw a woman off their regular cycle. I tried not to get pregnant; I don't want to have a baby here."

"Don't cry." He put his arms around her and held her close. "How far along are you?"

"Three months. Suppose I have another breech birth?"

"God will watch over you, and give us a healthy baby." He kissed her tenderly.

Eduardo came bounding out on the porch. His smile lit his whole face. "Missy Rennie having baby."

Jennifer's stared at him. "Shame on you for eavesdropping."

Bill laughed. "Let's keep this a secret for a while. Promise, you won't tell anyone."

Eduardo put his finger to his lips. "Okay, I won't tell anyone."

It was noon when Jennifer and Bill walked to the village. They could smell pork roasting on the spit. She sniffed the air and said, "That usually means a celebration. I wonder what the happy occasion is."

"Everyone's excited about something."

When the women saw Bill and Jennifer, they giggled and made a circle around them. Clapping their hands they started to sing.

"What's the big celebration?" asked Bill.

The woman danced and sang, "Missy Rennie have babe?" One by one they touched Jennifer's stomach and laughed.

"Where's that big mouth, Eduardo?" said Jennifer.

Bill pulled Eduardo aside. "I thought you weren't going to tell anybody."

"I only told chief. He told everybody," said Eduardo

The celebration was held under woven mats coated with slick oil from the Trogon birds.

Jennifer tried to eat, but felt sick and went to the infirmary.

Missia brought a warm drink in a coconut shell. "Drink this. It will make you feel better."

Jennifer smelled it and started to set it down. "No thanks,"

Missia pushed the shell to Jennifer's mouth. "It will take the agga's away." Missia pretended to vomit.

Jennifer laughed, but was still hesitant to drink it. "Maybe later."

"It won't hurt the baby. It will make you feel better."

Jennifer sipped it slowly and the taste was pleasant. "What's it made of?"

"Papaya, ginger and uga berries, drink it all."

Jennifer drank the rest of it. "Thank you Missia. I hope it works."

---

Three months later, Chief Melardo invited Bill and Jennifer into his hut. "Sit, sit. I have something important to tell you." They sat on the woven mats and Missia gave them a cup of cool coconut milk. The chief stood proudly with his staff in hand. "When your baby is born, I give you great honor. I will make your child my own."

Jennifer gasped and didn't know what to say. She stuttered, "I...I... don't..."

Bill touched her hand and said, "I'll handle this. Chief, we thank you for the honor, but we can't accept it. In our country, the child always remains with the mother and father."

Chief Melardo slammed his staff on the table and roared, "You are not in your country! You are in mine." His face turned red and his belly jiggled with fury. "You will not insult me."

Bill bowed his head. "I apologize. I did not mean to insult you. Thank you for the honor. We will go home and think about it."

When they got back to their house, they checked each room to make sure Eduardo was not around.

Jennifer sat on the bed sobbing. "I won't let him take my baby."

"Calm down, you're getting hysterical. Everything will work out. Maybe he just takes the baby in name only."

Jennifer took a deep breath, but started to cry again. "Oh, no, he keeps the babies. Why do you think all those children live in his hut?" She stood up and wiped the tears from her eyes. "We have to leave here right away."

"What! We still have over a year to go, before we can leave."

"Giving up our child is not in the contract. How much money do we have?"

Bill shrugged his shoulders. "Not very much, around fifty dollars."

"Only fifty dollars!" Jennifer started to cry again.

Bill put his arm around her. "Don't worry. I'll go to Cartagena and wire the Carters. I'll tell them we have an emergency. I'm sure they'll make arrangements for a freighter to take us home." Bill got down on his knees and pulled Jennifer down with him. "Let's pray and ask for guidance and we'll leave everything in God's hands."

The next day, Bill borrowed the old horse and rickety wagon and took the five-hour ride to town. He sent a wire to Reverend Carter and waited patiently for an answer. Three hours later the wire was answered: "Recession going on. Stop. Have no money for tickets. Stop. Stay in Colombia."

Bill lowered his head and prayed, "I have put our problem in your hands God. I know everything will be all right."

At 2 a.m. in the morning Bill arrived home and Jennifer heard him enter the house. "Did they say they'd arranged for a freighter to take us home?"

"He said they have no money. There's a recession at home, whatever that means. We have to stay until our commitment is up."

"What! Don't they understand? They'll take my baby!"

Bill rubbed her back. "Don't get so excited. We've put our problems in God's hands. He won't let Chief Melardo take our baby."

"Damn right he won't, because I'm not staying." Jennifer stamped across the room.

"What did you say? You should be ashamed using foul language."

Jennifer walked close to him, their noses almost touching. Her eyes narrowed as she said, "Find out when the next freighter leaves, and what the tickets cost."

"What! I just got back from there." Sinking into a chair he took a moment to control himself. "I can't get the horse and wagon tomorrow, the villagers need it. Why don't you calm down? Everything will work out."

"Don't keep saying that." She stamped her foot and glared at him. "If you won't go, I will."

"I can get the wagon again in two days. Now, I have to take the wagon back to the village. When Bill returned, he walked in the house picked up his Bible and read until bed time.

Two days later, at daybreak, he climbed in the rickety horse-drawn wagon and headed back to Cartagena. His bones still ached from the last trip. When he arrived at the port office, he went to the receptionist. "I'd like to see the Freight Master."

"Do you have an appointment?" asked Margo.

"No, I don't. It's urgent that I talk with him."

"I'm sorry, but he's very busy and can't see you today."

"I'll wait and maybe you could squeeze me in."

Margo pointed at the clock on the wall. "It's 5 p.m. and the office is closing." She read the disappointment that shadowed his face. "If you can be here by 8:30 a.m. tomorrow morning, I'll make sure you see him."

Bill smiled. "I'll be here. Thank you very much and God bless you."

He left the horse and wagon at a stable near the shipyard and walked around the crowded city.

He felt hungry and entered a tavern. When he sat down, a waiter came over. Bill asked, "Do you speak English?"

"*Si senior*. Would you like some good Chili with lots of beans?" said the waiter.

"Okay, I'll try a bowl and a cup of coffee. Oh! Do you know where I can get a room?"

"*Si, senior*, we have a grandee room upstairs."

"Who do I talk to about renting it?"

"Me! Not only am I the waiter and cook, but also the owner. I am Vajelo, and I will give you a special room cheap." Vajelo brought the chili. "When you are finished I'll show it to you."

Bill tasted the chili, and then put his spoon down. It was cold and so spicy, it burnt his tongue. He started to call the waiter, but felt so hungry he ate it.

Vajelo took the dishes away, then said, "Come with me and I'll show you the room."

They walked down the long dreary hallway. The paint was peeling off the doors and the walls were dirty with cobwebs hanging from the ceiling.

Vajelo opened one of the doors and said, "Look! This is your room. How do you like it?"

Bill looked at the rusty iron bed, the stained green walls, and thought, "it's only for one night." Water marks streaked the ceilings and cobwebs decorated each corner. Bill started to walk out, but hesitated. He didn't know where else to go. "How much?"

"Two bucks for you, because you are a nice man."

"I'll take it."

"Come down and have a drink on the house," said Vajelo.

"No thank you. I need to get some sleep."

"Then I'll see you Manana. Oh, the toilet is down the hall."

Bill went to washed up and when he returned he tried to turn the lamp on; it didn't work.

"I'm too tired to read anyway." Bill crawled in bed and fell asleep. An hour later, he was awakened by loud music coming from the tavern below. His body felt hot and itchy. Bill struck a match and cringed when he saw the bed bugs scatter. He jumped out of bed, shaking his underwear, in case any were stuck to him. Wearier, Bill sat on the wooden chair in the corner. When morning came, he skipped breakfast and hurried to the freight office.

The receptionist arrived at the same time and said, "Glad you made it. Mr. Mc Gonical will see you shortly."

Ten minutes later Margo said, "He'll see you now."

When Bill entered the office, the freight master asked. "What can I do for you, Mr. Rennie?"

Bill told him the story and they talked for an hour. When Bill left for the long journey home, he had five tickets in his pocket.

When he arrived home, no one was there. He was so tired, he barely made it up the steps. Bill flopped on his bed. Jennifer came home and found him sound asleep. She sat beside him on the bed, looking at the clear cut line of his profile. His handsome features were bronzed from the sun and age lines showed around his eyes. Her chest swelled with love and she knew she would do anything for him. She started to run her hand over his muscular shoulders, when she realized he was watching her.

Jennifer kissed him on the forehead. "I didn't mean to wake you. You were sleeping so soundly."

"I'm exhausted." He reached over and gave her a hug.

She snuggled against him as she asked, "How did you make out?"

"There's a freighter leaving next Tuesday, but the ticket agent said they were all sold out. The next one leaves in a month."

"A month? That's too long!"

"Wait let me finish. I told the freight master our story." Bill sat up and stretched.

"What did he say?" She sat up anxious to hear the rest.

Bill took off his sweaty shirt then said. "At first he didn't seem to listen. Then I told him I was a minister and you a nurse; he changed his mind. It seems they had a chaplain and doctor scheduled to sail with them. But they canceled." Bill reached for a clean shirt as he continued, "He said we could take their place."

"What! Are you serious?"

"Here's the schedule. I hold service on Sundays and handle the crew's personal problems.

"You, my Florence Nightingale, will take care of the crew when they get hurt or sick."

"What a lucky break! Wait a minute, how much are they charging us?"

"That's the best part. Not one penny. The chaplain and doctor travel free. We have the chaplain's room and the children have the doctor's room." Bill picked up his Bible. "It's not a lucky break, God is guiding us."

Jennifer put her arms around Bill and kissed him. "We're really leaving Tuesday. I'm so happy. Well, I'm sorry in a way we can't stay, the people are like family."

"Where are the children?" asked Bill.

"They're in the lagoon swimming with Rosa and Ramos. Let's join them."

They started to walked down the path until they saw the children walking home.

Jennifer walked between her daughter's with her arms over their shoulders. "Where's Rosa and Ramos."

"They went back to the village," said Margaret.

Bill and Joseph tossed a coconut back and forth as they walked. "You should have seen the fish I caught," said Joseph.

"You kids are free spirits in a jungle playground," said Jennifer as she laughed and tousled Cassie's hair.

The children ran up the porch steps and Bill called out. "Wait. We want to talk to you."

They saw the serious look on their father's face and sat on the tree stumps.

"We're leaving to go back to the states next Tuesday," said Bill.

Joseph stood up quickly, "What! I don't want to go to the states. I love it here."

"Cassie and Margaret together cried, "Why do we have to leave our friends?"

"Sorry kids, but it's not your decision. Your mother and I have made up our minds. I want you to pack your things and be ready to go by the end of the week."

"I know you'll miss your friends and all the animals," said Jennifer and then she laughed. "Hey, everybody goes home from vacation and ours is over."

The children walked into their room, murmuring, "We want to stay here. We don't want to leave."

"I know how they feel," said Jennifer. "If I wasn't pregnant, we wouldn't be leaving."

---

Bill woke up as the sun streamed in the window. He rolled over and tickled Jennifer's back, "Wake up sleepy head. We have to talk to the chief."

Jennifer yawned and stretched. "I hate telling him."

"Well, let's get the children up and get it over with."

Chief Melardo saw them coming and invited them into his hut. He smiled showing his white teeth. "I know you have something to tell me."

Bill gave him a questionable look. "How do you know?"

The chief laughed and pointed his finger at them. "You think you have a secret? I know everything. I know you're leaving Tuesday and taking the freighter home."

Jennifer stuttered, "How did you find out?"

"You can't keep a secret from me," he said puffing his chest out. "I'm glad you came to tell me."

"We never intended to hide it from you," said Jennifer. "We wanted to make sure we could get a freighter first."

The chief patted them on the back. "Why are you leaving?"

"I want to have my baby in my own country. Near our family," said Jennifer.

"I see. Well, I'm sorry you are leaving. My people will be very sad."

"We hate to leave your wonderful village. We have been happy here and will miss everyone," said Bill.

"Come with me and I'll tell my people." Chief Melardo walked to the door and signaled Uno, the hunter to comer. "Tell everyone to come to the community hut, I have sad news."

When the chief announced they were leaving, Missia ran over to Jennifer and grasped her hands. "I don't want you to go. You're like my sister."

"I feel the same way. We have taught each other so many healing techniques. You took the place of my sister, Caroline."

Eduardo walked over. "Don't go. Stay and continue to be family."

Bill placed his arm around Eduardo's shoulder. "I'm going to miss you. You've been a great help to us. It's time for us to return to the states."

"We will have a farewell celebration before you leave," said the chief. My hunters will kill the biggest pig they can find, in your honor."

Missia took Jennifer's arm. "Let's go over the herb supply that is in the infirmary. I want to see how much we have left."

"There's enough for at least six months," said Jennifer. "By then, another couple will come and bring more supplies."

"Take some of this tonic with you. It will keep you from getting the *aagh's* on the ship. It won't hurt the baby. Our women take it all the time when they are pregnant. You can give it to the children, if they get seasick."

Rosa walked into the infirmary, with tears streaming down her face and hugged Jennifer. "I will never forget how you saved my life. I love you like a mother."

Missia handed Jennifer the statue of the Blessed Mary. "I don't want you to forget her."

"How did you know about this," said Jennifer.

I saw you go in the woods one day and was going to walk with you. Then, I saw you stop at the giant rocks. You kneeled down and talked to this statue. I realized you were having a private moment."

Jennifer didn't want to explain why she had the Virgin Mary. "That is where I go when I want to be alone," said Jennifer. "Pastor Rennie doesn't know about my secret place."

"I too have secrets from my husband. Things he doesn't need to know." Missia handed her a bag one of the natives had weaved. "Put your secret in here and put the aagha on top to hide it," laughed Missia.

"With all that's been going on, I had forgotten about the statue. Thank you for not letting me forget it." Jennifer kissed Missia and Rosa. "I will always miss you."

The sun was setting when the family walked home. Jennifer sighed, "We've had a wonderful experience. We came to teach them, yet they taught us so much."

# Chapter Seventeen

They started to pack and Jennifer could hear the children banging the dresser drawers and complaining.

"I don't want to go home. I'll miss my friends," said Joseph.

"Maybe we can hide in the jungle. They'd have to leave without us," said Cassie.

"It won't work. They'd send Uno out to find us," said Margaret.

"Yeah, he's a good hunter. He'd find us," said Joseph.

---

On Monday, a celebration was held and the women circled Jennifer and her daughters. Puta, the Chief's number two wife, said, "We made gifts for you, so that you will remember us."

Several ladies handed Jennifer woven hats with bird feathers tucked in the bright woven band. Others presented her with colorful skirts.

Jennifer could feel the tears swelling in her eyes. "Thank you very much. We will cherish these forever."

Cassie and Margaret put their hats on. They hugged the women who had been like mothers to them. "Thank you we love them."

Uno walked over to Bill and Joseph. "You are like brothers. We will miss your prayers." He put the woven hats on Bill and Joseph's head and gave then each a pair of shoes made from the skins of the iguanas.

Bill held the shoes up and said, "These are the most beautiful shoes in the world." Joseph sat on the ground and put them on. Laughing, he danced around and said, "Perfect fit."

The pig was roasting over the fire and Jennifer walked over. "That's the biggest pig I have ever seen!"

"It's a wild boar," said Ramos. "I shot it for the celebration." He handed Bill a circled tusk. "This is for you."

"What a terrific gift. Thank you," said Bill.

"Wear it on your left wrist for good luck. Where is my hunting friend Joseph? I have one for him too."

"He's over in the field with the other children," said Bill

A special drink was served made from fermented mango juice and coconut milk. The natives played small wooden flutes, while the people sang and danced their ceremonial dances.

"I feel woozy from this drink," said Bill

The chief took another sip from his coconut shell. "We serve it only on sad occasions and we are not happy you are leaving."

As the sun set, Bill said, "I think we better go. We have some last minute packing." He stood up and staggered and everyone laughed.

Chief Melardo laughed. "Here, this will help you walk." He handed Bill his wooden staff with monkeys carved around it.

"I don't need that. I'm fine," said Bill.

"Keep it. I made it for you," said the Chief.

"This is a magnificent cane. Thank you."

Jennifer hugged Missia and Rosa. Then said goodbye to the rest of the people. "Thank you for everything. We'll miss you all."

"Hallelujah," yelled one of the men and everyone laughed.

Bill looked for his children. "Ramos, have you seen Joseph and his sisters?"

Eduardo called out, "They're coming. The children of the village are saying farewell."

They came out of the community center, carrying bows, arrows and small purses.

"Look at all the presents they gave us," said Margaret.

"That is so thoughtful. Come, we have to go home," said Jennifer.

"Can't we stay a little longer?" asked Cassie.

Bill looked at them sternly. "It's time to go."

The next morning Eduardo stacked their luggage on the wagon. When they left, twenty of the villagers followed them a short distance. They gave Jennifer and the girl's bouquets of flowers and threw petals on the ground, as the family walked alongside the wagon. Tears were in everyone's eyes, as they said their last goodbyes.

When they reached the port, they unloaded the wagon and Bill shook Eduardo's hand. "I don't know how we would have managed without you."

"Change your mind and stay. I will put everything back on the wagon."

"I wish we could, but we must go. Goodbye, good friend."

"The ships leaving in a half-hour, we better get on board," said Jennifer. She hugged

Eduardo. "I'll really miss you and so will the children."

Eduardo pulled JoJo out of a basket. "He wants to say goodbye."

"Can we take him with us?" said Cassie jumping up and down.

"I'm afraid not," said Bill. "Say goodbye and let's get on the ship."

The family climbed the gangplank and waved as the ship pulled away from the pier.

"I'm going to miss everyone, especially Rosa and Missia." said Jennifer.

"I know. I treasure the friendships we made in the past three-and-a-half years," said Bill.

The children wept. "I don't want to go. Why do we have to leave our friends?"

"We've already gone over that," said Jennifer. "Let's go to our cabins, I want to unpack before dinner."

As they walked into their rooms Jennifer said, "These cabins are much cleaner and larger than the last ship."

"I hope the food is better," said Bill, as he pulled his shirt off. "Babe, hand me a clean shirt. This one is filthy from helping Eduardo unload the wagon. We're eating in the officer's dining room again."

"Jennifer took a dose of the tonic Missia had given her. "I don't want to get seasick; I'll give some to the children too." She went to their room and gave each one a spoonful.

"What's that for? asked Margaret

"It will keep you from getting seasick. Missia says it works wonders."

"It tastes good," said Margaret. "Can I have some more?"

"Only if you need it. We only have one bottle and it has to last the whole trip," said

Jennifer. "Now stay in your room until I call you for dinner."

It would be a longer trip going back as the ship was scheduled to stop at three ports. The weather remained clear and the seas stayed calm, as they sailed through glass like sea. Jennifer tutored the children each morning, then they were free to play.

She sat on one of the lounge chair's looking out at the horizon. Her thoughts went to

Carnegie. "I wonder how Caroline and dad are? I can't believe I'm going to see them; it's been so long." She stood up and went to the railing and looked out over the horizon and thought, "Will I ever be able to make amends with Mother? I miss Nellie and William; they were so kind to me. I wonder what they'll say when they see I'm pregnant?"

Bill came on the deck and stood next to her. "You look deep in thought."

"We've been away so long. I'm wondering how everyone is."

---

They pulled into the first port and the crew rushed on deck, waiting for permission to go ashore. "I can't wait to have a beer and meet a tootsie," said Ralf, the chef.

"Me too. I'm tired of looking at you men. I want a female to hold," said one of the crew.

The captain voice came over the loud speaker, "Permission granted for those cleared to go ashore. Make sure you are back at twenty-four bells." The men rushed down the gangplank like captured prisoners.

At midnight, the parade of drunk and rowdy men staggered back, some were carried, others could barely walk. The singing and cussing could be heard throughout the ship, until they fell asleep in their hammocks.

In the morning, Jennifer found a line of men in front of the infirmary. "Good grief! You men look like a mess. You must have had a good time last night."

The first man in line had a two-inch gash on his forehead. "I'm really hurting."

"How in the world did you do this?" asked Jennifer, as she cleaned the cut.

"I got pissed off at some dumb bloke in the bar and I slugged him."

Jennifer stifled a laugh as she stitched him up. "Looks like he slugged you back. You know you are not supposed to fight."

The next man was holding his stomach. "I don't feel good, my stomach hurts."

"Here take a spoonful of this." She shoved the sassafras syrup in his mouth. "It will help your hangover." Jennifer looked at the line of men and shook her head. "This will be a busy day."

At the clergy's cabin, the line reached to the end of the hall. The first man sat down and with his head bowed. "Pastor. I'm a married man. I try to be true to the misses, but I get lonely." The crewman grabbed his crotch and continued, "Everything gets itching for a woman's body. I know it was wrong to bed that trollop last night, but I couldn't help it."

Bill placed his hand on the man's head and prayed, "Dear Lord, forgive this man in his time of weakness. Give him the strength to cast Satan away and stay true to his wife. Amen."

Each man confessed their sinful actions and felt better and swore they would never do it again.

Fifty knot winds churned the seas and the motion of the ship became intolerable. Jennifer and the children stayed in her room for safety.

"I don't feel seasick. That tonic really works," said Margaret.

Cassie looked out through the port hole and gasped, "Look how high the waves are!"

Captain Brown, knocked on their door and called out, "Mrs. Rennie, I'd like to talk to you."

Jennifer opened the door. "What is it?"

"I don't want the children to go out on deck in this weather. It wouldn't be safe."

"We won't. Mamma says we have to play inside." said Margaret.

"Don't worry, Captain Brown. We're staying in our rooms," said Jennifer.

They could hear the howling wind and feel the waves beating against the ship.

Joseph said, "This weather scares me. Will we be all right?"

Jennifer took his hand. "We'll be fine. Let's play a game of checkers?"

The next day, after breakfast, Jennifer went to her stateroom to get a sweater. The children were still at the breakfast. When she returned, they were gone. Jennifer went looking for them but couldn't find them. Her first thought was they had gone out on deck.

She ran to the captain's quarters and knocked on the door. When he answered she said, "I can't find my children."

He could sense the panic in her voice. "Calm down Mrs. Rennie, I sure they are safe." He called to his first mate, "Have you seen the children?"

"Yes Captain, they are down in the crew's dining room playing cards."

Jennifer and the Captain walked into the room. The children were sitting at the table with three men, playing cards.

"Look mamma," Joseph said, "We're learning to play poker! Look at all the crackers I won."

Margaret smiled and said, "This is fun, but Joseph's always winning."

"You scared me to death. I didn't know where you were," said Jennifer.

"Sorry, Mrs. Rennie. We didn't mean no harm," said one of the men." They were wandering around the halls and we didn't want them to go out on deck. Most of us have kids of our own at home; it felt good to entertain them."

"Thank you, but that's not a good game to teach children. Come children we have homework to do."

Two more weeks past with cloudy unpredictable weather and the ship stopped at another port. The wind blew so hard; the family didn't bother getting off, but the crew was eager. When they came back, it was the same. Very few were sober, and some needed medical attention.

Jennifer patched them up and Billed prayed for forgiveness of their sins.

The next day when Jennifer woke up, it was sunny and calm. Bill was still sleeping so she dressed quietly and went out on the deck. Streaks of red and orange slashed across the sky and stretched as far as the horizon.

"Look over to the starboard," shouted the mate at the wheel. "Look far into the horizon, you'll see land."

Jennifer kept scanning the horizon. "I don't see anything, but water."

"Look more to your right. Can you see it now?"

"No, I don't see anything…I see it. I do see it," she said, jumping up and down.

"That's Cape May, New Jersey," said the mate.

Jennifer ran to their cabin shouting, "Get up Bill. You can see land."

The children heard her and raced up to the deck, "Where? Where? Show us."

"Praise the Lord," said Bill lowering his head. "Thank you God for getting us home safe."

"We aren't there yet. We keep sailing till we reach the Delaware River and pull into the harbor of Philadelphia. That'll take three more days."

On October 1, 1929, after six weeks at sea, the ship pulled up to the dock. They stood at the railing looking at the swarms of people below.

"Everyone looks tired and nervous," said Jennifer. "Why are they pushing and shoving each other?"

The captain stood nearby and wiped his brow with his hanky. "It's very hot for October." He put his hand on Bill's shoulder. "Please be careful when you go ashore. Keep your belongings close to you."

"We will. Is there going to be trouble?" asked Jennifer.

"People are out of work and have no food or place to live," said Captain Brown.

"Our pastor wired there was a recession going on. I wasn't expecting anything like this," said Bill, wiping his brow with his sleeve. "What happened?"

The Captain took off his cap and wiped his forehead, as he said, "I'm not sure, but from what I hear on the radio, the economy is in bad shape. Thousands of people have lost their jobs. The market crashed and banks went under. People have been losing every dime they had. Banks and businesses folded and people have no way to pay bills or mortgages. They're killing each other for a few dollars and stealing whatever they can get their hands on."

"You're not serious?" said Bill.

"Dead serious."

They stepped off the gangplank and were overwhelmed by the lines of men waiting at the docks for work. People walked in a hypnotic state, begging for money or food. Bill huddled his family together, as strangers bumped and pushed up against them.

A woman approached, holding the hands of her two children. Desperation in her eyes she begged, "Can you spare a few cents? We're starving."

Bill reached in his pocket and handed her a quarter. "God bless you and help you."

Captain Brown said, "Fred and Toby will unload your luggage and stand guard until you decide what you're doing." He shook their hands. "It was a pleasure having you on board. Goodbye and good luck."

"Thank you." Bill watched the men unload their things. When everything was accounted for he asked one of the crew, "Will you stay with our children and watch our belongings for a few minutes? We want to make a few phone calls."

The crewman rubbed Joseph's head. "I'll take care of everything and they'll be safe."

Bill and Jennifer headed for the pay phone and Bill called his father. "Hi, Dad, we're in Philadelphia. I was wondering, how things are in Carnegie?"

William's voice sounded raspy. "It's bad, son. The mines are closed and the steel mill laid off half of its workers. Things weren't good before the crash, but after the banks went under I lost all my savings and my investments went down with the market. We sold livestock, everything. Even that money's gone. We've lost everything."

"Good heavens! That's terrible," said Bill.

"Things are bad, but right before the crash I was able to sell our house and farm. We're living in yours." William sighed.

"I hate to ask Dad, but could you wire me some money? We'd like to come home."

There was silence, and then Bill heard the deep sorrow in his father's voice. "I'm sorry, son. I don't have any money. We haven't been able to pay our bills. The phone company is shutting us off tomorrow." The words caught in his throat and Bill could tell that his dad was trying not to cry. We're living on what we can grow. Your mother is taking it hard."

"I understand, Dad. Don't worry, we'll figure out something. Give Mom our love."

When he hung up, he started to quiver and swallowed hard as he said, "They've lost the farm and everything".

"What! That's not possible." Jennifer reached for the phone. "I'll call my father at the bank, I'm sure he can help us."

She dialed the number and the operator said, "The line has been disconnected."

"What! It can't be." said Jennifer. "I'm sorry, but that line has been disconnected," the operator repeated sternly. Jennifer's hand shook, as she dialed the home number and the phone rang and rang.

As she was about to hang up a tired, withered voice answered. "Hello."

Jennifer thought she had a wrong number. "Is this the May residence?"

The quivering voice answered, "Yes, Who is this?"

"Father, this is Jennifer. Are you all right?"

"Jennifer! Is it really you? Are you still in Colombia?" Francis asked as his voice cracked.

"No, we're in Philadelphia," Jennifer said talking louder. "Can you send us money to come home?"

He sobbed, then cleared his throat and said, "Our bank went under. I've…I've lost everything."

Jennifer wiped the tears from her eyes. "This is hard to believe!" She blew her nose as she asked, "You've lost everything?"

"It's all gone, except your mother's house. That's going next." Francis whispered weakly. "I'm sorry, but I can't help you financially. You'd best stay there until things improve."

"Father, we only have forty dollars and no place to stay." She heard the click of the phone as her father hung up. Jennifer slammed down the phone and leaned against the wall. "Oh my Goodness! Father's lost everything, even the bank. This is horrible. What are they going to do?"

Bill put his arm around her. "God will help them."

Jennifer picked up the phone again. "I'll call Caroline. Maybe she can help."

"The line is disconnected," said the operator.

Jennifer put her hand to her mouth, trying to stifle a sob. "Her phone's cut off too. Now, what are we going to do?"

They walked back to the crewman and said, "Thank you for watching the children."

"Is it all right if we leave ya now? We gotta see our family," said the crewman.

"Sure, go ahead. Thanks for your help." Bill took Jennifer's hand. "Don't worry. We'll figure something out." He thought for a few seconds then said, "You and the children stay by the luggage, I'm going to see the dock master."

The dock master had been watching the family through his window and when Bill entered he said, "Heck of a way to come home, isn't it?"

"Yes, we certainly came back to a mess," said Bill. "Would it be all right if we left our luggage in your office until we find a place to stay?"

"Sure, I'll lock it up. If you leave it outside, it'll be gone in the blink of an eye."

"Thanks." Bill and the family managed to carry the luggage to the office. When it was safety locked away, he said, "I'll be back for it as soon as we find a place to stay."

The family tried to dodge the crowd as they walked the streets. "I've never seen so many people begging," said Jennifer. "I feel sorry for them." They walked through the park, looking at poor souls sitting on benches or on the ground, surrounded by their meager possessions. Their hearts went out to the children crying as their parents sat in a hopeless daze.

"I can't believe what has happened," said Jennifer.

They held their children's hands tightly as they continued across the street. They walked past the Marshall City Bank and saw people looking up. They glanced up and saw a man standing on the ledge of the twelfth floor. He jumped and let out a horrifying scream. He hit the sidewalk with a loud thud that echoed through the air. Jennifer turned away with the children, as his head cracked. His blood and brains splattered everywhere. Bill flinched as the blood splashed on his coat. Jennifer and the children screamed.

"Take the children around the corner," Bill shouted as he rushed to the man's side. A crowd gathered as he placed his hand on the man's chest and felt for a pulse. "He's dead, someone call the police." Bill placed his hand on the man's head and prayed. "Welcome this man into the kingdom of heaven. Forgive him for taking his own life."

A man reached over and grabbed the dead man's watch and stuffed it in his pocket. "He won't be needing this."

Bill grabbed another man's hand as he tried to untie the dead man's shoes. "Stop, leave the man alone. Have you no respect for the dead?"

"Get out of my way," snarled the man, pushing Bill aside. "I need them more than he does."

The crowd went through the dead man's pockets, stripping off his coat and pants. Bill shook his head in disgust and moved back before he was knocked over.

Saddened by the crowd's reactions, he continued to pray. "Have mercy on him, O Lord and welcome him. Amen." Exhausted, Bill walked around the corner where Jennifer and the children were huddled together.

Jennifer sobbed as she said, "I can't believe that man jumped from the building! There are too many horrible things happening."

"I don't like it here," cried Margaret as she hugged her sobbing brother and sister.

Bill knelt beside his children. "That was a terrible thing for you to witness, but everything is going to be all right."

Jennifer trembled, but held back the tears. "What are we going to do? Where are we going to find a place to live with only forty-five dollars to our name?"

Bill shook his head. "Reverend Carter mentioned there was a recession, but I didn't know it was this bad." He picked up a newspaper from the street and read the headline. "Country in mist of Great Depression! Unemployment Out Of Control!" Bill let the paper slide back down to the sidewalk and leaned against the brick wall.

He stood thinking for quite a while and then said, "I know who can help us. Let me find a phone book first."

"What! Tell me," said Jennifer pulling on his shirt sleeve.

He walked to the phone booth on the corner as he said, "I will in a minute." He looked through the phone directory and found the address he wanted, then hailed a taxi. Three cabs took off at the same time, blasting their horns, as they cut each other off, trying to get the fare. Bill opened the door of the first taxi that reached him.

They climbed in as Bill said, "Take us to Third and Susquehanna Streets."

Jennifer held Joseph on her lap and said, "Why are we going there?"

"Pastor Markus told me about a reverend he knew at the Church of Faith. Let me think. What is the name of the Reverend? Thatcher, that's it!"- Jennifer couldn't stop trembling and her voice shook as she asked, "What makes you think he'll help us?"

"Pastor Markus said Reverend Thatcher was the kindest man he ever knew. I'm sure he'll help us."

A service was in progress when they arrived and they sat in the last pew listening as

Reverend Thatcher gave his sermon.

"There's a terrible shadow passing over this part of the world," shouted the reverend. "It is God's way of punishing the wicked, the greedy. Those that lust after women, the immoral people of the devil"

"Amen," chanted the crowd.

In a bold, rasping voice the reverend continued, "But fear not! That's right, fear not! He will watch over his people and help them through this time of famine. But only, now listen to me, only if you have faith in Him."

"Hallelujah!" shouted the congregation.

When the sermon was over, Bill introduced himself. "I'm Pastor Rennie, from the Saviors Church in Carnegie. That was a wonderful sermon you delivered."

"Thank you," said the reverend. "What can I do for you?"

Bill told him about their missionary work in Colombia and why they had to leave early.

The reverend sat next to Jennifer. "Don't you fear little mother; the Lord will take care of you and your children."

Jennifer's eyes swelled with tears. "My baby is due in five months and we have no place to live!"

When the children saw their mother crying they started to weep and they clung to her.

Reverend Thatcher thought for a few minutes then spoke, "Come into the back room. There are comfortable chairs and a pot of tea. You can rest and have a cup, while I make a couple of phone calls." In a short time the reverend came out smiling. "I have a house for you and there's a public school about eight blocks away. "A kind lady from our parish has a house that she hasn't been able to rent. She'll let you have it rent free, for six months. By then you should be on your feet. You can discuss the amount you'll pay at that time."

Jennifer let out a sigh and said, "How can we ever thank her?"

"Don't worry about that now," said Reverend Thatcher. "Right now we'll hop in my bus and go to the docks for your belongings."

"Reverend Thatcher," asked Jennifer. "Is the Church of Faith the same as the one Pastor Markus runs?"

"In most ways. The only difference is that we believe in faith healing until there is a problem. Then the lord needs a helping hand."

"Such as?" asked Jennifer.

"When it's a matter of life or death, it's time to call a doctor."

Bill was listening and said, "That's against our religion. We believe God will heal.us."

"The way we see it," said the Reverend. "The good Lord put doctors on this earth to help him. When he's ready to call you to heaven, no medicine on earth will stop him."

"I can't abide by that thinking," said Bill.

Reverend Thatcher pulled up at the dock masters office. "Well, here we are. Let's get the luggage and I'll drive you to your new home."

As they drove down Germantown Avenue, the Reverend said, "We're looking for Camac Street. Ah, here it is." He turned and they came to a row of brick houses. "That's it," he said, stopping at number 1332.

"Why isn't the lady living in it?" asked Bill.

"Her sister died and left her the house and all the furniture. Now the economy is so bad, it's impossible to rent, let alone sell it."

"We are so grateful. How can we thank the lady who owns it?" asked Bill.

Reverend Thatcher handed him the key. "I'll tell her how grateful you are, but I'm the grateful one. The Lord brought you to me when I needed a new pastor." He helped them unpack then said, "Get settled and come see me the day after tomorrow, that is if you still want to."

"Yes I do. We believe in faith healing; the doctor part is something we won't abide by."

"Fine. I'll see you in a couple of days."

———————————

When they entered the house, Jennifer couldn't believe her eyes. "Everything is exquisite. I can't believe we're going to live in such a lovely house." She walked into the parlor. "I love the French Provincial furniture."

"Look, there's a piano," shouted Margaret.

Joseph sat down and banged on the keys as he tried to sing "Get along little doggie."

"Don't do that; you'll ruin it," said Jennifer, closing the lid of the piano. She walked into the dining room. "My mother had a cherry mahogany dinning set like this." Jennifer rubbed her hand across the table and smiled at the china closet, filled with exquisite dinnerware.

Margaret called out. "Mamma come look! The pantry has food in it."

Jennifer sat in a red velvet, upholstered chair and took a deep breath. "After what we were living in, this is a true blessing."

The children ran upstairs to the bedrooms shouting, "Yippee, we have our own rooms."

They carried the luggage up and Bill said, "Quiet down. You're making too much noise."

Joseph ran into the largest room. "This room is mine."

"No. I'm the oldest. I get to pick first," said Margaret.

Joseph slammed the door and locked it. "It's my room and you can't come in."

"All right, that's enough out of you." Jennifer knocked on the door. "Joseph unlock this door." Joseph opened the door a crack and peeked out. Jennifer pushed open the door. "Let me see the bedrooms." She inspected both rooms and said, "Margaret, you and Cassie will sleep in this large room. Joseph, you can sleep in the room across from them."

Joseph's mouth puckered as he whined, "Not fair. Why can't I have the big room?"

Jennifer knelt down and hugged him. "Because there are two of them and only one of you. Okay children, unpack your clothes."

Jennifer started to open her suitcases and heard the children run down the steps.

"Let's see what the rest of the house is like," said Margaret.

They opened the door of the pantry and Joseph said, "I wonder where this goes? I want to see what's down there."

They ventured down and Margaret said, "It's dark and I can't find a light."

"I could play hide and seek down here and you'd never find me," said Joseph.

"I don't like being in the dark. I'm going upstairs," said Margaret.

"Yeah, it scares me," said Cassie. The girls ran up the steps and slammed the cellar door.

"Ha, ha, we locked the door. The boogie man's going to get you," said Margaret.

"Stop that racket. Get up here and unpack your clothes," yelled Jennifer.

"Ha, ha, you're locked in and the bogeyman coming after you," teased Margaret.

"Mamma, Daddy, help me," screamed Joseph.

Jennifer and Bill ran down and heard them say, "Here comes the boogeyman."

Bill slapped them on their backside. "Get up to your room now." He opened the cellar door and paddled Joseph. "That will teach you to behave. Get upstairs."

Jennifer was shocked. "Bill, that's the first time you ever laid hands on our children. That wasn't necessary."

Bill was out of breath and his face turned red. "It's time they learned to behave. The Lord says, spare the rod and spoil the child."

The children were crying as they ran up to their bedrooms. Bill called out to them, "If you don't shut up, I'll use the strap on you."

Jennifer grabbed his arm. "Whoa, wait a minute. I won't let you beat our children."

Bill's eyes bore into hers and they stared at each other. He started to say something, but walked out of the room.

Jennifer followed him. "I know coming home to this mess is nerve racking, but we can't take it out on the children."

"I guess my nerves are bad. Why wouldn't they be? We come back from living a quiet life into a big city full of turmoil and noise. We have very little money, our parents are broke and we can't get back to our house in Carnegie."

Jennifer started to answer him but stopped when she heard the children crying and went to calm them.

"Why did Daddy hit us?" asked Margaret sobbing.

"Daddy is worried and tired."

"He's been tired before and never hit us," said Joseph.

Jennifer wiped his nose with her handkerchief and dried his eyes. "Unpack your clothes and try to be quiet while I see what I can find for dinner. After we eat, I'll play the piano and we can sing and have fun."

"Ok," they sniffled as they began to unpack.

---

Sunday morning they went to the Church of Faith for the first time. They arrived early, before the congregation. Reverend Thatcher introduced them to Mrs. Claudia Runderson, a heavy set woman who played the piano. She had a round pudgy face that held a constant smile. "Claudia is always the first one here," said Reverend Thatcher. "She loves playing the piano and never misses a service." Jennifer smiled, shook her hand and noticed her staring at Bill.

"I'm so glad to meet you, Pastor Rennie," she said smiling sweetly at him. When you give the service. I'd be delighted to play for you."

"Thank you. That's very kind," said Bill gently pulling his hand from her grip.

Bill and his family sat in the first row and watched Mrs. Runderson walk down the aisle. Her body waddled like Jell-O under her sack dress, as she approached the piano. When the service began, Jennifer felt a warm relaxed feeling and felt comfortable there. She was pleased that the congregation was much quieter than the church in Carnegie. When the Reverend prayed, Jennifer put her hand in the pocket of her dress and held her rosary beads. Silently she said the Hail Mary. When church was over, Mrs. Runderson came scurrying up to Bill. "Mr. Rennie it was so nice having you here. I do hope you will become a member of our church."

"Don't worry, Pastor Rennie will be giving the service here shortly," said Reverend Thatcher.

"Oh, I'm so delighted. Well, I must be going. Tod aloo."

On the way home, Jennifer winked at Bill. "I think the piano player has a crush on you."

"I don't think so. She's just lonely. I understand she's a widow and lives alone."

# Chapter Eighteen

It was the end of November and the winter winds rattled the windows. It was hard keeping the house warm as they were low on coal. Jennifer went through the children's closets looking for warm clothing. Most of the things were for the summer weather. She went down to the parlor where Bill was reading. "We have to get the children some warm clothes. All they have is summer clothes. They need coats and warms shoes."

"I'm going to church to see if Reverend Thatcher has any work for me. While I'm there, I'll check to see if anyone donated warm coats. Then I'm going to the unemployment office."

"Oh! Have you registered the children for school?"

The children were playing checkers on the floor and Margaret said, "Why do we have to go to school? Can't Mamma teach us at home, like she did in Columbia?"

Jennifer poured a cup of chicory coffee and looked out of the window. "No I haven't. I don't how they'll make out in school. I've been teaching them for over three years."

"I know but they still have to go to school," said Bill.

She took a sip of coffee and said, "I've been busy trying to unpack. I haven't had a chance." She sat at the table next to Bill. "Time is going so fast. March will be here before we know it. That's when the baby's due."

"Maybe you should register them today. He kissed her goodbye. I've got to go."

Jennifer watched him walk down the street. She wondered what they were going to do when their money ran out. They only had ten dollars left. She carried the dishes to the sink and stared out of the window. The leaves had turned shades of red and brown and were blowing in circles around the yard.

"Mama, can we go out to play?" asked Joseph.

"No, I have to register you in school." Jennifer went through their drawers and found several sweaters and light jackets. "Maybe," she thought, "If I put enough layers on them, it will keep them warm."

The cold wind blew against them as they walked down the street. "Stay close to the buildings, it will protect you from the wind," said Jennifer.

"I'm cold," said Joseph. "I can't walk anymore."

"We've already walked six blocks. You can make it. We only have two more to go. Look! You can see the school," said Jennifer. "Let's hold hands and run."

They stopped at the corner for the light to change and a trolley car went by.

"Why can't we ride on the trolleys?" asked Margaret

Jennifer tucked her scarf into her collar as she said, "We can't afford it. Come on, the school is just across the street."

The school nurse was sitting at her desk when Jennifer and the children walked in. "Can I help you?"

"The principal sent me," said Jennifer. "He said you had to examine them before I can register them for school."

Nurse Jennings handed Jennifer two papers and asked. "Have the children been vaccinated?"

Jennifer took the papers and said, "No, they haven't."

"Okay. I can examine them. However, they'll need small pox vaccinations before they can attend school. The nurse picked up a fine-toothed comb and searched through Cassie's hair.

"You don't have to do that. My children do not have head lice," said Jennifer.

"We have to do this with each child entering school." The nurse looked through Margaret and Joseph's heads, then continued with the examinations. "I've checked them over and everything seems fine. They can start next Monday as long as they're vaccinated."

Jennifer smiled and said, "Thank you. We'll see you Monday."

She thought about going to the clinic, but knew Bill would be furious.

Jennifer pulled the children close to her, trying to shield them from the cold wind. The sun was behind the clouds and the cold seeped through their light clothing. "Stamp your feet when you walk, it will warm them. Stay close together."

She shivered in her light spring coat and said, "Let's stop in this store for a moment to warm up."

The clerk looked up as they entered and asked, "May I help you with something?"

"I wanted to look at your infants wear," said Jennifer. "I'm five months pregnant and will need some baby clothes." Her legs and back ached and she looked for a chair.

The clerk could tell she was tired and said, "Why don't you rest for a moment?"

Jennifer legs wobbled as she walked to the chair. "Thank you so much."

Margaret loved everything in the store and picked up a tiny garment. "Isn't this cute. It looks like it would fit my doll."

"Don't touch anything." Jennifer saw a baby carriage in the corner. "Oh, this is lovely." She pushed the carriage back and forth visualizing her baby in it. Then she said, "Thank you so much. I'll be back soon."

The walk home seemed endless and Jennifer wasn't sure she was going to make it. She kept her mind occupied with the children's vaccination. What was she going to do?

Bill was home when they arrived. "How did you make out? Are they registered?"

Jennifer collapsed on the sofa beside him. "Yes, but they can't go without being vaccinated." She rubbed her swollen ankles. "I'm so glad to get off my feet, I ache all over.

How did you make out? Did you find work?"

Bill ran his hands through his curly hair as he let out a sigh of exhaustion. "I worked two hours for Reverend Thatcher doing paper work. Then I went to the employment office. I was one of the lucky ones to get a job. I worked four hours today, and will work the next three days."

"What does it pay?"

Bill took off his shoes and wiggled his toes. "Three dollars a day."

"At least we'll be able to pay the electric bill." Jennifer reached for his hand and saw the open blisters on his palms. "Your fingers are raw; you're not used to hard labor. I'd better put something on them."

Bill put his arm on her lap. "Don't get up; I'll take care of them later." He leaned against the back of the soft couch and closed his eyes. "I have no choice. We need the money." He yawned and asked, "Are you sure the children have to be vaccinated?"

Jennifer rubbed her ankles, trying to relieve the pain. "Yes, and I don't know what I'm going to do about it."

"Didn't you tell them it's against our religion to go to doctors?"

Jennifer hesitated before saying, "Of course, but they don't want to hear it. It's getting late, I'd better start dinner. Oh! Were you able to get any warm clothes for the children?"

"Yes. There was a box of children's clothes in the back room. I found two coats for the girls and a boy coat. They might be a little big, but it will keep them warm. Got a couple kid hats too. They are on the chair in our bedroom."

"Good, I'll check them out in the morning."

Jennifer crawled into bed right after dinner. She felt exhausted, but couldn't sleep. Her mind searched for a way to get the children into school. "How am I going to get them vaccinated? Margaret's already vaccinated, but Cassie and Joseph aren't." Finally she fell asleep.

After Bill left for work, Jennifer went to the hardware store and bought a small bottle of muriatic acid. When she came back, she told Margaret and Joseph to play in the living room and took Cassie to her bedroom. Jennifer put her arms around Cassie. "Honey, sit on the bed next to me."

"Why, what are you going to do?"

Jennifer took Cassie's right arm and said softly, "Hold real still while I touch you with this cork, it will sting a little."

Cassie started to cry before Jennifer even touched her. "Don't hurt me."

Jennifer took a small cork, the size of a nickel, and dipped it in the acid, then lightly touched Cassie's upper arm. The child screamed and Jennifer held her close, blowing on the sizzling burn. She dabbed the burn with an herbal lotion and coated it with a salve.

"It hurts! Look how red it is," cried Cassie.

"It will stop hurting in a minute." Jennifer kissed her child's forehead. "Now, you'll be able to go to school."

She vaccinated Joseph the same way and by late afternoon scabs formed on their arms. At the end of the week, the scabs fell off, leaving a mark resembling a vaccination scar.

The next morning Jennifer tried the coats on the children. They needed a little altering, but she was able to fix that with her sewing machine.

They were a lot warmer as they walked to school on Monday morning. The school nurse examined their arms. "The scabs are healing well. Go down the hall to the principal's office. Someone will tell you what class they belong in."

After they were safely in their classes, Jennifer walked to Saint Bonaventure church a few blocks from the house. It had been a long time since she had been in a Catholic church. She sat in the front row, holding her rosary beads and praying. The smell of the incense relaxed her and she lit a candle. "I must come to confession soon," she thought. As she left, she noticed the times for the morning masses. I'll start coming to Church again.

# *Chapter Nineteen*

The family went to church twice a week as well as Sunday morning and evening service. Each time they attended, Claudia would pull Bill aside to ask questions about Columbia. It was Thursday night service and Jennifer and the children walked down to their seat and soon Bill joined them. He sat down. "Mrs. Runderson can really talk. It's hard to get away from her."

"Why don't you just excuse yourself and leave?"

"I feel sorry for her. God bless her lonely soul."

When service was over, they said a quick goodbye to the reverend and made a dash to the door. Mrs. Runderson came scurrying after them. "Goodbye, Pastor Rennie. I'll see you next week."

---

It was six in the morning and the sun just began to rise. The family was still snuggled in their beds when Tessie Morgan pulled up to the

Rennie house. She got out of her car and reached for the wide black bag on the back seat. Her ample body prevented her from getting it. Tessie crawled in. "Darn, I've got to lose some weight." She grabbed the bag and got out. She slammed the car door and felt the tug as her cape ripped. "Now, doesn't that beat all? It always happens when you're in a hurry." Tessie released her cape and walked up the front steps. When she knocked on the door of the Rennie house, no one answered. She banged hard with her fist as she shivered in the cold morning air. Tessie turned the knob and the door sprang open.

"Well how about that, they don't lock their doors." She walked into the house and threw her blue cape on a nearby chair and bellowed out, "Anyone home?" She walked halfway up the stairs, banging her pocketbook on each step. "Hey, is anyone up there?"

Bill threw off the covers. "Who the heck could that be?" He walked out in the hall and shouted, "How dare you burst into my house? Get out. Get out now."

"Take it easy, Pastor Rennie." Tessie straightened her flowered dress. "You'll have a heart attack."

Her high-pitched voice grated on Bill's nerves. "Who are you and what are you doing in my house?"

"I'm Tessie Morgan, the midwife. Reverend Thatcher said your wife is pregnant?"

"What's that got to do with you barging in, waking us up at this unthinkable hour?"

"Reverend Thatcher said I should stop by this morning." Bill started to say something, but she stopped him. "Maybe I should have come a little later, but I don't have time. Mrs. Robertson is having labor pains, and I figured once I got there I'd be tied up with her the rest of the day." Bill walked down the steps, Tessie slapped him on the back and laughed. "I apologize for waking you. I know I'm too abrupt and do things without thinking."

Then she touched her head and added, "Especially when I have a lot on my mind."

Bill laughed at her truthfulness. "Okay, I'll forgive you this time. Do you want some coffee?"

"Yes, I would. Maybe you should put your pants on, before you make coffee."

Bill's face turned standing there in his underwear. Oh, I'm sorry." He ran upstairs and returned, tucking his shirt in his trousers. Come out to the kitchen, while I make coffee. My wife will be down in a while."

Tessie's thighs swished together as she walked and flopped down on the kitchen chair. Bill heard the legs of the chair crack and waited to see if it would collapse.

"I could do with a cup of java and a piece of toast," said Tessie, leaning back on the chair as it creaked under her weight.

Bill glanced over as he put the coffee pot on the stove. Watching to see if she was going to land on the floor.

"Nice house you got here, said Tessie. I knew the old bitty that owned it." Bill set a cup and saucer down in front of her as she continued. "Had money coming out of her ears. It all went to her sister when she died. I think her sister is pretty well-heeled too." Bill poured the coffee and set the toast and margarine on the table. Tessie squinted. "I see you can't afford butter. Neither can I, but how about jam or honey?"

Annoyed, Bill grabbed the grape jelly from the cupboard. He was saving it and didn't want to put it out. It was a luxury they used sparingly. He slammed it on the table and bowed. "Does the queen wish anything else?"

"Don't get huffy just because I asked for jelly." She took a sip of coffee. "They say the old lady didn't trust banks and stuffed her mattress with money."

"Tessie, it is sinful to talk against your neighbors."

"Oh, come on now, Pastor. I'm not talking against the old bitty. I'm just telling you what I heard."

Jennifer sniffed the air as she walked into the kitchen, "Hmm, that coffee smells good. Who was that ignorant pers…?" Jennifer stopped when she saw Tessie sitting at the table.

Bill went to the cupboard to get Jennifer a cup. "Babe, this is Tessie Morgan. She's the midwife from the church."

Tessie stuffed her mouth with a chunk of toast and mumbled, "I'm here to examine you."

Jennifer sat down. "Can you at least wait until I have breakfast?"

Bill poured Jennifer a cup of coffee. "My wife gets sick if she doesn't eat right away." He gave Jennifer a caring smile. "I have the oatmeal cooking."

Tessie let out a big burp. "Matter a fact; I could stand a bowl myself."

Bill shook his head. "Okay, I'm the chef today. Two bowls of oatmeal coming up."

Tessie banged the table and laughed. "One thing about me, I'm not fussy."

Bill dished out the oatmeal. "I help out once in a while, but my Babe's a good cook. Now let's bow our heads and say grace."

Before the prayer was over, Tessie dug in and ate half of the oatmeal. She eyed Jennifer curiously, as she poured herself another cup of coffee.

"Your names Jennifer. So what's this Babe, a nickname?" Smacking her lips she said, "Good coffee. I can't taste any chicory."

Jennifer took a spoonful of cereal. "Bill likes to call me Babe, it's a pet name."

"Pet name?" Tessie laughed and cracked Bill on the knee. "Aren't you the lover boy?"

Jennifer gave Tessie a dirty look and walked to the sink. "Can't you come back later?"

"No, siree. It's like I told the pastor, I don't have any extra time today." Tessie pushed her dishes aside. "Don't have any time tomorrow either. Reverend Thatcher said it's been a while since you've been examined and I'm here to do it."

"Okay, okay," said Jennifer. "Let's go up to the bedroom and get it over with."

Tessie followed Jennifer. "I'm not as rough as I sound. You'll find my touch as gentle as an angel. Tessie washed her hands in the bathroom and when she returned, Jennifer braced for the worse. She stiffened when Tessie started to examine her. Then relaxed when she felt how gentle she was. "Doesn't seem like the baby turned yet," said Tessie feeling around. "Are you in your eighth or ninth month?"

"Beginning of the ninth," said Jennifer.

"How was your last birth?" asked Tessie, a bit concerned.

"I had a breech birth. My baby was stillborn."

Tessie continued to examine her, then pulled Jennifer's gown down. "Okay, I'm finished. We got to watch this little one. See if I can turn it."

"Thanks, Tessie, you are very gentle."

"Told you so," laughed Tessie as she hurried out of the house. "I'll be back in four days."

The children came downstairs as Tessie was leaving. "Who was that funny lady?" asked Margaret.

"Margaret, don't call people names," said Bill. "They are all God's children, big or small."

The children saw the expression on his face and sat down quickly.

After breakfast, the children left for school and Jennifer went through the clothes that were too small for them. She found some that could be taken apart and made into baby clothes. She was busy sewing when the children came home. Margret and Joseph ran to the bread box for a piece of stale bread and Cassie laid on the sofa.

"What's the matter? Don't you feel well?" asked Jennifer.

"No, my throat hurts."

Jennifer placed a spoon on Cassie's tongue, pressing down to look. "Your throat is all red and you have a fever." Jennifer took her up to the bedroom and removed her shoes and stockings. She took one of the stocking and placed the foot section against Cassie's throat. She tied a small scarf over it to hold it in place.

"Why are you putting that stinky thing on me?" asked Cassie.

"The sweat in the stocking will help cure your throat. Get undressed and get in bed. I'll get you an aspirin and a cup of hot tea."

Cassie slept through dinner and Jennifer checked on her several times. She remembered when Andrew was sick and how he died from the fever. "His fever was much higher," thought

Jennifer. Before she went to bed, she kissed Cassie's forehead. Thank God her fever has broken.

When Jennifer woke the children for school, Cassie said, "Mama, my throat is all better."

"Let me see." Jennifer used the spoon again to look at her throat. "You're right. It's not red, your fever has gone," said Jennifer. She fixed their breakfast and sent them off to school.

The church sent over a crib that someone had donated and Jennifer decided to scrub it, making sure it was free of germs. She took an old sheet and cut it in squares to make sheets to fit the crib. She found an old cotton blanket that had holes in it and made baby blankets.

When the children came home from school, she fixed a snack for them. That's when the first pain hit her.

She was just able to make it to the chair when another came on stronger. "Margaret, come quick, I'm having labor pains."

She rushed to her mother's side. "What do you want me to do?"

"Call Tessie. Her number's on the wall over the phone. Then call the church and tell your father."

Jennifer was ten days overdue and knew it could happen anytime. She had hoped Bill would be home when the pains started.

"Tessie said she'd be right over," said Margaret, "and Daddy's coming too."

Jennifer patted Margaret's head. "You're a big help, honey. Now, when your daddy and Tessie get here, I want you to take care of your sister and brother."

Margaret's eyes filled with tears. "I will, Mama."

Tessie arrived and said, "Margaret, take the children outside and play. We don't get these nice March days often." She walked them to the door. "See, the winds are calm and the sun is shining just for you. Stay outside until you hear the baby cry."

Margaret handed Cassie her jump rope. "Go play." Joseph had a ball and was tossing it against the wall while Margaret sat on the steps watching her brother and sister.

"Margaret, come play with me," said Cassie.

"I don't want to. I'm worried about Mamma and the baby."

"Daddy said God was helping Mama with the baby," said Cassie. "Come, play with me."

Joseph looked bewildered as he asked, "Where do babies come from?"

Margaret propped her arms on her knees and tucked her chin in her hands as she mumbled, "God puts it in Mama's stomach."

"Why?" asked Joseph.

Cassie stopped jumping and asked, "If God has to get the baby out, why did he put it in there?"

"Shut up! Shut up!" Margaret shouted putting her hands over her ears.

As their mother's moans echoed through the screened windows, Cassie and Joseph started to cry.

"Why does Mamma have to hurt?" asked Joseph.

"Shut up and listen," said Margaret. "I think I hear the baby crying."

They ran into the house shouting, "Is the baby here?"

Bill had been sitting outside the bedroom praying, and Joseph climbed on his lap. "I want to see the baby."

Tears streamed down Margaret's face as she asked, "Is Mama okay?"

Bill patted Margaret's head. "Yes, she's fine; you have a new baby sister."

"A baby sister," squealed Margaret and Cassie. "I can't wait to hold her."

"Aw phooey, I wanted a brother," said Joseph.

Tessie dried her hands on her apron as she came out of Jennifer's room. She grabbed Bill's arm and whispered, "I had to cut her in several places, so she wouldn't tear. She's going to hurt for a while. Okay kids come on in."

Jennifer was sleeping with a peaceful look on her face. Bill kneeled and prayed, "Dear God, thank you for giving us this healthy child and keeping my Babe alive. Amen" He stood up, took the baby in his arms and kissed her forehead. "I name you, Faith Louise, after the church that helped us."

Tessie walked into the room and handed him a tiny piece of sheer pinkish substance. Bill looked at it blankly. "What's this?"

Tessie smiled and said, "Faith was born with a veil on her face."

"What in the world are you talking about?"

"It's a piece of skin that covers the face. They call it a veil. The child born with it has Gods special blessing."

"Well, I'll be doggone," said Bill, cuddling the baby. "I never heard that before." He thought about it for a moment, then said, "Hmm, a special blessing from God!"

He knelt down to let the children see the baby. Cassie and Margaret were mesmerized by their new sister, "Oh, isn't she beautiful!"

Joseph looked at the baby and said, "I wanted a baby brother to play with."

Jennifer opened her eyes and saw her family with the baby. She loved them so much. They reminded her of her childhood with her mother, father, especially Caroline. She missed them so!

# Chapter Twenty

The children just left for school and Jennifer and Bill finished their breakfast. Jennifer refreshed Bill's coffee as she said, "The principal sent a note home with the children yesterday. He said that I did a fine job with their home studies, their grades are at the top of the class. It's only been three months since the children started school. I'm so proud of them."

"I'm proud of you because you taught them," said Bill. "Oh! I forgot to tell you. Reverend Thatcher is letting me give both the morning and evening services on Sundays."

"When will Reverend Thatcher give the services?"

"He's taking the week nights, so I have time to work other jobs."

"Well at least we can depend on the five dollars a week he's paying you."

"The church can't afford to pay me a salary anymore. Fewer people are coming to the church. Those who come only give a few pennies."

"What! I was counting on the five dollars to buy food."

"I'm trying to find work and I'll look again today." Bill put on his coat. "Don't worry, everything will work out."

"You keep saying that but things aren't getting better."

_____

Jennifer wanted to get the baby christened at the Catholic Church. She had to do it now before Bill had the baby baptized at his church. She had already met with Father Ryan and explained the circumstances. He agreed to have one of the nun's stand for her. After Bill left the house, Jennifer hurried to the church. Baby Faith was anointed into the Catholic religion. On the way home she thought, "Now all my children have been christened in the Catholic Church. I know Bill will want to have her baptized into his religion, but that won't change things."

_____

Three weeks went by and the family still had very little food and no milk. Jennifer searched the trash bins at the grocery stores for whatever wilted vegetables she could find. She gave the food they had to the children and drank water to fill her own stomach.

Faith started to cry and Jennifer placed the baby at her breast. The baby started to suckle and then screamed.

"What's the matter honey?" Jennifer squeezed her nipple and nothing came out. "Oh no, what am I going to do now?" Jennifer fed Faith a bottle of warm water with a few sprinkles of sugar, but it didn't satisfy her.

Jennifer walked the floor trying to sooth the child. She started to sing, "Hush, little baby, don't you cry. Mama's goanna buy you." She stopped when she heard a knock on the door. She opened the door and was surprised to see Reverend Thatcher.

"What's the matter with the baby?" he asked.

"She's hungry." Jennifer forced back the tears. "My breasts have dried up and I have nothing to feed her."

"Can't you feed her regular milk?"

"We have no money. No one will give us credit."

"Where's your husband?"

Jennifer felt dizzy and sat down. She patted the baby's back as she said, "He's out looking for work."

"I didn't know your situation was this bad, I'll go back to the church and see if I can get some food sent over."

"Please try. We are so hungry!"

After Reverend Thatcher left, Jennifer continued to walk with the baby trying to comfort her. She put a little more sugar in the water and tried again. Faith drank it until she fell asleep. As she placed the baby in the crib she thought, "I never remember being this hungry. We had so much and I took everything for granted. Now we're starving. I wish we were in Carnegie with our families."

———————————

Bill roamed the streets looking for ways to make money. He stopped at every business asking for work. His strong, muscular body was now scrawny and he felt desperate. The rent was due soon and he didn't want his family to be put out on the street. He never thought he would ever have to beg or ask for a hand out. He swallowed his pride and approached a man who was dressed in an expensive looking overcoat. He stood tall and proud and his white hair and distinguished face reminded him of Francis May. Unlike the others nearby, the man did not look hungry.

"Sir, could you please help me? I can't find work and my family is hungry. Can you spare a little money so I can buy milk for our three children and newborn baby?"

At first the man thought he was just another beggar, but then noticed that Bill spoke like a well-educated man. He was clean, well-mannered, but with a desperate look in his eyes. "Where do you live?"

"On Camac Street, 1335. A woman from our church has been letting us live there free. Now, she wants us to pay rent." Bill told him about arriving from Colombia.

The man listened intently and then reached into his pocket. "Here's ten dollars, buy some food for your family." He placed the money in Bill's hand and walked away.

Bill stared at the money in awed and then shouted, "Thank you and God bless you." He looked up to the heavens and whispered, "Thank you for your help, God."

He could hear the baby crying when he walked into the house. Bill's arms were loaded with groceries. "Babe, I have milk. Bring the baby downstairs."

Jennifer ran down holding the baby. When she saw all the food, she gasped, "Where did you get all this?" She laid the baby in the cradle and pulled everything out of the bags. She was looking for milk. Faith's little face was red from screaming and her tiny legs flailed in the air.

Jennifer grabbed the bottle of milk as she said, "Hush, Baby, Mama's fixing you some milk." Jennifer held the bottle to the baby's mouth and squeezed the nipple, letting drops of milk splash on the child's tongue. She then placed the nipple to the baby's lips. When Faith tasted the milk, she drank so fast she choked. "Take it slow, honey. Poor baby, you look like a scrawny bird." Tears came to Jennifer's eyes. She held the baby close, until the child was content.

When the children came home and saw the fruit they grabbed for it. "This is a better treat than the stale bread," said Joseph.

"Stop grabbing and sit down. I'll give you each a banana," said Jennifer. As the children devoured the fruit, Jennifer hugged the package of ground beef. "I can't believe we're going to have meat tonight. I'm only going to use a quarter of this meat, that way I'll get four meals out of it. I don't know when we will get this much food again. I'll make hamburger stew for dinner that will fill us up."

Margaret and Cassie were washing the dinner dishes, when someone knocked on the door.

"It's late. I wonder who that could be?" said Margaret.

Jennifer opened the door and there was a large basket of food sitting on the step. She looked around, and no one was in sight.

"Holy mackerel," she squealed as the family came running to the door.

Bill carried the heavy groceries into the kitchen and put his hands together in prayer. "Thank you, God."

Jennifer unpacked the basket. "There are a dozen cans of condensed milk, two boxes of cereal, some vegetables, meat, and even some soap!" Setting the things on the counter she said, "Look children there's candies and cakes. I wonder who left it."

"Can I have a Hershey bar?" asked Margaret.

Bill took one of the candy bars and broke it in three pieces. "Take this and go get ready for bed." He yawned, "I'm tired; I think I'll turn in too."

Faith started to cry and Jennifer held the baby in her arms. "I'll be up shortly," she said, rocking the baby. When Faith fell asleep, she took the baby up to her crib. Bill was still awake and she said, "I hate being poor. In Colombia, we had plenty to eat."

"I know we just pick the bananas or papayas off the tree. Roasted boar and chicken. We had all we wanted. It was like a hidden paradise."

"When I was young, I never went without a meal. Oh, the dinners our cook used to prepare!" Her mind drifted to her sister and mother. "I wish my mother wasn't angry with me. I'll never get that angry with my children, I swear."

"Jennifer, please go to sleep, I'm too tired to talk."

The next day Jennifer checked the mailbox. She was hoping for a letter from her family. She threw the mail on the table, "Nothing but bills. I've written two letters to Caroline and my father and they never write back."

Bill picked up the mail. "Take it easy. Maybe they're busy."

"I wonder how my father is doing. He might be sick or even dead."

"Don't be so dramatic. They are fine. If they weren't, someone would have called."

"Aren't you worried about your mother and father?"

"Of course I am, but I know God is watching over them." Bill went through the mail, mentally calculating how much money was needed. He slammed his fist on the table. Jennifer almost jumped off her seat. "How much longer is this depression going to last?"

"For heaven's sake, what did you do that for? You scared me."

"I'm just frustrated. The rent is due and we didn't pay the gas and electric last month. I was hoping 1931 would be better, but things are worse." Bill picked up his bible and whispered, "Forgive me for the loss of patience, dear Lord, but I really need the money. Please help me find some kind of work."

Bill got up at 5 a.m. in the morning and trudged to the unemployment office. It was still dark as he walked along the railroad tracks. This area was called Hooverville. Families slept along the streets in crooked shacks made of odds and ends of wood and cardboard.

"I'm thankful we have a roof over our heads," he murmured.

He glanced up the street and saw the unemployment line filled with desperate, hungry people. He got in line and moved slowly along. He was near the front when he saw a brawny man standing in front of the line. His legs spread apart, hands on his hips, he eyed the men.

"My names is Mr. Broady. I'm the foreman for the Public Works Department. I'm looking for twenty strong men."

He picked over the men like a cannibal ready to eat. Bill was finally getting near the head of the line when Mr. Broady eyed the three men in front of him. He pointed to two of them. "I can't use you, there's not enough meat on your bones."

"Hey, I'm stronger than I look," said one of the men. The foreman continued to ignore him. The man called out again, "Please let me work, my family needs to eat."

"Get out of line!" roared the foreman. Then he looked at Bill. "Can you handle five days building railroad tracks? The pay is a buck fifty a day do you want it?"

Bill's face brightened. "Yeah, sure."

"Okay, that makes twenty," said Mr. Broady. "Climb in that black pickup on the

Corner. We're leaving in ten minutes."

He was hammering spikes into the tracks. It was strenuous work. Bill took a minute to stretch his aching back, then went back to work. He knew if he was a good worker, they would keep him on. Bill hadn't eaten breakfast and didn't think to bring lunch. By the end of the day, he felt weak and exhausted.

The 5 p.m. whistle blasted and the foreman called out, "You're done." The men piled into the truck and were driven back.

When they arrived at the employment office, Mr. Broady paid them a dollar fifty each and said, "See you tomorrow, 7 a.m. sharp."

"I'll be there," said Bill. His back ached and his biceps throbbed as he limped home, happy to have money for his family.

When he opened the door, Jennifer was shocked. "You looked exhausted. You better lie down on the couch and rest. I'll get you a cup of tea."

"No, I'll be all right after I eat." She poured him a cup of tea and he asked, "Where are the children?"

"They're playing out back."

The back door opened and the children came in. Their arms were filled with grey, square boxes.

With a half full mouth Margaret mumbled, "Look what we got."

Joseph's mouth was so full. He couldn't close it and chocolate seeped down his chin. "We found all this candy in the trash at the Five and Ten Cent store."

Cassie said between chews. "They threw out all this good candy."

Jennifer opened the boxes, "These two are filled with broken and smashed chocolates." She took a bite and said, "There's white on the edges from age, but they taste all right. This other box is full of gumdrops all stuck together."

"Can we keep it?" asked Cassie, stuffing her mouth with the gumdrops.

"Yes, but stop cramming your mouths," said Jennifer. "You have to eat dinner." She put the boxes in the cupboard. "I'll dole these out slowly to make them last."

"Why can't we keep them in our room?" asked Margaret. "We found them."

Bill laughed and said, "Oh no! The candy would be gone in a day and you'd all be sick."

The family sat around the kitchen table, eating beef stew and relishing the fresh vegetables.

"For dessert, you can each have two pieces of candy," said Jennifer.

"Hurry and get ready for church," said Bill, getting up from the table. "We have to leave in thirty minutes."

"Bill, you're so exhausted. Why don't you stay home tonight?" said Jennifer.

"That's no reason to stay home. Worshipping God will help me feel better."

It was snowing out and the six-block walk was almost unbearable. When they arrived, Bill sat in the warm church listening to Reverend Thatcher give the sermon. He felt so tired; he could hardly keep his eyes open. When it was over, hot tea was served to warm the family for their walk home. As they neared the house the children started to throw snow balls at each other and stopped to make snow angels in the snow.

"Come, children, it's time for bed," said Jennifer.

Margaret ran toward the house then stopped and said, "What's that big dark thing on our step?"

"There's another basket of food here," said Joseph, "I wonder who's leaving them. Oh boy! This is great. More cookies."

Bill picked up the basket and carried it into the house. "It's a blessing from God." "I'm too tired to unpack it. I'm going to bed."

---

Saturday afternoon, Jennifer sat quietly on the couch. Bill was in his favorite overstuffed chair, reading a day old newspaper he picked up off the street.

He looked over at Jennifer. "What's the matter? Is something bothering you?"

"Christmas is coming and it won't be a merry one. We don't have a penny to spare to buy a

Christmas tree."

"I won't have a Christmas tree in this house. We are not going to celebrate the birth of Jesus that way. We'll have a quiet Christmas reading the Bible and praying." Bill turned the page of his newspaper.

Jennifer pushed his paper aside and sat on his lap. She put her arm around his neck and kissed his cheek. "We can celebrate Christmas your way, but still have a tree."

"No, that's a heathen's way to honor Jesus."

"There's nothing heathen about it. A little bit of Yuletide cheer will make the children happy."

"We are not having a tree and that's final." Bill pushed the paper between them and started to read again.

Jennifer stood up. "We'll talk about this later. When you're more reasonable."

Jennifer went to bed, but lay awake trying to understand Bill's attitude. "Sometimes he's weird," she thought. "I don't know where he gets these ideas. We've always had nice Christmases, even_in Columbia. If he believed in doctors, I'd take him to a psychiatrist. Oh well, he's not going to spoil the holidays for the children if I can help it. I better think of some ways to make extra money." She tossed and turned and thought, "Maybe I could get a job? I'd love to get a nursing job in a hospital, but I'm sure Bill wouldn't hear of it. Besides I have to take care of the baby. She's too young to leave all the time. But I could get something for a half a day and ask my neighbor if she could take care of Faith. Oh well, I'll think of something." She finally fell asleep.

The next day, Jennifer left the baby with a friend and walked to the neighborhood store. She went into the dark drab building that sold candy, cigarettes, sundries and newspapers. The owner, a short, dark-haired woman was standing behind the counter.

She smiled at Jennifer and with a French accent asked, "Can I help you, madam?"

"I...I'm looking for work. Do you have anything I could do?" asked Jennifer.

"Madam, everyone's looking for work," said Mrs. Freyland.

Mr. Freyland was sitting in the corner of the store smoking a cigar. The smell made Jennifer's nose twitch and she sneezed twice.

He walked over and smiled at Jennifer, then said, "God bless you. He chewed his cigar and brown saliva leaked from the corners of his mouth. It dribbled down his chin and he wiped it with his shirt sleeve. He said to his wife, "She's a nice lady, give her some work."

Jennifer watched the nicotine juice drip down on his blue shirt that looked a size too small. It stretched over his watermelon stomach.

Mr. Freyland relit his cigar. "The house is a mess; give her a dollar to clean it."

"A dollar!" Mrs. Freyland looked Jennifer up and down. "I'll give you seventy-five cents if you do a good job."

"Thank you. I'll work real hard."

"Come with me." She led Jennifer into their living quarters.

Two small dogs yapped at Mrs. Freeland's feet, then ran wildly around the house. Their smelly mess dotting the floors.

Jennifer picked up the newspapers and trash that was scattered around and asked, "Where are the cleaning things?"

"The bucket and mop are in the pantry," said Mrs. Freyland. "I'll be in the store if you need me. Make sure you don't steal anything."

The smell of dog poop and stale food caused Jennifer to gag and she wondered if they ever emptied their trash. The stove was crusted with burnt food and Jennifer put the dirty pots and pans in the sink. She swept the sticky floor, then mopped it clean.

"Wow! This house is filthy. How can they live in this mess?"

When the main floor was finished, she went upstairs to the bath-room. A wooden tub sat in the middle of the floor. Jennifer started to clean it, but the paint on the tub had blistered.

When she scrubbed it the paint chipped off breaking into tiny pieces. Jennifer did the best she could with the rust-stained toilet and washed all the yellow urine stains that coated the floor.

When she entered the bedroom it looked like a cyclone hit it. "I'm sure these sheets haven't been changed in weeks," she thought.

She found clean sheets in the closet and started to put them on the bed. She raised the mattress to tuck in the sheet and Jennifer gasped. Bundles of five-ten and twenty dollar bills lay in front of her.

"Look at all that money," she thought. "I could really use some of this. Why do they have it under there? Did they steal it? I guess they can't trust the banks yet." Jennifer quickly made the bed and went into the hallway, before she was tempted. As she swept the bedroom rug, the stiff broom caught the corner of the rug, pulling it over showing more money. "Ooh," screamed

Jennifer as she slapped the broom several times against the floor. "They have all this money and wouldn't pay me a dollar for cleaning this filthy place." When she was finally finished, she looked around at the rooms; they was spotless. Jennifer let out a deep breath. "It looks much better now." She opened the door that led to the store and waited while Mrs. Freyland took care of a customer.

When the lady left, Jennifer said, "I'm finished and I think you'll be satisfied."

Mrs. Freyland stomped into the house. "I'll be the one that says if it's clean or not." She went into the house and looked around. "You didn't steal anything, did you?"

"Of course not," answered Jennifer sharply. "Could you pay me now, I have to get home to my baby."

"I'll pay you tomorrow," said Mrs. Freyland as she walked into the store.

"I want the money now; I worked hard and need my money."

"Don't give me your lip, I said come back tomorrow."

"You promised I'd get the money when I finished, so give it to me. I really deserve more than seventy-five cents for cleaning up that filthy mess."

Mr. Freyland walked over and handed Jennifer a dollar. "Thank you. I'm sure you did a good job." He puffed on his smelly cigar and patted her backside. "Come back and help us again."

Jennifer ignored the pat, grabbed the money and left.

For the last two months Jennifer had walked the streets on trash day, collecting soda bottles. She had thirty bottles and returned them to the grocery store for the two cents each.

Jennifer sat at the kitchen table, adding up her money. "I have sixty cents from the bottles and two dollars I've saved from Bill's pay. With the dollar I just made, gives me three dollars and sixty cents."

The next day, she bundled up with two sweaters and her light spring coat and headed for Abby's wholesale store on Germantown Ave.

The store owner watched as Jennifer scanned the aisles. "Can I help you Madam?"

"I'd like to buy as many boxes of Christmas cards I can for three dollars and sixty cents."

"Hmm, three dollars and sixty cents. You can have twenty-five boxes of these," he said holding up a box of cards.

"No. They are not colorful enough." She picked up a box with angels and white doves on a gold background. "I like these much better."

"They are more expensive. You get eighteen boxes for three dollars and sixty cents."

"The other ones won't sell as well. I need the money for my children's Christmas."

Jennifer calculated how much profit she would make. She thought, "Twenty-five boxes for three dollars and sixty cents comes to about fourteen cents a box. If I sell them for twenty-five cents a box, that gives me a profit of eleven cents a box. Wow!"

He held up the cheaper ones again. "These are good cards. Everyone likes them."

"I don't. Can't you please let me have twenty-five boxes of the ones with the angel for three dollars and sixty cents?"

"You drive a hard barging lady," Abby saw the sad expression on her face, "Okay, I'll give you twenty boxes." Jennifer shook her head no and Abby sighed. "Okay, twenty-four boxes and don't tell anybody the price I am giving you."

"Thank you very much."

Jennifer's smile melted Abby's heart. "I never could resist a pretty woman," he said, as he packed the cards into a large box.

"You are very kind," said Jennifer.

She carried the heavy box down the street, stopping every other block to rest. Until she reached her house. When the children came home from school, Jennifer held up a box of cards.

"Look what I've got."

"Oh, what pretty angels," said Cassie.

"What are you going to do with all these cards?" asked Margaret.

"I want you to help Santa Claus," said Jennifer smiling. "You can go around the neighborhood and sell them."

Margaret looked bewildered. "How much would I sell them for?"

"Twenty-five cents a box. You can go to the houses on one side of the street for five blocks and then work your way home on the other side."

"That sounds like fun. Can we do it now?" asked Cassie.

"Yes, but don't stay out after dark," replied Jennifer.

Jennifer handed them each a knapsack with five boxes of cards in each sack. "Make sure you're dressed warm and carry this over your shoulder. Be careful crossing the streets."

They rang the doorbell of the first house and waited until someone answered. A grey-haired lady opened the door. "My goodness children, what are you doing out in this cold?"

"Would you please buy some Christmas cards?" said Margaret.

The lady had grandchildren of her own and felt sorry for them, "Come in and I'll give you some hot chocolate to warm you up, while I look at the cards." They eagerly drank the hot chocolate, as she examined the cards. "They are pretty. I'll take two boxes."

Sympathy for the children shone at every house. A young woman expecting a baby saw

Joseph and said, "What are you carrying in that big sack?"

Joseph shivered, as he said, "Will you buy some Christmas cards, please?"

"Well, come in and warm up." She led them into the parlor. "How much are they?"

"Twenty-five cents a box," said Joseph.

"Yes, I'll buy a box." She handed Joseph three dimes and said, "Keep the change."

The children liked the attention people gave them. Soon all the cards were sold and they arrived home with empty bags.

Jennifer gasped and said, "You sold all the cards that I gave you?" She counted the money. "Where did the extra money come from?"

"Some people said keep the change," replied Margaret.

Jennifer hugged her children. "I'm so proud of you."

"I liked doing it," said Joseph. "Can we do it again tomorrow?"

She helped them off with their coats. "Yes, tomorrow's Saturday."

The next morning while the children were selling cards Jennifer crocheted doilies, vanity scarves, head and arm pieces for upholstered furniture. Her mother had taught her to crochet when she was in high school. Her mother always complemented her on the scarf and dollies she made. She started crocheting again two weeks ago, hoping she could make extra money. On Monday, when the children were in school, she searched for stores that would sell her pieces. She was lucky that several stores agreed to sell her pieces on consignment.

---

Bill stayed late at the church on Christmas Eve helping Reverend Thatcher with the Christmas sermon. Jennifer took the children to mass and then to buy a tree.

The stands were closed and all the trees were gone. "Darn, what will I do now? I shouldn't have waited so long."

"What will we do without a tree?" said Margaret.

"I don't know, honey." She spotted a thin scraggly tree lying by the curb. Jennifer picked it up and shook the snow off of it. "I guess they couldn't sell this one. Well, it's better than nothing."

When they got home, she put the children in bed and said, "Santa Claus won't come until you're fast asleep. Close your eyes, stay in bed and be very good."

"Will he bring me a truck?" asked Joseph.

"I want Santa to bring me a doll," said Cassie.

Margaret just snickered; she knew there was no Santa. "I just want a book."

Jennifer kissed them goodnight and went downstairs. She placed the tree in a bucket and put bricks inside to hold it straight.

Bill entered the house and called out, "Babe, where are you?"

"I'm in the parlor."

He walked in and stared at the tree and yelled. "What is that thing doing in my house?"

Jennifer put a ginger bread cookies on the tree.

Bill threw the books he was carrying on the floor. "I told you I would not have that heathen thing in the house. Take it down immediately."

Jennifer strung the popcorn strings along the tree as she sang, "Deck the halls with boughs of holly."

"Did you hear what I said?"

"I heard you and I'm not taking it down."

Bill stomped over and reached for the tree. "It's coming down now."

Jennifer grabbed his arm. "You're not going to spoil Christmas because of your silly belief."

Bill reached out again and Jennifer stepped in front of him. "Get out of my way."

Her eyes blazed as she stared at him. "Don't you dare touch it?"

They stood staring at each other, neither giving in. Then Bill kicked the box near the tree and stomped upstairs.

It was late by the time Jennifer finished decorating and putting the gifts out. She was exhausted, from the weeks of buying toys and making things. She crawled into bed for a few hours, knowing the children would be happy in the morning.

They woke early to see what Santa had brought. Their faces beamed when they saw the tree. It was trimmed with strings of popcorn, home-made gingerbread cookies. A cardboard angel sat on the top, smiling down at them.

"Oh, the angel is so pretty," said Cassie.

The presents were wrapped in the comic sections of newspapers and Margaret read the name tags, as she gave out the gifts.

"Santa left me a Little Orphan Annie doll and a book about her," said Margaret.

Cassie hugged her doll, "Its Raggedy Ann. I wanted her so bad."

Joseph jumped up and down when he saw the little red truck, "Zoom, zoom," he said as he rolled it along the carpet.

Faith sat quietly on the floor, chewing on a cookie she pulled from the tree. A puppy made from rayon stockings laid beside her. One by one, the children opened the rest of the presents, squealing with joy when they saw their new clothes. Bill watched quietly from the hallway, then sat next to Jennifer on the sofa.

She smiled at him. "Merry Christmas."

"Where did you get the money to buy all those clothes?"

"I took apart some of my old dresses and made them. There was a box of used winter coats and hats at the church. I took the best ones and altered them. If you look, you'll find something nice for you, under the tree."

Smiling, he opened his present. "I needed a new white shirt. Oh! I think I recognize the material the ties are made from."

Jennifer laughed as she said, "Yes, one of my dresses."

"I'm sorry I was nasty. The children look so happy." He hugged her as he whispered, "You're a miracle worker."

Christmas dinner was chicken giblets, potatoes and pumpkin pie for dessert. After the children had their baths, Jennifer tucked them in bed and said, "Bill, there is just enough water for a quick wash for us. I turned off the hot water heater to save on the gas bill."

"Good idea. I'll bank the furnace before we go to bed," said Bill.

Jennifer yawned. "I think I'll go to bed now. I'm really tired." She quickly undressed and washed up before snuggling under the blankets. She was half asleep when Bill snuggled up close to her.

"Babe, are you awake?" he whispered.

"I'm almost asleep," she mumbled turning toward him.

He nibbled her ear and said, "Christmas was terrific. I love you." He kissed her, then caressed her breast.

Jennifer pulled away, "I love you too, but I'm so tired."

"I'll wake you up," he said, pulling her on top of him.

Jennifer tried to pull away, but he held her tight. "Stop it. It's the wrong time of the month. I don't want to get pregnant."

"We don't believe in that Catholic stuff." He said cupping her breast with his hand. His lips kissed the soft mound and she could feel his hardness against her thighs.

Jennifer pushed his hand away. "Please stop."

Bill continued to caress her and as he entered her, she couldn't resist anymore. Their bodies moved together in a symphony of sighs and moans, as they climaxed together. Jennifer ran to the bathroom and douched twice with water so cold it took her breath away. Shivering, she crawled back into bed. "I hope I don't get pregnant."

# Chapter Twenty-One

Jennifer had thought last winter was bad, but the beginning of 1932 was worse. She bundled the children in layers of clothes to keep them warm and sent them to school.

Jennifer sat next to Bill at the table. "It's so cold. I hated to send the children to school."

Bill poured a cup of chicory coffee. "I know. Maybe someday we will be able to afford a car. Then I can drive them."

"I get depressed when I walk to the store and see people sitting on the park benches in this cold. They have no way to keep warm."

"I'm thankful God led us to Reverend Thatcher," said Bill. "Well, I have to go to work.

Got to pound those railroad tracks if we're going to eat."

As he walked to work, he passed groups of men huddled around blazing fires built in steel drums. Their clothes were worn and not nearly warm enough. Makeshift huts made from scrapes of wood and tin stood in rows along parking lots and by the railroad station.

"Will you buy an apple, Mister? Only two cents," said a young boy shivering in the cold.

Bill gave him two cents. He would eat the apple for lunch.

He worked through the day and despite the cold developed a sweat from the strenuous labor.

Jennifer went to the grocery store, while the children were in school. She walked to the back of the store where the wilted produce was on sale. Jennifer picked up some assorted shriveled vegetables and two loaves of stale bread. She was putting the groceries away when the children came home.

"I'm hungry," said Joseph. "Can I have something to eat?"

"There are still a few pieces of the candy you found," said Jennifer. "Here's the box. Share it with your sisters."

They started to fight over the candy and Jennifer said, "Give me the box. I'll give you each two pieces."

"That's the box I found," said Margaret. "I should get the most."

"You'll share equally or you get nothing."

Bill walked in the door. "What's all the fussing about?"

"It's nothing; they're just fighting over the last of the candy."

Cassie grabbed the candy from Joseph and he hit her. Cassie screamed, "He hurt me."

"She was stealing my candy," said Joseph.

"You should be ashamed of yourselves, fighting over candy," said Bill. "You should be thankful you have candy and a warm house to live in. Now go do your homework."

The children went to their rooms and Jennifer let out a big sigh. "I'm thankful we have a warm house to live in, especially since I'm pregnant."

Bill smiled and patted her hand, "It's God's blessing."

Jennifer pulled her hand away. "I don't want to be pregnant. Look how skinny I am. I don't have the strength to live through another pregnancy."

"Don't talk like that. It's God's blessing, I told you."

"It's not God's blessing. It's your insistence on sex when it wasn't safe. You don't care. It's not you who is pregnant."

"Everything will be all right."

"You can say that when there's barely enough food to go around. Let alone another mouth to feed."

"Don't get so riled up." Bill put his arm around her.

Tears rolled down her face. "I don't want to hear my baby cry from hunger, like Faith."

"Everything will work out, I promise."

"There you go again, don't tell me that. Oh God, I don't want another baby and I don't want the pain."

"Shame on you for saying such a thing," yelled Bill. "May God forgive you."

She wiped her tears away. "I'm going to see what the children are doing."

Jennifer helped the children with their homework, then prepared dinner. When the meal was over, she sat on the couch in the parlor.

"I feel so exhausted," she said, stretching her arms out.

Bill was going over their expenses and in desperation said, "There's not enough money to cover our expenses. We have to find a cheaper house to live in."

"What will we do about furniture?" asked Jennifer. "All this belongs to the owner."

"Yes, that's right." Bill thought for a moment. "I only work a half day tomorrow at the Highway Department. I'll ask around about a furnished place."

"I don't want to move, it's so comfortable and happy here."

"I know, but we just can't afford it. Let's call it a day, I'm tired."

The next day Bill put in four hours of exhausting work, and then stopped by the church. "Good Afternoon, Reverend Thatcher."

"Good to see you, how are the children?"

"The children are fine, but I have a problem." Bill took off his jacket.

"Maybe I can help," said the reverend.

"The house we're living in is too expensive for us. I wondered if you knew of a cheaper place we could rent."

Reverend Thatcher scratched his head and said, "There's a smaller house not too far from here. It's across the street from a park."

"Is it furnished?'

"Let me call the owner and see." He smiled when he hung up the phone and said, "It's available and furnished. The owner will meet you there if you want to look at it."

"Thank you. You came through for us again," said Bill. "I'll go over right now."

When Bill went home, he found Jennifer in the basement scrubbing the clothes on the wash board. He hugged her. "I found a place and the rent is a lot less. We move in next week."

"What, you took it without letting me see it first?"

"I had to grab it before someone else did."

Jennifer pinned the wet clothes to the line she had strung across the basement and asked, "Couldn't you have called me? I could have met you there."

"I got so excited when Reverend Thatcher told me about it; I never thought to call you."

Jennifer dried her chapped hands. "How many rooms does it have?"

"Just as many rooms and even closer to the school."

"What's the neighborhood like?"

"You'll love it. It's across from a park with swings and picnic tables."

"Well, I'm not moving in unless I see it first. Then we'll see."

"Okay. Okay. I'll take you there tomorrow after work."

The next afternoon Bill took her to see the house. "This is it. It's smaller than the one we're in, but it has the same number of rooms."

Jennifer looked around. "The parlor is much smaller and so is the dining room." She sighed and said, "The furniture is nothing like the other house, it's worn and scratched."

Bill pushed her toward the kitchen. "Look how large the kitchen is and the afternoon sun comes in the window."

"Yes, it does brighten the kitchen." Jennifer inspected the black iron wood stove, sitting in the corner and opened the white icebox. "This house has the old stove, the other had a gas one. The paints chipping off the icebox, we'll have to paint it."

"I like the slatted wood cupboards, but they could use a paint job too," said Bill.

Jennifer sighed and said, "At least it's clean."

Bill took her arm. "Come on, I'll show you the upstairs."

Jennifer walked down the hallway checking the rooms. "The bedrooms are small."

"Let's just thank God I found a place we can afford. I'll borrow a truck from the church and we can move into the house on the weekend."

It was Saturday afternoon, March 10, 1933, when the truck pulled up in front of the house. They carried their things inside their new home and Jennifer took the children upstairs.

She said to her daughter's, "I'm putting you and the baby in the biggest room. Joseph you can have a room of your own."

"That's swell, I have a room all on my own." He slammed the door and said, "Ha, ha, Margaret you can't come in."

Margaret banged on her brother's door. "That's not fair!"

"Cut that racket out," shouted Bill. "Margaret, go put your clothes away."

She stamped into her room and threw her clothes in the drawers, slamming each one shut. "Why does Joseph get a room of his own? I'm the oldest I should have my own room."

"You're not getting my room," shouted Joseph through the door.

"Listen to the racket they're making," said Bill. He walked to the stairway and called out, "Quieten up there, or I'll take the strap to you."

When they finished unpacking the dishes and kitchen utensils, Bill said, "I'm exhausted. I'm going to take a nap."

"I'm tired too, but I want to put these last few pieces away."

The children came down and Jennifer said, "Dad and I are going to take a nap, and I want you to play quietly. Your books and games are in the kitchen."

Bill was asleep when Jennifer lay down and as she started to doze off, she heard the children playing. She tried to ignore them but their tempo got louder. Jennifer went to see what they were doing. Joseph and Faith were sitting on Margaret and Cassie's back. They were crawling around the floor, laughing so loud, they didn't hear Jennifer.

"Giddy up horsy," yelled Joseph.

"Children, quieten down, your father is trying to sleep." Jennifer smiled, as she watched

Margaret fall on her side laughing.

"I'm a dead horse," said Margaret.

Joseph fell off her back, giggling so hard he couldn't stop. He pulled Margaret's arm and said, "Get up, horse."

"Children, you're making too much noise! Play cards or something quiet."

Bill was snoring when she crawled in bed and they slept until shouts of laughter woke Bill. He leaped out of bed and hurried down the steps.

"I told you kids to be quiet," he said pulling the leather belt off his pants.

The children yelled, "We're sorry, Daddy."

He grabbed Margaret and whacked her hard on her bottom. "You're the oldest and you know better." He whacked her again.

The buckle cut into her tender skin and she screamed, "Stop! Daddy stop!"

Bill growled, "That will teach you to listen to your mother." He grabbed Cassie and Faith screamed and ran into the corner quivering. "Don't hurt me Daddy."

Bill stopped and looked at her for a second; he knew he could not touch her. Cassie tried to wiggle free, but Bill gave her a hard whack with the belt, and reached for Joseph.

Joseph ducked under the table whimpering, "I'm sorry, don't hit me."

"Get out here now," yelled Bill.

Joseph stayed under the table, trembling and crying, "No, no, I'm sorry."

Jennifer rushed down and grabbed Bill's arm, "Don't you dare hit them again."

Bill yanked his arm away. His face was beet red as he shouted, "You kids get up to your rooms. I don't want to hear a sound out of you."

The children sobbed as they scurried passed him, "Ooh, I'm bleeding and it hurts bad."

Bill was breathing heavy, his face red and sweaty. "You'd better listen to me from now on."

Jennifer stood in front of him, blocking him in case he went after them. She tried to stay calm. "Why did you get so upset, they were just playing?"

She watched him gasp for breath. "I'm not putting up with insolence."

"You look like you're about to have a heart attack. You'd better go back to bed." Jennifer gave him a glass of water.

Bill laid down, holding his hands over his eyes. "All that noise really got to me. I can't take their screaming and hollering."

Jennifer lay beside him. "They're so little compared to you. It doesn't seem right for you to hit them that way." When he didn't answer, she thought he was asleep and got up.

"Don't you dare go to those children, they are being punished."

Jennifer stared at him defiantly. "What in the world is the matter with you? They were just having fun in a world that has very little laughter. You hit them with your belt. Does that make you feel like a big man?"

Jennifer turned to leave and Bill shouted, "Don't you dare go to their room or I'll take the strap to you."

"You'll what?" Something near hatred showed in her eyes. "I'll leave them alone for a while, just so they realize they have to behave." She pointed her finger at him. "Don't ever think that you can lay a hand on me?" She walked close to the bed. "Be careful just how far your discipline goes. I won't ever let you abuse our children."

Bill lowered his eyes. "Lie down and get a nap while they're quiet."

Jennifer fell asleep, but woke up with severe cramps. She turned over on her stomach, waiting for the pain to subside.

When she felt better, she went into the children's room. "Come help me fix dinner," she said cheerfully.

"Don't let Daddy hit us again," cried the children.

"He won't, but be quiet. He's still asleep." Jennifer took them downstairs.

---

They had a meager dinner of soup meat and potatoes, followed by some stale cookies.

"I'm glad we found these cookies in the Five and Dime trash," said Cassie.

"Yes. Before someone else did," said Margaret. "They throw out good stuff."

Jennifer stood up holding her stomach, she still didn't feel well. "Margaret, you're in charge of cleaning the kitchen, and Joseph and Cassie will help you."

Jennifer was sitting in the parlor crocheting, when a pain cut through her lower abdomen. She doubled over with pain and her underpants felt wet. She touched herself to see why she was wet.

Bill put his paper down. "You're white as a sheet. What's the matter?"

Jennifer staggered toward the steps. "I'm bleeding, I'm losing the baby."

Bill jumped to his feet. "Let me help you upstairs."

She sat on the commode holding her stomach. A sharp pain went through her and she moaned. "It feels like my insides are falling out."

Bill held her hand. "Is there anything I can do to help?"

There was a splash in the toilet and she muffled her cries. "Oh! I just lost the baby, quick, hand me a towel."

"I think you ought to lie down." Bill lifted her in his arms and carried her to the bed.

Jennifer sobbed, "I lost my baby."

"Rest now, Babe. I'll take care of the children."

She laid in a fetal position and thought, "God. Forgive me, but I'm glad I lost it. Now at least my baby won't be crying from hunger."

Bill went down to the kitchen and helped the children do their homework. He hugged each one as he said, "Mother's not feeling well, so be quiet."

Margaret closed her book and asked. "What's wrong with her?"

Bill whispered, "I'll tell you later."

"Let's play Monopoly. That will keep us quiet," said Cassie.

"Me don't know how to play Monopoly!" said Faith, as she stood on the chair.

Margaret laughed at Faith and lifted her onto her lap. "If you're good, I'll let you be the banker."

Bill let them play for a while and then held Faith on his lap. "Mom's lost the baby and she needs to rest."

"Oh no!" said Margaret. "Will she be all right?"

"Yes she will be fine, she wasn't that far along."

"I didn't want another baby anyhow," said Joseph. "It would probably be another girl."

Bill lifted Faith off his lap. "Get ready for bed and I'll come tuck you in."

Cassie looked at him timidly. "You're not going to be mean to us, are you?"

"Not as long as you listen to me." As he kissed each one goodnight, he said, "I only punish you when you misbehave. That doesn't mean I don't love you. I love you very much."

# Chapter Twenty-Two

Just as life had become financially better, the railroad job ended. Bill was out of work again. He searched for work each day, but found nothing. He lined up at the unemployment lines, but things were slow. Bill walked the streets talking to the homeless trying to convert them to his church. He handed out leaflets that read, 'Repent and Be Saved.'

Bill walked up to a man, who was sitting in the park. He shook his hand as he said, "Have you talked with Christ lately?"

The man shivered and looked at Bill. "Are you nuts?"

"Fear not. The Lord God is waiting to welcome you to his flock. Put your fears aside and remember the Lord will take care of you."

The man scoffed and said, "Yeah sure. If you know God so well, ask him to give me a warm coat. It's goddamn cold."

Bill took off his winter coat and handed it to the man. "Take this as a token of God's love. Come meet Christ at the Church of Faith tonight."

The man grabbed the coat and put it on. "Thanks buddy. Hope you don't freeze your ass off," he said, as he ran down the street.

"Don't forget to come to The Church of Faith tonight."

The cold wind blew against him and his teeth chattered as he headed for home.

A pot of tea was simmering on the wood stove and Bill poured a cup. He lingered there, letting the heat warm his body.

Jennifer noticed him trembling. "Are you sick?" She placed her hand on his head. "Well, at least you don't have a fever."

"No! I'm fine. I'm just cold. I gave my coat to a man who was freezing."

"You what? You gave your only coat away? How are you going to keep warm when you find work?"

Bill refilled his tea cup. "Don't worry, the Lord will provide?"

"Sometimes I think you are out of your mind. How can you give your coat to a perfect stranger when it's so cold?" Jennifer stared at him, while she stirred the stew, wondering why he did it. Then shook her head in confusion and said, "Go take a hot bath it will warm you up."

———————————

The day was grey and snowy. Frost painted icy patterns covered the windows and icicles hung from the rooftops. Bill heard they were hiring at the Public Works Department and he bundled in layers of clothes. He walked, in the freezing weather, to the company. They hired him for strenuous work outside. The wind showed no mercy, as it blew against him, seeping through the layers of clothing. When the day was done, he was tired and cold. He stopped at the church. And as he walked in the back room, Reverend Thatcher was pulling clothes out of a box.

"Anything new happening?" asked Bill.

"Someone just dropped off a box of winter clothes and a hundred dollar donation."

Bill looked through the pile and found a black cashmere overcoat. There were a few stains on the front of the coat and the sleeve and the pocket was torn. "Do you mind if I take this coat? I gave mine away yesterday."

"You gave your winter coat away?"

"Yes. The man was freezing and had no place to stay. I gave him mine."

"God bless you. You're so kindhearted. Take it and praise the Lord for these bounties."

When Jennifer saw him, she smiled. "That's a nice coat. Where did you get it?"

"I told you God would take care of me." Bill took off the coat, "It needs a few repairs."

"Give it to me, I'll make it look like new," said Jennifer.

---

It was a beautiful morning and Jennifer was enjoying a cup of chicory coffee. Bill was at work and three of the children were in school. She could tell it was March, the tulips had started to show. She took Faith's hand and went outside. They stood by the forsythia tree looking at the beautiful yellow blooms. "I love springtime," she said to Faith. "It makes me so happy to see the first signs of spring." She picked her daughter and let her smell the yellow flowers. Jennifer spent a few hours digging and planting her vegetable garden, while Faith played. After lunch, she started to clean the house. Faith seemed to be underfoot at every step.

Jennifer picked up an old magazine and said, "Sit down next to me. I'm going to make you some paper dolls to play with." She cut out pictures of a women and a child, and some clothes. Jennifer made sure to cut tabs at the top and sides. "See, you can dress these paper dolls in different clothes."

Faith start playing with them. "This is fun," said Faith. She played with them until she looked out of the window. Her friend was across the street in the park. "Look, Mama. Katie's playing in the park. I want to play with her."

"I can't stop now. I'm busy taking down curtains." said Jennifer. "You'll have to wait until I'm finished."

"Why can't I go now?" asked Faith.

"Just because Katie's at the park, doesn't mean you have to go," said Jennifer, as she continued taking down the curtains.

"Please, Mama. You can watch me from the window. Please, please," whined Faith.

"Let me get this last curtain down, then I'll take you across. I have to see if Katie's mother, Claire, will watch you."

When Jennifer finished, she took Faith's hand and walked across the street to the park. Katie came running to meet them. Jennifer and Katie's mother talked for a while and Grace agreed to watch her.

Jennifer knelt in front of Faith and said, "Promise me, you won't go out in the street."

"I promise," said Faith, as she ran to the swings with her friend.

Grace said, "I'll call you when I'm ready to leave."

"Thank you so much. I'm cleaning the parlor and I can see you out of the window. As soon as you wave, I'll come get her."

Jennifer finished washing the windows and started to wipe the wood work. Then she saw Faith jumping up and down at the curb.

"Mama, I have to go wee, wee," said Faith holding herself.

Jennifer ran out of the door, as Grace ran after the child. "Faith wait. Come back here."

Faith ran into the street just as a truck sped around the corner.

"Stop! Go back!" screamed Jennifer.

Faith ran into the truck and bounced off the fender.

"Oh my God," screamed Jennifer, as she raced to her daughter. She knelt beside her and held her head. "Faith, wake up. Please God, don't let her die."

Grace kneeled beside her. "I'm so sorry. She was playing with Katie and all of a sudden she ran in the street."

The truck driver jumped out of his cab and picked up the unconscious child. His expression was twisted with sorrow. "Let me take her to the hospital."

"No, bring her over to my house," said Jennifer.

He carried the child into the house and said, "I'm sorry Lady. I didn't see her." He laid the child on the couch and asked, "Where's your phone? I'll call an ambulance."

Jennifer looked desperately at the driver and wanted to, instead she said, "We don't believe in doctors."

Her nursing experience had helped her all these years. She really had to rely on it now. Jennifer checked Faith for broken bones and cuts. There was a bruise on her cheek and arm, everything else seemed normal. It was late afternoon and she knew Bill would be finishing work. He always stopped at the church on the way home so she called and left a message.

As soon as Bill got the message, he rushed home. "How is she?"

He could see the tears on Jennifer's cheeks as she answered, "She's unconscious, but doesn't seem to have any broken bones. It's a miracle that she's not dead."

The truck driver grabbed Bill's arm. "I'm so sorry, I didn't see her. She ran right into my truck."

"I understand," said Bill. He got down on his knees. "Dear Lord, we come to you for your mercy. Please heal this innocent lamb. Protect and bring her back to us. Amen."

As the prayer ended, Faith opened her eyes. "Mama, why are you crying?"

"Oh, thank God you're all right." Jennifer held her close.

"Well, I'll be damned," said the driver. "That's a miracle if I ever saw one."

Jennifer ran her fingers through Faith's hair. "I'm going to touch you in different places and I want you to tell Mama if it hurts." She pressed Faith all over her body, as the child giggled, wiggling on the couch. "Does your head or neck hurt?" asked Jennifer, maneuvering Faith's head back and forth.

"No, nothing hurts," Faith said giggling.

"She seems to be all right," said Jennifer holding her daughter on her lap.

"That big bad truck hit me," whimpered Faith.

"I'm sorry, little girl. Really sorry," said the driver.

"She's going to be fine. Maybe you should go," said Bill, as he walked him to the door.

As the day went by, Jennifer watched Faith closely, wanting to be sure there were no after effects. She examined the child's body, while she was in the tub and found a few small bruises.

"You're a lucky little girl and I'm grateful that you're not hurt." Jennifer tucked her in bed and kissed the other children goodnight.

She joined Bill in the kitchen, he was going over their household budget. "I thank God our child wasn't killed. I've checked her over and can't find anything wrong."

Chewing on his pencil he said, "I don't think he hit her. She ran into the truck. Otherwise she would have been in a bad condition."

"How's the money situation?

"Well, I added up what I make at my job, the little bit the church gives me and what you make from your crocheting. It barely covers the household expenses." He tapped the pencil on the table. "That leaves nothing left for groceries."

"I can't cut back anymore on our food money. We're on a starving menu already. Small bowls of oatmeal for breakfast, stale bread spread with mustard or ketchup for lunch. Weak soup, made from soup bones and wilted vegetables for dinner. I have to get to the market early to buy them before someone else gets there. I'm lucky if the soup bones have meat on them."

"Thank God the food basket is still showing up every so often. We eat better then," said Bill.

"I wonder who keeps putting the basket on our steps."

"It's just another one of the Lord's blessings. I don't know what we are going to do." Bill shook his head in despair and studied his figures again.

Jennifer started to work on the scarf she was knitting, when Bill let out a deep sigh.

"What's the matter?"

"Our electric bills are atrocious and we are almost out of coal for the furnace."

"It's the end of March, the electric bills will be lower and we won't need to buy coal until fall," said Jennifer.

Bill sat silent for a while, then said, "Maybe we should pull Margaret out of school and let her get a job. She's fourteen. It would give us enough money to buy food."

Jennifer stopped knitting. "It sounded like you said you wanted Margaret to quit school."

"She's a big girl aged fourteen; she could get a job."

"Jennifer in a stern voice said, "That child stays in school; I'll get a job."

"Calm down, it was only a suggestion." Bill stacked the bills together and put them away.

"Ask Reverend Thatcher, if he has any work I can do." When Bill didn't answer, she stood up. "Did you hear me?"

"Yes, I heard you. I'll ask him tomorrow."

Jennifer wondered who would take care of Faith if she went to work. They couldn't afford to pay anyone to watch her. She wouldn't be old enough to go to school until August.

A week later Jennifer took Faith's baptismal certificate and found a pen that matched the written words. Carefully she changed the birth date to make her a year older, then brought out the cork and acid.

As she touched Faith's arm with the cork, she screamed. Holding her daughter close she said, "I'm sorry, honey. It will only hurt for a little while. You're going to have a big girl mark, like Cassie and Margaret."

The burn formed into a blister and later a scab and again she convinced the school nurse that Faith had been vaccinated.

Margaret held Faith's hand, as the four of them walked to school. When they left,

Jennifer turned off the hot water heater to conserve gas and cleaned the kitchen. As she cleaned, she tried to think of ways to make money. Jennifer walked to the nearby clothing store; she saw very few clothes hanging on the racks. The sales woman sat reading a magazine.

She looked up and smiled, "Can I help you?"

"Yes, I was wondering if you needed any help?" said Jennifer.

"Lady, if things don't pick up soon I won't even have a job."

"Things are that bad?"

"Worse. I'm the owner. If I close the business, I'll lose everything." Tears filled her eyes and she quickly wiped them away.

"Well, thanks anyway, Good luck."

Jennifer walked a few blocks, feeling the chill in the air, but the warmth of the sun felt good.

Jennifer sat on a park bench across from her house and tried to think. "I can't stand being poor like this. I have to do something." She went into several more stores and realized that she was wasting her time.

Depressed, Jennifer went home and started to cut up the gizzards and chicken wings for a chicken potpie. She threw wood and coal into the stove to get the oven hot and rolled out the dough. The stove warmed the house, but after the sun went down, the house cooled off.

Everyone went to bed early and Jennifer snuggled under the covers feeling the warmth of the blankets. It was late, but she couldn't sleep. Bill tugged at the covers pulling them up to his chin.

"Are you awake?" asked Jennifer.

"Hmm," he murmured.

"Did you ask Reverend Thatcher if he had work for me?"

Bill moved over and cuddled close to her. "I talked to him; he said there was nothing right now. Maybe later."

"I heard there's an opening at the Jefferson hospital. They need nurses and the pay is good."

"No." Bill ran his hand over her warm breast.

"No? No, what?" Jennifer pushed his hand away.

"No, I don't want you working in a hospital." Bill caressed her nipple.

Jennifer pulled his hand away again. "You'd rather our children wear rags and holes in their shoes? You'd rather eat the slop I serve you than have me work at the hospital?"

"Let's talk about this tomorrow. Right now, I want to make love to you," he whispered pulling her on top of him.

She rolled off. "Stop it. I don't want to get pregnant. It's the wrong time."

"Come on, Babe," he urged, as he tried to kiss her. "I'll pull out. I promise I won't come inside you."

Her body stiffened. "Don't you understand? We can't afford to have another baby." She sat up and her lips thinned in anger. "You want me to stay home, have babies and go hungry. But I can't work at the hospital. I don't understand your reasoning."

"That's enough, not another word. The Lord watches over us and provides. We'll take whatever child he gives us."

Jennifer had to have the last word. "Have you ever heard the expression, the Lord helps those who help themselves?"

Instead of their argument turning Bill off, it heightened his lust. He wanted her. "You're right; the Lord does help those who help themselves. He also says, wife, honor and obey your husband." He slid on top of her. "I need you, Babe."

"Get off me," she tried pushing him away, but he was too heavy.

She dug her fingernails deep into his bare back making long bloody gashes. Bill let out a howl and Jennifer pushed him off.

"I told you, I don't want to get pregnant."

Jennifer ran into the bathroom and when she came out Bill was asleep on his stomach. She could see the bloody lines across his back, but he deserved it.

# Chapter Twenty-Three

Jennifer got up early, cooked the oatmeal and set the table. She was sitting at the table when Margaret came down for breakfast.

She looked curiously at her mother. "Why are you all dressed up?"

"I'm going job hunting; I can't live like this any longer."

Bill came in the room. "Hey, what's going on here?" He sat down and Jennifer scooped oatmeal into a dish and handed it to him.

Bill ruffled Margaret's hair. "You look pretty with those ribbons in your hair."

"What's keeping the other kids?" Jennifer went to the steps. "Get a move on up there. You're going to be late." They clamored down the stairs and raced to the table.

"What, oatmeal again?" said Cassie.

Bill leaned over and slapped her lightly on the head, "Thank the good Lord you have food. Think of all the people who have nothing to eat." He glanced at Jennifer. "Why do you have your good clothes on?"

"I'm going to look for a job."

Bill frowned. "What kind of work are you looking for?"

Jennifer shrugged her shoulders. "Cleaning houses, waiting on people."

Bill got up from the table. "I went to the unemployment agency yesterday, I have a job on Market Street. It is new construction so I better not be late." He tried to kiss Jennifer, but she bent down to tie Faith's shoe. He slapped his hat against his leg. "See you at dinner."

The trolley car dropped Jennifer off at the unemployment office at Seventh and Market Street. Bill had told her about the long lines, but she didn't expect fifty people to be ahead of her.

"It's 8 a.m., why don't they open the doors?" said the woman in front of Jennifer.

"Stop complaining, they're opening them now," said the woman standing behind Jennifer.

"They're only letting seven people in at a time, it's going to take all day," said a man at the back of the line.

Two hours later, Jennifer walked into a large office. The walls were a drab steel gray. The sun shone through the big glass windows, lighting up the dreary place. Twenty wooden desks stood in rows of three and a guard directed her to one in the front row. A wooden chair sat beside the scarred wooden desk that was piled high with papers. Jennifer sat facing a thin, blonde woman. Her sour expression made Jennifer feel uneasy.

"I'm Mrs. Schwartz." The veins bulged out on her scrawny hands as she handed Jennifer a paper. "Fill out that form and be sure to list your qualifications and what type of work you're looking for."

Jennifer stared at the paper and looked around the desk.

"What's the matter, can't you read?" asked Mrs. Schwartz.

"Yes, I can read. I'm looking for something to write with."

Mrs. Schwartz handed her a pencil. "Sorry, I thought I gave you one."

Jennifer's hands shook as she filled out the form and gave it to the counselor.

She studied it. "Hmm, hmm, you have nursing experience." She took her glasses off and peered at Jennifer. "Tell me why you want to scrub floors, when you could apply for work in a hospital or private duty?"

Jennifer fiddled with the pencil. "My husband doesn't want me to work in a hospital."

"Come on, lady, let's be sensible. Scrubbing floors will get you a dollar a day and there are hundreds of women available for that." Mrs. Schwartz leaned back in her chair. "Now nursing, that's different. They're in demand. You can earn ten dollars a day, sometimes more."

Jennifer's eyes lit up. "Ten dollars a day?"

"Close your mouth, I can see your tongue flapping," laughed Mrs. Schwartz. "If you don't want to work in a hospital, I have a couple of private duty jobs. Let's see. One pays twelve a day, one pays ten, interested?"

"I…I don't know, what are the hours?"

"The night job pays twelve. The day one pays ten." Mrs. Schwartz waited for an answer.

"We desperately need the money."

"Does that mean you want it?" When Jennifer didn't answer, Mrs. Schwartz said, "Come on lady. You have to make up your mind; there's a bunch of people waiting."

"Where's the day job?"

"Germantown section. Three days a week, 8 a.m. in the morning to 3 p.m. in the afternoon. It's an old lady that needs care, until her husband gets home from the office."

Jennifer sat quietly thinking, "Should I take it? Bill won't let me, but I want to. That's more money a day than he sometimes makes in a week."

Mrs. Schwartz shook her head. "You're a strange one. Most people grab the jobs right away, but you act like you don't want one." Mrs. Schwartz put her hand up and yelled, "Next!"

"No, wait, I want it. Give me the address."

The counselor sighed, "Okay, I'll call and set up an interview. When can you go?"

"Tomorrow afternoon."

Mrs. Schwartz made the phone call, then said, "You're to be at Mr. Clancy's house at 2p.m. Here's the address and directions, good luck."

Jennifer was overwhelmed with what she had done. Her legs felt like rubber as she walked outside. She let out a deep breath and thought, "I need a cup a coffee to think about what I just did." Jennifer walked to a restaurant and took a booth in the back.

"Can I help you?" asked the waitress.

"A cup of coffee please." She leaned back against the booth. She knew Bill wouldn't allow her to do this. She sat there thinking, "I'll have to lie to him. No. No I can't do that. I'll tear up the address and go home." Jennifer stirred the hot coffee, sipping it slowly as she continued to fight with herself. "I know I'll make a lot more money nursing than scrubbing floors. We're barely surviving now." With a decisive look on her face, she said, "I'm going to do it."

The waitress stopped. "Did you want me to get you something?"

Jennifer replied, "No. Thank you."

With a new determination she boarded the trolley, knowing she made the right decision. She felt light hearted, as she thought. "From now on things will be better. When she arrived home, she made lunch, cutting the ketchup sandwiches into diamond and heart shapes. She placed a flowered oilcloth over the scratched wooden table, then put a jelly jar of dandelions in the middle."

When the children came home, Margaret smiled. "The table looks pretty."

Cassie picked up a heart shaped sandwich and whined, "Do we have to have the ketchup sandwiches again?"

Margaret bit into the diamond shaped piece and between bites said, "I wish we could eat like we did in Columbia."

"I do too," said Jennifer. "Guess what. I'm going for an interview. If they like me, I'll be working for some rich people in Germantown."

Faith started to cry, "I don't want you to work. Who will take care of us?"

Jennifer put her arms around her. "Don't cry, precious. I'll be home by the time you get out of school. I'm only work three days a week and I'll make enough money to buy you good food and a nice dress."

Faith smiled. "Would you buy me a pretty blue dress?"

"Yes. A blue dress with satin ribbons. Now eat your lunch." Jennifer poured each a cold glass of watered-down condensed milk. "I'll buy some real milk too."

---

Jennifer waited for the trolley in the chilly March weather. She shivered as the cold seeped through the layers of her sweaters, underneath her light coat. The trolley screeched to a stop and Jennifer took a front seat. As the trolley moved along, she watched for the street signs. She had to transfer to another trolley. Mesmerized by the clacking of the metal wheels, Jennifer's eyes started to close, but she forced herself to stay awake. The reflection of her hair curled loosely around her face, made her smile and she took out the rouge from her purse and applied a little to her cheeks. The trolley car stopped at Indiana Street, and her transfer was waiting. The only seat available was in the back between two men.

"Pardon me, I'd like to take that seat," she said.

The man never moved or answered. She squeezed past him and sat watching for her stop.

Jennifer leaned forward to look out the window and the man next to the window stared at her purse.

"Nice pocketbook," said the man, smiling.

Jennifer gripped her purse tightly and sat rigid in her seat. The man pressed his thigh against her and she pulled away.

"What stop are you getting off?" asked the stranger.

His words frightened her and she said, "Washington Lane."

The conductor called out, "Next stop Germantown Avenue."

Jennifer got up and pushed passed the man on her right and headed to the side door.

When she got off, Jennifer made sure no one was following her. As she hurried along the street, she thought, "What a lovely street. I like the way the tall oak trees shade the houses." Jennifer checked the numbers and found the house and a strange feeling crept over her. "It's just like my house in Carnegie! Big, white two story, with the same tall columns and wide porch." Jennifer's legs wobbled as she went up the steps and rang the bell.

A tall, distinguished-looking man with white hair opened the door. He was neatly shaved and dressed in an expensive blue striped suit. "He looks something like my father," she thought.

"You must be Mrs. Rennie. I'm Mr. Clancy, please come in."

Jennifer stepped into the marble foyer and gazed at the magnificent chandelier. The curved staircase of walnut was carved with cupid figures around each post.

"Everything is so lovely," said Jennifer.

"Thank you. Come in the library."

He led the way to a high-back leather chair by the fireplace. Just like the one her father had in his library. A fire was burning in the fireplace and she sat forward to warm herself.

Mr. Clancy sat across from her, and crossed his legs, as he leaned back in his chair. "Where did you work before?"

Jennifer was nervous and gripped her purse so tight, it hurt her fingers. "I'm a registered nurse, but I haven't worked in the states for years. I worked as a missionary in Colombia, South America, for three years. I took care of the sick and injured." She told him about their mission.

Mr. Clancy listened intently. Wondering where he had heard the story before.

"I'm very good at healing people and have great patience," said Jennifer. When he didn't say anything, her mouth quivered as she quickly added, "I need the work and I won't let you down. I promise."

Mr. Clancy uncrossed his legs and asked, "Do you have references?"

"No sir, but if you give me a try, you won't be sorry. I'm a very hard worker."

"You have a sincere way about you and I like the way you handle yourself." He stood up smiling. "I'll give you a three week trial and see how things work out."

Jennifer clasped her hands together. "Thank you so much."

"I expect you to be on time and wear a clean white uniform."

"White uniform, hat, stockings and shoes," she answered wondering where she was going to get the money to buy them.

He led Jennifer to the hall. "My wife had polio a few years ago and it left her weak and unsteady on her feet." As they reached the staircase he said, "I can't leave her alone because she loses her balance and falls. She needs someone to help her bathe and dress."

"That's no problem," said Jennifer.

"Come upstairs, I want you to meet her. I expect you to prepare her meals. We had a cook and butler before the depression, but we had to let them go."

"I won't mind that at all."

As they walked down the hall, a hoarse voice called out, "Roger, is that you?"

Mr. Clancy opened the bedroom door. "Marsha, I have a new nurse I want you to meet."

"Hope she's better than the last lazy bum," slurred Marsha. "What's your name?"

"Have you been overdosing on your pain medicine again?" asked Mr. Clancy. Then he looked at Jennifer and winked. "When she takes the medicine herself, she doesn't measure it, just sips it from the bottle." He laughed. "You can always tell, because she slurs her words."

"Well, are you going to tell me your name or not?" asked Marsha.

"Jennifer. My name is Jennifer." She walked over and shook Marsha's hand.

"You're a pretty one. Much nicer than the last one." Marsha patted the chair next to her. "Sit and tell me about yourself. Do you have any children?"

"I have four children and they're all in school," replied Jennifer shyly.

Marsha stared at Jennifer, taking in her complete appearance, then she grabbed Jennifer's arm and felt it. "You're pretty skinny. Do you have any strength in those arms?" Jennifer started to answer, but was interrupted as Marsha said, "Rodger, I like her."

"Good, that's settled," said Roger Clancy. "We'll need you three days a week; Monday Wednesday and Friday. The salary is ten dollars a day, is that agreeable?"

"That's swell," said Jennifer.

"Your hours will be 8:30 a.m. to 3:30 p.m." Roger walked her to the door. "If I'm ever held up at the office, our neighbor will relieve you."

Jennifer walked over to the wheelchair. "Mrs. Clancy, its nice meeting you. I know we'll get along."

"Call me Marsha, it sounds friendlier." She wheeled her chair toward the closet. "Roger, open this door and get that brown coat out. The one with the little mink collar." He pulled a thick, wool coat out of the closet. "Don't stand there looking at it, give it to Jennifer. She can't come to work on cold days with that thin thing she's wearing. She'll freeze to death."

"Oh no, I couldn't take it." Jennifer pushed it away.

"What's the matter, don't you like it?" asked Marsha.

"Like it! It's the most beautiful coat I've ever seen."

"Then take it girl, before I change my mind." Marsha wheeled the chair to the center of the room. "I won't wear it again and you'll look lovely in it."

Jennifer took off her thread worn coat and put on the brown one. She hugged herself to feel its soft warmth and smoothed the fur at the neck. Her eyes gleamed with happiness.

"Thank you so much," said Jennifer.

"Might as well have the hat that matches it," said Marsha. She opened the drawer of the dresser and pulled out a brown felt hat. It had an ostrich feather at the crown. "Put it on. Let's see what you look like in it."

Jennifer stepped in front of the mirror and placed the hat on her head. "Oh I love it."

"You look like something out of a magazine," said Mr. Clancy.

Jennifer started to thank her again, but Marsha stopped her. "Get on with you gal. Take it and go home to your children."

Mr. Clancy led Jennifer down to the front door. "Wait here a minute," he said and walked out to the kitchen. When he returned, he handed her a shopping bag. "These belonged to our last nurse. You might be able to use them." Jennifer's eyebrows lifted in surprise. Mr. Clancy said, "She washed her uniforms here and when she quit, she forgot them."

"Won't she come back for them?"

"No, she's moved to another state."

Jennifer was so happy to get the uniforms. She wanted to hug him, but instead said,

"Thank you so much for everything. I'll see you Monday."

---

The trolley was empty and she sat behind the conductor feeling happy about her new job. At least there would be money coming in each week.

Her smile turned sad as she thought. "What am I going to tell Bill?"

The trolley slowed and Jennifer knew it was the transfer stop. She stepped off and stood waiting for the next trolley. Jennifer saw a crowd watching a man, standing on a crate. She walked over to see what was going on. The person looked a lot like Bill, wearing the same black felt hat and black coat. "That is him!" She thought. "It's him! What's he doing way out here?" She heard him yell at the top of his voice, "Repent you sinners and give up your drinking, fornicating and lying. The thunder of God will come down upon you, sending you into hell and damnation." His face was red from exertion and a stern expression covered his face. "The devil has you by the coat tails. Dragging you deeper each day into his clutches. Repent and come into the glory of God."

A man in front of the crowd yelled, "Go home you bum, you're crazy."

"Yeah, we don't want to hear it," yelled another man.

"Did you just escape from the nut house?" heckled the crowd.

Bill pointed to the man in front. "Give up your drinking." Then he pointed to a young woman. "Stop your fornicating and using your body in sinful ways."

Jennifer watched the crowd making fun of her husband and she held back the tears. She cringed when the tough looking woman walked up to Bill.

The woman shouted, "Maybe you need a little nookie to calm you down. Come back to my room, and I'll save your soul, while you fill my hole."

The crowd laughed and Bill said, "The wrath of God will come down on you for your sinful ways."

A policeman broke through the crowd, blowing his whistle and waving his club. "Come on, break it up." He pulled Bill off the crate. "Move it along buster and don't come around here again."

Bill waved his hands. "You're all sinners. Repent and be saved. Come to the Church of Faith tonight and have the Lord wash away your sins."

The policeman grabbed his coat collar and pushed him forward, "Get on your way buddy, before I throw you in jail."

Bill picked up his crate and shouted at the officer, "The wages of sin are death Hallelujah, Praise the Lord."

The policeman noticed Jennifer. "Are you all right lady, you're white as a sheet? Don't worry about that preacher man, he's a little loco."

Jennifer walked back to the trolley stop and sat on the bench. She didn't know Bill preached on the street; he sounded so fanatical. The streetcar pulled up and she handed the conductor the ticket and thought, "I'm not going to tell Bill I saw him."

# Chapter Twenty-Four

Jennifer arrived home a half hour before the children. She changed her clothes and sat on the couch trying to relax.

As they opened the door the children said, "Hi, Mama. Can we have something to eat?"

"How about a peanut butter sandwich?" asked Jennifer.

"There's peanut butter?" they shouted.

"Yes. Now that I have a job, the corner market extended me credit."

Margaret reached for the jar and spread a slice of stale bread. "You got the job?"

"Yes, I start Monday morning at 8:30 a.m. It's in a lovely home in Germantown."

"I don't want you to work, but I know how worried you are," said Margaret. "Maybe I should quit school and help out too."

Jennifer put her hands on Margaret's shoulders. "You are going to finish school."

"Oh, I love you." Margaret hugged her mother. "I'll help with the housework, and even take care of the kids. If you're late getting home, I'll cook dinner."

"You're thirteen now, old enough to be a big help honey." Jennifer held her tight; she loved her children dearly. "I'll only be working three days a week."

"What smells so good?" asked Cassie.

A five cent bag of chicken heads, tails, and gizzards simmered in a pot of water. "Chicken and dumplings," said Jennifer. "Homemade biscuits are in the oven. As soon as your father gets home, we'll eat."

Bill was late getting home and Joseph said, "I'm hungry. When are we going to eat?"

"Your father should be home soon. Let's play a game of cards until he comes."

They waited for Bill for two hours and gave up. Jennifer put the steaming chicken on the table and Bill walked in.

"Why are you so late?" asked Jennifer

"Let's say grace and eat."

"Did you run into trouble at the church?"

"No. I was out recruiting for the Lord," he replied. Bill lowered his head. "Let's pray." The family bowed their heads as Bill started his prayer. Instead of a grace he went into a sermon on the wages of sin. Faith kept her head bowed, but her eyes were on the biscuits. Her stomach growled and her mouth watered. She started to reach for one, but stopped. Her father continued his sermon and temptation became too much. The smell of the warm biscuits was overwhelming. Faith reached for the warm biscuits and Bill's hand swung out. He slapped her across the face and she fell off the chair.

"I'm sorry, daddy," cried Faith.

"The Lord gives us these bounties and we do not touch them until we thank him."

Jennifer picked up Faith and held her close. "There's no excuse for being that rough." She placed Faith on her chair. "Look at the bruise on her face."

Bill slammed his hand on the table. "I won't have you interfering when I discipline the children. Take your seat immediately."

"Who do you think you're talking too?" When Jennifer noticed the children had tears in their eyes, she sat down.

"Bow your heads," said Bill. "Thank you Lord, for the food we are about to eat, amen."

Faith sobbed as she held her bruised cheek. "My jaw hurts."

"Stop crying this instant, do you hear me?" said Bill.

Faith choked back her sobs and wiped the tears with her napkin. "Yes Daddy."

Everyone ate quietly. Bill ate two helpings, and then pushed his chair back. Jennifer put her hand on his arm. "Wait, I want to talk to you,"

"I'm going down to the basement. I can't talk now."

Jennifer let out a deep breath and started to clear the table. "Children, come help me do the dishes."

When they finished cleaning the kitchen, she helped them with their homework. The clock started to chime. "Good grief," said Jennifer, "It's 9 p.m. Children get ready for bed."

Jennifer went to the basement to see what Bill was doing. He had papers in his hand, feeding a mimeograph machine reams of paper.

Jennifer gasped and said, "Where did you get that?"

"I brought it home this afternoon from church. Reverend Thatcher told me I could."

Jennifer picked up one of the sheets of paper. "Why are you printing Psalms and passages from the Bible? What are you going to do with them?"

Bill turned the arm of the roller. "I'll pass them out in the streets and speakeasies."

"Who's paying for all this ink and paper?"

"Why? It's none of your business." He opened a fresh ream of paper and loaded the machine. "Your business is to take care of the house and kids. I say where the money goes."

She placed her hands on her hips. "Bill, I'm asking you again, who is paying for all this?"

Bill stared at her, then continued to turn the handle. "If you must know, I'm splitting it with the church."

"Splitting it with the church? We can't afford food, let alone all this paper and ink."

"The Lord provides. He will see that we are justly rewarded for our efforts and sacrifice."

"I'm tired of your commanding tone. Your holier than thou behavior. It's too much for me to handle. She wanted to scream but said, I don't feel like arguing about this. You know darn well we can't afford it. I'm going upstairs."

She started to walk away and Bill said, "How dare you say things like that to me. I'm the master of this house. Don't you dare go upstairs, I need you to stay and help me?"

She shook her head in despair. "I can't. I have things to do. When you come up, I want to talk to you."

"I don't want to hear you nagging me about the children."

"What I have to talk to you about is something just as important."

Jennifer got the shopping bag Mr. Clancy had given her and went into the parlor. She opened the bag and pulled out two white uniforms, two caps, two pair of white stockings, and a pair of shoes. She held the uniforms up to herself. I can alter these easily, just take in the waist a bit. Jennifer tried the shoes on and they were a size too large. I'll make them fit by stuffing paper in the toes. She wiggled her toes. There, that will do until payday, then I'll buy a pair. She opened her sewing machine and altered the uniforms. When everything was put away, she called down to Bill. "How much longer are you going to be?"

"The machine keeps jamming; I have to finish this last batch."

"I'm going up to bed. Don't be too late. I still need to talk to you."

She lay in bed wondering why Bill changed so much. He's so stern and strict with the children? I've never known him to be so mean. He's been like that since we came back from

Columbia. Maybe it's all the stress of having no money, trying to provide for us. Jennifer fell asleep and as the clock struck midnight, Bill crawled in bed.

---

The children's laughter woke Bill and he hurried down to breakfast. "I overslept."

"You were up so late. I thought you should sleep as long as you could." Jennifer served him his oatmeal as she said, "The children already ate and are ready for Sunday service."

"I have to run downstairs for a minute, be ready and at the door when I come down."

Jennifer got her new coat out of the closet and was putting it on when Margaret walked into the parlor. "Where did you get that beautiful coat?"

Jennifer stood in front of the mirror and put on her new hat. "The people I'm working for gave it to me. Don't mention it to your father; I want to see if he notices it."

Bill came up from the basement with his arms piled high with the flyers. "Each of you carry a bundle," he said, spreading the load between them. "Hurry, we're going to be late."

Bill put the flyers in Reverend Thatcher's office, then stood by the front door. He welcomed his parishioners as Faith stood next to him. As each person came in, they shook Pastor Rennie's hand, then patted the child head gently. "Hello, little Faith, hope and charity."

Faith stomped over to her mother. "I hate my name."

"Why? You have a pretty name."

"I wish people wouldn't say that every time they see me."

Jennifer looked at her curiously, "What are you talking about?"

"Every time we come to church, people pat me on the head and say, little Faith, hope and charity. I hate it."

"Hate is not a nice thing to feel." Jennifer put her arm around her daughter. "They're just trying to be nice."

"I don't want them to be that nice to me."

"Go get your brother and sisters for me."

Faith went running. "Margaret, Joseph, Cassie, mamma wants you."

They went over to where Jennifer was sitting and Margaret said, "Is it time for service?"

"No, I want to give you each a nickel for the collection, don't lose it."

"We won't," said Joseph.

"Can we go outside until service begins?" asked Margaret.

"Yes, but just for a little while."

Joseph kept looking at the candy store across the street. "Let's go buy some candy."

"Suppose mom and dad catch us?" said Margaret.

"They won't. They're busy talking," said Joseph. "Come on, let's go."

As they entered the store, they gasped when they saw all the different types of candy.

"Wow, look at all the gumdrops and licorice sticks," said Cassie.

"I like the jaw breakers and lollypops," said Joseph.

"Only buy two cents worth," said Margaret. "We have to save some for the collection."

They huddled in a corner of the church eating their goodies. When they heard their mother call, they took their seats.

Jennifer noticed the mischievous look on their faces. "What's so funny?"

Before they could answer, Mrs. Runderson started to play the piano. When the collection basket was passed around, the children put their fist in the basket and dropped the three pennies.    Their eyes went directly to their mother and Cassie whispered, "She never noticed."

They started to giggle and Jennifer reached over and whispered, "Don't utter another sound or I'll take you down to the bathroom and smack your bottoms."

Jennifer sat back and listened to Bill deliver the sermon. She noticed how spellbound the people were. He didn't seem as demonstrative as he was on the street.

When they returned home she hung her coat in the closet and thought, Bill never noticed my new hat and coat.

––––––––––––––––––––

Jennifer finished making the children mustard sandwiches for school lunch and placed them in brown bags. She kissed them goodbye and said, "I want you to stay in school for lunch. Here's the money to buy milk. I start work today, but I'll be here when you get home."

Bill came down after the children left and Jennifer smiled. "Margaret is really maturing. Look at the way she takes care of her sisters and brother."

"Yes, she's becoming quite the young lady. Where does the time go? It seem like yesterday she was just a little tyke."

Jennifer poured him a cup of chicory coffee. "I have something to talk to you about."

Bill drank down the coffee. "I'm sorry, I'm late. I have to work at the highway department." He kissed her goodbye. "They're still digging that trench for the new water pipes by the river. After work, I'm going to stop by the church."

She sighed. "Okay, I'll talk to you later." Jennifer grabbed the shopping bag with the uniforms and ran to the trolley stop.

Mr. Clancy opened the door before she rang the bell. "You're early that pleases me. Let me show you where everything is."

When he opened the icebox, Jennifer gasped at the amount of food. "You have plenty to choose from."

"Marsha needs a full lunch. Fix her whatever she wants and make sure you eat too. Oh, ice gets delivered every day at 11 a.m. Come upstairs and I'll give you instructions on what medicines my wife takes. Some days she may be a little cranky, but most of the time she's very pleasant. Give her a bath each morning and be careful she doesn't fall."

Marsha smiled when they entered the room. "You came back, I was afraid you might change your mind."

Jennifer took her hand. "Don't worry; I'll be here whenever you need me." She turned to Mr. Clancy. "Where can I change into my uniform?"

"Call me Roger." He pointed across the hall. "Use the guest bedroom."

Jennifer walked into the warm, tastefully decorated room and took her coat off. She admired the bedspread and drapes that were in light tones of blue, trimmed with white. The dark blue carpet felt thick and plush under her feet. It reminded her of her home in Carnegie. Jennifer changed and walked over to the mirror.

As she pinned on her white hat, she looked at her reflection. "I've always loved nursing."

When Roger saw her, his eyes lit up. "My, you look just like the nurse on the Red Cross posters."

Jennifer blushed. "Thank you. Are there any last minute instructions?"

"No. I think I told you everything." He picked up his briefcase. "I've got to leave." He handed her a card. "Here's my phone number in case you need me." He started walking towards the door, then said. "Oh, I also wrote our neighbors name and number on the back of the card. Call her in case of an emergency."

Jennifer walked into Marsha's room, smiled and said, "Are you ready for your bath?"

"That the highlight of my day," Marsha said, as she wheeled her chair towards the bathroom.

The day went fast and before she knew it, Mr. Clancy was home.

———————————

Jennifer arrived home and was surprised to find Bill in the basement. She watched him print the flyers.

She started to stack the papers that covered the desk and asked, "How was your day?"

"I worked at the railroad and I'm exhausted, but I have to finish these flyers."

Jennifer tapped the pile on the desk to straighten the papers. "Did they pay you? I need money to buy food for dinner."

Bill, glanced up at her, but didn't answer.

Jennifer raised her voice a notch. "Did they pay you? They owe you for five days."

Bill kept his eyes on the machine. "They paid me."

Jennifer put out her hand. "Can I have some money?"

He reached in his pocket as he kept working. "Here's two dollars."

"Two dollars, is that all they paid you?"

Bill kept his eyes on the machine. "No, that's not all they paid me. I needed the rest to buy ink and paper."

Jennifer stepped closer to him. "You spent almost fifteen dollars on paper and ink?"

"No, I was handing out flyers and came across three homeless boys." This time he looked up as he continued, "I talked to them for a while and converted them to the Church of Faith, then I gave them some money for food."

Jennifer sat on the couch by the wall. She shook her head. "I can't believe you did that knowing how little we have."

Bill continued turning the arm of the machine. "God will repay our generosity."

Her voice quivered. "I need to talk to you. I have a few things I need to discuss."

He waved his hand as if he was dismissing her. "Okay, as soon as I'm finished, but right now I'm busy." Jennifer kept staring at him. He looked at her, "What! What do you want to tell me? Can't you see I'm busy?"

"I took a job, I'm working."

"You took a job without talking to me?"

"I tried to talk to you, but you're always busy printing flyers." She slapped her hands down on her lap in frustration. "I'm working three days a week for an elderly couple in Germantown."

"Call and tell them you quit, you won't be in tomorrow."

Jennifer held back her tears. "There's no food in the house and no money to buy any. The children's shoes have holes in them and so do mine. You've got to let me work until you get a better job." He started to say something, but she walked over and placed her fingers gently on his lips. "Please, please Bill let me work for a while." She laid her head on his shoulder and wept. "I'm so tired of struggling for every morsel of food. You've got to let me help."

He felt her tears soaking through his shirt and he put his arms around her. "How are you managing with the children?"

"They eat lunch in school and I'm home by 3 p.m. Margaret and Cassie have been helping with the housework."

"As long as the children aren't neglected, I'll give you my consent."

She felt better now that Bill knew she was working and was glad he hadn't asked what she was doing.

She started walking up the steps and said, "I'm going to see what I can find for supper."

Jennifer searched the cupboard and wracked her brain trying to figure out what to have. She had to save the two dollars for the trolley fare and for the children's milk at school. The only thing on the shelf was a package of cornmeal.

"What am I going to make out of this?" She thought of all the food in Mr. Clancy's icebox and wished she had some of that delicious meat. "Oh well, let's see what I can make with this." Jennifer mixed the cornmeal with water and boiled it for ten minutes, then poured it in a bread pan. When it cooled she cut the cornmeal into slices and fried it in leftover fat from yesterday's soup. She poured sugar into a small amount of water and cooked it until it started to thicken.

Jennifer scraped the almost empty jar of strawberry jam into the syrup. She placed the fried cornmeal on the table, then spread the syrup across the top. She called everyone to supper.

Joseph ate two helpings. "This is a great dinner."

"I think we should have this every night," said Cassie.

## Chapter Twenty-Five

Jennifer had roasted a chicken the day before for Marsha's lunch. Today, she pulled the rest of the meat off the carcass and prepared a hot chicken sandwich and a salad. Marsha took a bite and smiled. "This is delicious."

"Thank you. Would it be all right if I took the bones of the chicken home?"

"Certainly, dear. Take the giblets too, we never eat them." Marsha wiped her mouth with the napkin. You can take any of the leftovers in the ice box as well."

With a grateful smile, Jennifer said, "Thank you so much." She knew what the children would have for dinner that night.

"Put the radio on," said Marsha. "I'm in the mood for music."

Jennifer loved the radio, but Bill wouldn't allow one in the house. She turned the small knob and a song came on. "Who is that singing?" asked Jennifer.

"That's Al Jolson. I love the way he sings Mammy," said Marsha.

Jennifer took the lunch dishes to the kitchen and when she returned she said, "That's such a catchy tune."

"That's a new song out, 'If you knew Susie.' Boy, I loved to dance before I got sick."

Marsha sang along, "If you knew Susie like I knew Susie, Oh, oh, oh, what a gal."

"That's such a happy song," said Jennifer, humming along with the tune.

When she went home, Jennifer was still humming the song. The children asked, "Mama, what's that you're humming?"

"It's a new song I heard on the radio. I'll try to remember the words. Let see it goes, 'If you knew Susie like I know Susie oh, oh, oh, what a gal.'" She started to dance around the kitchen and the children joined her. "There's none so classy as this fair lassie. Holy mackerel what a chasse."

Bill walked in and stood watching for a moment. "What kind of rubbish are you teaching our children?"

"It's a song I heard on the radio at work; it's such a fun tune."

"It's a trashy song and I won't have my family listening to such garbage. Shut your ears to those sinful songs and don't repeat them at home."

"But there's nothing wrong..."

"The subject is closed. Put the dinner on the table."

Jennifer slammed the pot of stew on the table. "There! Dinner is ready."

The children stared at their father. Bill lowered his head. "Let's all say grace."

---

Living conditions had improved now that Jennifer brought home a salary. Bill kept his job working four mornings a week, and the church paid him a few dollars. With the food Marsha gave her, they were meeting their bills and eating better.

"Today is the end of my three week trial," thought Jennifer. She had enjoyed the work immensely and hoped they were satisfied with her. She didn't want to lose the job.

Roger came home early that afternoon and took Jennifer's hand. "My dear, you have been with us three weeks and we're very satisfied with your work. I hope you stay with us for a long time." He handed her a white envelope and a paper bag. "Here's your salary and some cookies for the children."

Jennifer's face brightened. "I enjoy working here. Martha is a gem to take care for."

"It's such a lovely spring day; I decided to come home early." Roger pressed an extra ten dollars in her hand. "You can leave now. Go shopping, buy yourself something nice."

She smiled and thought, "I could use a new dress, but we need so many other things."

As Jennifer left she said, "Thank you for the extra money. I'll enjoy the time off."

She walked down the street and heard the birds chirping in the trees. Spring is really here, she thought.

She walked past the trolley stop to an exclusive section on Germantown Avenue. A red linen dress with white buttons caught her eye. She looked at the price tag hanging on the side of the dress. "Darn! It's way more than ten dollars. I used to be able to afford anything I wanted. I long for the good old days." Jennifer stretched her arms, then took a deep breath of the fresh air. She felt happier than she had in a long time. She walked toward an area that had large shade trees and benches. She sat down to enjoy the afternoon, then noticed a crowd on the side street. They were gathered around a man wearing a black suit. "Oh no! Don't let it be Bill." She walked a little closer. It was Bill.

He stood on a wooden crate shouting to the crowd, "Change your ways, and give up your sinful habits. Come under God's hands." Pointing at two men, he said, "God sees you sneaking in speakeasies, fornicating with the devil's prostitutes. Lying, cheating and taking God's name in vain."

"Go home, you old drunk," shouted a man in the crowd.

"Yeah, if the likes of you are saved, I don't want no part of it," yelled another man.

"Here, save this," said someone throwing a rotten apple at him.

Bill ducked and the apple missed him. He held his arms in the air and looked up at the sky. "Hallelujah! Praise the Lord. Get down on your knees and ask forgiveness." Bill stepped off the crate and fell to one knee. "The wages of sin are death."

A husky man pulled him to the ground. "He's on his ass now and I'm going to kick it." The people up front laughed, as they pushed Bill back and forth, slapping his head as they said, "Hallelujah."

"Stop!" shouted Jennifer, trying to make her way through the crowd.

Two police officers ran toward them blowing their whistles. "All right. Break it up.

Everybody, go home."

The crowd started to disperse and one officer grabbed Bill by the collar, hauling him to his feet. "I told you yesterday to stay away from here. I'm taking you in for disturbing the peace."

Bill tried to pull away. "Let go of me. I'm doing God's work."

The policeman pulled him toward the police car. "Well, I'm doing my work, getting trouble makers off the street."

Jennifer ran over to them. "Officer, please…"

He put his hand up. "Not now lady. I'm busy."

Her voice quivered as she said, "I'm his wife. Please let me take him home."

Bill brushed his pants off and looked her up and down. "What are you doing here and where did you get that coat?"

The officer looked at Jennifer's expensive coat and tipped his hat back. "You're his wife?"

"Please don't take him to jail. We have four children at home."

The officer looked at Bill for a moment. "I'll let him go this time, but don't let me catch him here again."

Jennifer took her husband's arm. "Thank you Officer. Bill, let's go home."

They walked down the street and Bill said, "What are you doing in this neighborhood?"

"I work just a couple blocks away. I should be asking you the same thing."

"Where did you get that expensive coat?"

"The people I work for gave it to me. I've been wearing this for weeks. You're so busy with the Lord's work that you don't notice anything. When you're not working for the city, you spend all your time at the church, on the street or in the basement. You're getting carried away with your religion."

"That's blasphemy against God." Bill stopped in the middle of the street. The passing cars swerved around him blowing their horns. "I've been called to do His work."

Jennifer saw the streetcar coming. "Hurry! We don't want to miss our trolley."

"I'm not going home. I'm going to the church." He stepped on the trolley. "You should come with me and pray for forgiveness."

Jennifer sat by the window. "Oh for heaven's sake Bill, sit down and shut up!"

"No, I'm going to talk to people." Bill walked down the aisle and stopped in front of a man staring into space. "You look lonely and confused my friend. God, can save you if you ask forgiveness for your sins. Come to the Church of Faith and be baptized in our Father's name."

The other passenger's watched Bill and one man said, "Another nut case."

When the man didn't respond he went over to another man, dressed in dirty, torn clothes. He placed his hand on the man's shoulder. "You look like you've fallen on hard times. Come to church with me and God will take care of you."

The man pushed Bill's hand away. "Listen, buddy, I'm broke and my family's starving. I'll come to the church if you promise me enough money to buy food."

Bill reached in his pockets and pulled out five dollars. "The Lord placed this in my pocket for someone who is reaching out to Him. Take it and buy food, but first come to the Church of Faith and be saved."

"Hey buddy, I'll go anywhere with you for five bucks," yelled another man.

"If you got anymore fiver's in your pocket, I'll go too," yelled a woman.

Jennifer's heart sunk, as she watched him hand out his money. She wanted to scream, "you stupid man, don't give our money away. There goes most of his salary again and the extra money Roger gave me. God help us. I think my husband is mentally ill. What do I do now?"

The trolley started to slow and she walked to the front of the car. Bill pushed ahead of her, pulling the man behind him. Jennifer went home and Bill went to church with the man.

By the time Bill came home, Jennifer and the children were in bed.

———————————

Jennifer was up early and cooked breakfast. The smell of bacon and eggs flowed through the house.

Bill came down sniffing the air. "Smells like bacon and eggs. Is that real coffee?"

"It's Saturday and we don't have to go to work. I wanted to surprise everyone."

When the children came down, Cassie said, "We're not having oatmeal!"

Jennifer placed the platter on the table and Joseph said, "Wow! Bacon and eggs."

Bill sat at the table and said, "Bow your head, while we say grace."

Jennifer placed a basket of toast and marmalade on the table and sat down. She watched her family enjoy the meal. She took a bite of the bacon and said, "We haven't had a breakfast like this in a long time."

While they were eating, Joseph said, "Some kids from school are going to the movies to see Charlie Chaplain. I've never been to the movies. Could I go too?"

"My friends are going. They say it's really funny," said Margaret.

"Sounds like a dandy idea," said Jennifer. "Something we could all do together. What do you think Bill?"

His brows drew together and his voice hardened. "No one in this family is going to a movie house. It is a den of iniquity."

"Aw! Come on Bill. It's a comedy. It would give us a good laugh and God knows we need it," said Jennifer.

The children looked at their father's face and Margaret said, "Guess we can't go."

Bill slapped his hand on the table. "That's right. I forbid it." He threw his napkin on the table and went down to the basement, slamming the door behind him.

"Can I have Dad's eggs?" asked Joseph.

Jennifer began to clear the table. "Sure, go ahead, I don't want food to go to waste." She felt aggravated and threw the dirty plates in the sink, breaking a cup. She reached to get it. "Ouch! I cut my finger." Jennifer dried her hands. "I'm going to get a bandage. Margaret, you and Cassie finish the dishes for me. When I come down, we'll go shopping."

---

The shoe store was the first stop where Joseph got his much needed shoes. The three girls waited outside while Jennifer and Joseph went in.

The salesman tied the laces of the new Buster Browns shoes on Joseph's feet and asked, "How do you like your new shoes?"

A bright smile was on Joseph's face. "They're swell! Wait till my friends see them."

"Good," said Jennifer. Now let's go buy Faith her new dress."

After choosing a blue dress with ribbons, Faith ran outside to show her sisters. "Look

Cassie and Margret! It's the most beautiful dress in the whole world."

"Okay. Next stop the grocery store," said Jennifer.

As they got near the store Joseph and Margaret spotted their friends. "Look, there's Harry and Audrey. Can Joseph and I walk home with them?" asked Margret.

"Sure, but make sure you go right home."

When Jennifer was finished shopping, she gave Cassie and Faith each a small bag to carry and carried two big ones herself. Jennifer's legs ached and the bags felt like lead in her arms.

Faith said, "I'm tired. Can we stop for a while?"

"All right." Jennifer put the bags down, as she sighed. "I didn't realize how heavy these bags were."

They rested for ten minutes, then continued. Cassie started complaining, "This bag is too heavy."

"We're almost home," said Jennifer. "Look, there is our house." When they arrived, she put one of the bags on the step and turned the door knob. When the door swung open, painful cries came from the kitchen.

"Good grief! What's going on?" She dropped the bag of groceries. "Girls, stay here until I come back." She ran to the kitchen and saw Margaret on the floor sobbing. Her dress was torn and her back and arms were bloody. Joseph's shirt was ripped and blood streamed down his back. "Bill! What are you doing? Stop it!"

"Daddy, please don't hit me again," screamed Joseph.

Bill lifted his arm and swung the rubber hose as Jennifer jumped in front of him. She deflected his arm, but the hose hit her shoulder.

Jennifer gasped from the pain as she called out, "Run up to your rooms and lock the doors."

They ran like deer as Bill reached out to grab them. Jennifer grabbed his shirt and he shoved her away, knocking her to the floor.

He raised the hose above his head. "I'll teach you not to interfere."

Her eyes flashed with anger as she stared at him. "Go ahead. Hit me. I'll get even with you, when you sleep."

Bill saw the hate in her eyes and a chill went through him. He threw the rubber hose down. "From now on, keep your distance when I'm punishing the children."

Jennifer stood up and spat out, "Don't you ever strike our children again with anything except your open hand. What could they have done to deserve such cruel punishment?"

Bill's face was red and dripping with sweat. He wiped it with his handkerchief. "They defied me. I caught them coming out of the movies."

"They never went to the movies. They were with me almost all afternoon." Jennifer pushed back the hair that had fallen in her face. "I let them walk home with their friends. They were probably looking at the posters in the lobby."

"I told them not to step a foot in that house of inequity."

"What's the matter with you? You never used to be so short-tempered and cruel."

Bill's hands went up in the air, "God says, spare the rod and spoil the child. The family should unconditionally obey the master of the house. When you interfere or do not obey me, you choose the side of the devil."

"There's no reasoning with you. Is there?" She felt sick over what he had done.

She heard Faith and Cassie sobbing hysterically and realized she had forgotten them. "Oh my God, I forgot my babies." She ran to the door, they were huddled together crying.

"Hush now. Everything will be all right." Jennifer hugged them to soothe their fears. "Help Mamma, carry the bags in."

When they saw their father, they grabbed their mother's skirt. "Don't hit us Daddy."

Jennifer put her arms around them and guided them into the parlor. "Sit here and eat a cookie, while I go upstairs to see your sister and brother."

"Don't go! Daddy might hit us!" cried Cassie.

"Okay, come upstairs with me."

Margaret and Joseph had red welts and cuts on their shoulders, arms and back. Jennifer started to take Joseph's shirt off, but he cried out holding his right arm.

"Don't touch it. It really hurts," said Joseph.

"Let me see it. Your arm is a funny shape. I think it might be broken." Jennifer tried to straighten it, but Joseph screamed with pain. "I'm sorry; I didn't mean to hurt you." Jennifer kissed his head. She broke apart two wooden coat hangers and padded them with rags. Jennifer placed the padded pieces under his arm and wrapped it tight.

"Ouch, that's too tight," yelled Joseph.

"I need it tight." Jennifer loosened it a bit. She made her scarf into a sling and put it around his neck. "Keep your arm in there until it feels better." She kissed their tears away and washed their lacerated skin. Jennifer applied a soothing lotion of horse chestnut oil on their bodies.

"Why did Daddy beat us?" asked Margaret. "We didn't do anything wrong."

"I don't know, dear," she said, giving each child an aspirin to ease the pain. "Lie down and rest. I'll bring your dinner up later."

No words were spoken at the evening meal and right after dinner Bill went to the basement. Jennifer put the younger children to bed and went to see how the other two were doing. How could she explain why their father beat them? She wasn't sure herself? Jennifer laid down between them with her arms around each child. In a few minutes, they were asleep.

Jennifer went down to the basement. "You broke Joseph's arm."

"God will heal it."

"What! Is that all you can say?" She stepped closer, her eyes flashing with anger. "If you ever hit the children again…"

He had a smirk on his face. "What! What are you going to do?"

Her eyes blazed as she said, "You better not go to sleep after you do."

He was about to laugh until he saw the flash of determination and strength on her face. He turned and started to stack papers.

# Chapter Twenty-Six

By March 1933, Bill was working full time at the Philadelphia Navy Yard. He was shoveling coal into the fire box on trains. Reverend Thatcher paid him six dollars a week as Pastor of the church. Jennifer still worked for the Clancy's who gave her a two dollar raise. Without Bill knowing, Margaret had made her confirmation, and Cassie and Joseph had made their holy communion at the Catholic Church. Once a week, they rode the subway to the church for preparation for their confirmation. Instead of the children paying five cents each for the ride, they snuck under the subway turnstile on their bellies. Saving the nickel for candy.

Saturday morning Bill sat at the kitchen table paying their bills and Jennifer set up the ironing board and heated the iron.

"I'm going to iron everything in this basket if it takes all day," said Jennifer.

"I need my white shirts ironed," said Bill, sipping his coffee. "Well, this is amazing!"

"What's amazing?" asked Jennifer.

"This is the third month that I paid all our expenses and still have money left over." He closed his accounting book. "One of the parishioners wants to sell his car. What do you think about buying it?"

Jennifer put the iron down. "Can we afford it?"

Bill leaned back in his chair and stretched. "Not a new one."

"It would be nice to have a car."

"It's a classy looking Packard. I think he said it was five years old."

Jennifer put one of Margaret's dresses on the ironing board. "You're getting me excited, what does it look like?"

"It's navy blue and has four doors with plenty of room in the back for the children. It even has roll down windows."

"Sounds swell. But why's he selling it?"

"He hurt his leg and isn't able to work. He needs the money."

Jennifer put the clothes she ironed in the basket. "Whew, I only have five more pieces and I'm done." She poured a cup of coffee and sat next to Bill. "Is the car in good shape?"

"Motor runs like a top. The right fender has a few dents and the heater doesn't work, but that's easily fixed. Oh and it needs new tires."

"Sounds like it would be expensive to fix."

"Nah. I could get Higgins to help me repair the heater and he knows a place where they can knock out the dents."

Jennifer laughed. "Seems like you researched this pretty thoroughly. But what about the tires?"

"I can pick up four used tires cheap."

Jennifer poured another cup of coffee. "How much does he want for it?"

"Last I heard he wanted fifty-five dollars."

"Well, you handle the money. If you think we can afford it, I'd love to have a car again. Sure beats walking all those blocks. Maybe we could drive to see our parents in Carnegie."

Sunday night, after church, Bill pulled Judas Oglesby aside. "Are you still interested in selling your car?"

"I sure am, Pastor Rennie. I'm in a bind. If you want to buy it, I'll let you have it for forty-five dollars."

"Will you take twenty-five dollars down and five dollars a month?"

"I was hoping to get it in a lump sum."

"I'd give it to you, if I had it. Twenty-five is all I got."

Mr. Oglesby thought for a moment. "All right, it's a deal. I'll bring the car over to your house tomorrow night."

Bill pulled Jennifer aside from the group of women. "Oglesby is bringing the car over tomorrow night. If you like it, we will be the proud owners of a 1928 navy blue Packard."

Jennifer took Bill's arm and squeezed it. "I can't wait to ride in it. No more walking long blocks, lugging groceries."

"I can just see us driving to and from church."

The next night, they were waiting on the front step for Mr. Oglesby. He drove up in the dark blue Packard.

"It's a pretty color," said Jennifer.

Margaret ran to the car. "I want to ride in it."

Joseph opened the door and climbed in the back. "Me, too."

"Calm down, kids," said Bill. "Go sit on the steps and let me talk to Mt. Oglesby."

Jennifer walked around the car. "It does have a few dents like you said, but it's a nice looking car."

"Well, what do you think, do you like it?" asked Bill.

"Jennifer climbed behind the wheel and ran her hand over the seats. "The leather seats are in good condition." She slid over. "Start the engine and let me hear how it sounds."

Bill climbed in. Bill turned the key and the engine turned right up. "Sounds like its running smooth."

"Sure beats the cranking we used to do. I think we should buy it," said Jennifer.

Bill laughed. "Women don't know anything about engines. Okay, Mr. Oglesby, it's a deal.

Here's your money. Do you have the title?"

"I thought I'd ask you to sign this paper stating our terms. When the balance is paid, I'll give you the title." Mr. Oglesby blushed. "It's not that I don't trust you Pastor Rennie. It just makes it legal and binding. You know, real business like."

"I understand." Bill took a pen from his pocket. "Let me read it… Looks okay to me."

Bill scribbled his name at the bottom. "Hop in, kids. We'll give Mr. Oglesby a ride home."

"After we do that, can we take a ride? I want all my friends to see our new car," said Cassie.

"I can't believe we really have an automobile." Jennifer ran her hand over the leather. "It's almost brand new inside." She took a deep breath. "I love the smell of leather."

Mr. Oglesby shook his head. "The Misses loved this automobile. She always took good care of it, but we just can't afford to keep it."

Bill pulled up in front of Oglesby's house. "Here we are. Got you home safe and sound."

Mr. Oglesby climbed out and patted the car, "Well, she's all yours now. Take good care of her."

"Thanks, we will. See you in church," said Bill.

As they drove off, Mrs. Oglesby peeked out of the window. "Guess she's upset at losing this pretty car," said Jennifer.

"I'm sorry she is unhappy, but I'm glad it's ours now." Bill stepped on the gas.

"I can't believe its September already. Tomorrow the children start going back to school," said Jennifer.

"Can Daddy drive us to school in the mornings?" asked Joseph.

"Sounds like you want to show off our new car," said Bill.

The next morning the children were up and ready to go before Bill was dressed.

---

Jennifer was tired when she came home from work and stretched out on the couch. She had twenty minutes to herself before the children came home from school. She was almost asleep when they came charging in the house.

Joseph shouted, "I'm starving. Can I have a sandwich?"

"There's peanut butter in the cupboard. Help yourself." Jennifer picked up their school bags. "How much homework do you have? Maybe you can do it yourselves." She spread their work on the table. "You have all this to do?"

"Yes, it's twice as much as last year," said Margaret.

"You better start now. I'll help you with the rest, when we get home from church."

The children were asleep in the back seat of the car when they got home. Jennifer shook them, "Wake up, we're home. You have to finish your homework."

"Ah, do I have to? I'm too tired," said Joseph.

"Come on! Get in the house. I'll help you," said Jennifer.

The children staggered in and sat at the table. Jennifer gave them their books. "The sooner you get started, the quicker you can go to bed."

Bill looked at their homework. 'That's too much work for children their age. Hurry up and get it done. I'm going to bed."

"Oh! To be a man," thought Jennifer. When they finished, it was 11:30 p.m. and she hustled her sleepy children upstairs. "It's hard enough getting you up for school, but tomorrow will really be tough."

In the morning, Jennifer woke the children and went down to fix breakfast. When she didn't hear them, she went up and pulled their covers off. "Get up! You're going to be late."

Each weekday, she worked with them before and after dinner to get them in bed by 9 p.m. On the nights they went to church, they never got to bed until 11 p.m. Thursday night after the children were in bed, she fixed a cup of coffee and sat in the living room exhausted. She heard Bill working in the basement and went down. He had drawn a picture of the devil on a stencil and wrote under it, "The devil is taking over your soul, leading you to hell and damnation. Repent now and be saved." At the bottom, he had printed the name and address of the church. He laid the stencils on the mimeograph roller and started to print.

"Come sit on the couch with me, you look tired," said Jennifer. "I brought you some coffee."

He shut off the printer and sat beside her. His shoulders fell forward as he sighed, "My bones ache, I feel worn out."

Jennifer rubbed his back. "Why don't you take some time off?" Her hand moved up to his neck and she rubbed it gently. "

"I can't, I have too much to do." Bill wiggled around so Jennifer could get his neck. "Hmm! That feels good."

"Jennifer rubbed his lower back. It's late, let's go to bed."

"I can't. I have to work on my Sunday sermon. Let me go over the different subjects I'm thinking about and see what you think."

Jennifer listened intently. "They're all good. It's hard to choose."

Bill leaned back on the couch and closed his eyes. Jennifer ran her fingers through his dark hair. "Got a few grays coming in," she laughed. When Bill didn't answer, she rubbed his shoulder. "You know the children have so much homework this year. It takes three hours to do it. The nights we go to church are really late nights. It's hard getting them up in the morning."

Bill opened his eyes. "I know all this, what are you getting at?"

Jennifer took a deep breath. "I don't think they should go to church during the week. They need their sleep to be attentive in school."

He studied her for a while. "What about you?"

Jennifer took his hand. "I'd have to stay home to help them, make sure they get to bed."

Bill stood up and stretched. "I'm glad they gave me a different job at the Navy Yard. I'm getting too old to do hard labor. Working on the trains is much easier." He rubbed Jennifer's shoulder. "I'd like you to go to church with me, but if you think it's best for the children, I'm in no mood to argue."

"Whew!" she thought, that was easy, almost too easy.

―――――――――

It was Tuesday night and Bill went to church, while Jennifer stayed home with the children. After they were in bed, she fixed some tea and fresh baked cookies for Bill. A few candles were lit for a romantic atmosphere. Jennifer laid her head back on the sofa and thought, "It's been a month since I've gone to church during the week. The extra time with the children helps a lot."

Bill came home exhausted and sat next to Jennifer. "Ah. It's good to be home."

She handed him a cup of tea. "This will help you relax." They sat talking for a while until Bill started to fall asleep.

# Chapter Twenty-Seven

Claudia Runderson always arrived at church early and sat at the piano. She fondled the keys, waiting for Pastor Rennie to give the signal to play the opening hymn. Claudia loved Pastor

Rennie's handsome face and his body made her loins ache.

When church was over, Claudia stood beside Pastor Rennie at the door and said, "Since your wife isn't here, I'll help you say goodnight to the parishioners."

"Why, that's very thoughtful."

When the congregation left, she smiled at Bill, blinking her eyes. "I'm going to the back room. If there's anything I can do for you, just let me know."

As Bill started to put his coat on, Claudia scurried out from the back room. "Pastor Rennie, I made you some hot tea. It will help you relax before you go home to your family."

Bill took the cup and sipped it slowly, "Thank you. It's delicious, has an unusual taste."

Fluttering her eyes she said, "It's my special brew. Sit down. You work so hard."

"It does feel good to relax." Bill took another sip. "Aren't you having any?"

"I already had some." Bill set the cup down and started to get up, but Claudia grabbed his hand. "There's still a little more tea."

"No thank you. I'd better get home before my wife starts to worry."

"Too bad your family can't come to church during the week. I want you to know, I'll be right by your side whenever you need a helping hand."

Bill put his coat on, "Good night Reverend Thatcher and Mrs. Runderson."

"From now on I'll have a cup of tea waiting when the service is over," said Claudia.

Jennifer was on the couch reading when she heard the door open. She called out, "I'm in the parlor Bill."

"I'm sorry I'm late," he said kissing her.

"You look flushed, don't you feel well?"

Bill sat on the couch and leaned back, "I'm exhausted."

"Your eyes look glassy. Do you have a fever?" She felt his forehead.

"I almost fell asleep at the wheel." He took his coat off and hung it on the rack in the hall. "I feel like I'm burning up inside."

"Your head is not hot. I don't think you have a fever. Sit down and have a cup of tea, I made your favorite cookies."

"No thanks. Mrs. Runderson gave me a cup, before I left church. I'm not hungry. I just want to go to bed."

"Why don't you stay home tomorrow and sleep? I don't have to work and we could spend time together."

Bill yawned. "I can't. I have too much work. I'm going to bed."

She followed him upstairs and Bill went in the bathroom. Jennifer took off her red velvet housecoat, propped her pillows and started to read.

Jennifer heard him come in the room and gasped. "You're naked! Do you want me to get your pajamas?"

Bill mumbled something that Jennifer couldn't understand and he crawled in bed.

"What did you say?" she asked pulling the covers over him. "You'll catch cold laying there without covers."

Bill was so still; it frightened her. She felt his chest for a heartbeat and he let out a big snore. "You're really exhausted," she said, as she rolled over and went to sleep.

In the morning the aroma of coffee filled the air and the sun lit up the kitchen. Jennifer sat watching the birds peck at the seed she left for them. When the children came down for breakfast, she gave each a bowl of oatmeal.

"Your father can't drive you to school this morning. So eat fast or you'll be late for school."

"Okay. Hmm…The coffee smells good. Can I have a cup?" asked Margaret.

"No. You're too young for coffee. I'll make you a cup of tea."

Cassie said, "Do we have to have oatmeal every morning?"

"You say that every day," said Margaret.

Jennifer finished packing their lunch. "Eat your oatmeal and be glad you have food to put in your belly."

After the children left for school, Bill came rushing down. "I'm going to be late. Why didn't you call me?"

Jennifer poured him a cup of coffee. She laughed and said, "I did call you, but you didn't wake up. I was just coming up to check on you. Last night you were so tired you forgot to put your pajamas on. At first I thought you had ideas, but then you started to snore."

"You're kidding! I wondered why I didn't have any clothes on this morning. I don't know why I felt so tired; I didn't work that hard yesterday." He finished his cereal and grabbed his coat. "I have to go. The job at the Navy Yard is pretty steady and I don't want to lose it. I'll see you tonight."

When Jennifer came home from work, she started dinner. Then, she helped the children with their homework.

Bill walked in and smiled as he ruffled Margaret's hair. "You look pretty today."

Then he kissed Jennifer. "What's cooking? It smells delicious."

"Chicken and dumplings. You're in a good mood."

"I feel terrific; I had a good day at work and tonight I'm home with my family."

---

Thursday night, Claudia hurried to church. She wanted to stand beside Bill at the door. "Good evening Pastor Rennie, how are you feeling?"

"I feel fine. Why do you ask?"

"When you left Tuesday night, you seemed tired. I hope the tea helped."

"I was. When I got home I felt completely drained, but I'm okay now."

"Glad to hear that. I'll put a pot of tea on to brew. You can have a cup before you leave." She stood close to him, as he greeted the parishioners. "I see your family didn't come to church again tonight. Is someone sick?"

"No. The children have a lot of homework. They have to get up early for school. If they come to church on week nights, they get to bed too late."

Claudia gave him a questioning look. "Surely the children are old enough to take care of themselves."

"We don't like to leave them home alone. You know how kids like to clown around. Their homework might not get done."

"Not if they're properly disciplined." Claudia cocked her head. "The Bible says spare the rod and spoil the child."

"That's what I try to tell…," Bill stopped, it didn't seem right to discuss his affairs with someone outside the family. "It's time to start the service." Bill walked to the podium.

He stared out at the congregation and in a loud piercing voice said, "You're all

Guilty. Guilty of not loving your Savior, being selfish and self-centered. Let me ask you, how many people have you helped today? How many souls lie shivering on the ground that you passed by?" Hands raised, he continued, "How many have lied, cheated, committed adultery, thought you got away with it? Well, you didn't. Because the Lord knows what you do."

"Amen, hmmhmm, amen," shouted several people.

"Get up on your feet and come forward." Bill put his hands out to beckon them. "I said get up on those God-given feet and ask forgiveness."

Seven people walked toward the alter shouting, "Forgive me, Lord, forgive me."

"Shout it out. Let the Lord know you're calling Him," said Bill, waving his arms high.

"Get down on your knees, ask for forgiveness. Praise the Lord and hallelujah."

Three women and a man wailed and threw their arms up as they rushed up the aisle pleading, "I've sinned, oh Lord, forgive me." They knelt in front of the podium as one of the women fainted.

Bill knelt beside the woman and placed his hand on her forehead. "Have mercy, dear Lord. Forgive these people for their iniquities." The woman opened her eyes and Bill helped her up. "Go back to your seats. Your sins have been forgiven. Praise the Lord."

Breathing hard from exertion, the parishioners shuffled to their pews shouting, "Hallelujah. My sins are washed away. Thank you Lord, thank you."

After the congregation left, Bill started to put the songbooks away and Claudia brought him a steaming hot cup of tea.

"It was such an inspiring service. This will help you relax," said Claudia.

Bill sat in a pew and sipped the tea. "This is really good. It has more of an almond taste than the cup you gave me the other night."

"I put a bit more in it this time to give it added flavor," said Claudia smiling.

Bill drank the tea, then put his coat on and said, "Goodnight everyone."

---

Jennifer knew Bill wouldn't be home for dinner and fixed the children's favorite meal, hot dogs and beans. When dinner was over, she said, "Finish your homework, I'm going down to the basement to do some washing. Call me if you need help."

The children worked on their papers until Joseph got angry and threw a pencil across the room.

"I can't do this. It's too hard."

The pencil hit Margaret on the arm. "You hurt me!" she cried, throwing a book at him.

Cassie rolled up papers and threw them at Joseph. "That's because you hurt Margaret.

Faith sat giggling and their laughter reached a high pitch.

Jennifer ran up from the basement. "What's going on here?"

Joseph and Margaret lowered their heads, pretending to read.

Cassie said, "Joseph started it."

"No I didn't," said Joseph.

"I don't care who started it. Shut up and finish before I smack your bottoms."

By 9:30 p.m., the children were in bed and Jennifer felt tired. She sat on the sofa with her feet up, waiting for Bill and she dozed off.

Bill felt dizzy as he got out of the car. He made it to the front door. When he opened it, then he fell against the door. The noise woke Jennifer and she went out to the hall. Bill was leaning against the wall.

"What's the matter? Are you sick?" She put her arm around his waist. "Let me help you to the couch."

His eyes were glassy and his breath smelled of almonds. Bill tried to walk, but staggered and fell against her. "I need to lie down."

Jennifer helped him up the stairs. When they reached the bedroom, he collapsed on the bed.

"Bill, what's wrong?" She could smell that strange odor. "What did you eat that had almonds in it?"

He breathed deeply and seemed to be in a sleep-like coma. Jennifer felt his head and then checked his pulse. It was normal. She guessed he was overtired and removed his coat and shoes. Jennifer crawled in beside him. When she woke in the morning, Bill was gone and she wondered why he left so early.

After she sent the children off to school, she ran for her trolley. When she arrived at work

Mr. Clancy asked, "You look worried. Is something wrong?"

"I'm just tired; I didn't sleep well last night."

The day dragged by and when she arrived home, she sank into a tub of hot water for a half hour, then prepared dinner.

Bill came home and hugged her. "What's for dinner?'

"Kidney stew. How are you feeling?"

"Fine. Why?" said Bill.

"Why! Because last night you came home so tired, you could hardly walk. You fell asleep with your clothes on."

"I don't remember that! I wondered why I was all dressed this morning. Hmm! Sorry

I left early because I had an early shift at the Navy Yard."

Faith came in the kitchen. "Ugh! Kidney stew! I hate it."

Jennifer put the food on the table. "Too bad, but you're eating it."

Bill took a bite of the stew and said, "This is really good."

"Thanks. I wonder what makes you so exhausted on church nights. It's almost like you're drugged. You never used to get that tired."

"Maybe I'm coming down with something. If so, the lord will take care of me."

She looked closely at his eyes. "How are you feeling now?"

"I'm fine. I have to do some work in the basement before I go to bed."

"Well, I didn't sleep last night worrying about you. I'm going to bed right after the children finish their school work."

———————————

Tuesday night Jennifer helped the children with their homework, then sent them to bed.   She decided to read in bed until Bill came home. Jennifer felt tired, her eyes kept closing. Soon the book was lying on the bed and Jennifer was asleep.

Church was over and Bill said goodnight. He put on his black wide-brim hat and started to leave.

"Pastor Rennie!" Claudia called out. "Pastor Rennie, wait."

"Yes, what can I do for you?"

"Could you give me a lift home? It looks like it's about to rain and in April it can rain anytime."

"Why, certainly," said Bill. "I never refuse anyone that needs help."

Claudia grabbed her coat. "Where is your coat?"

"I gave it to a poor unfortunate man today."

"You're such a caring man. Didn't you do that a couple of months ago?"

"Yes and the lord delivered me a coat the next day."

Claudia took his arm. "Thanks for giving me a ride. The trolleys are never on time and it's so dark." Bill opened the car door and helped her in. "What a gentleman! My house is ten blocks from here. Too far for me to walk." Claudia sat back and said, "I just remembered. I have a wool topcoat in my closet. It belonged to my late husband. God rest his soul. I'd like you to have it. I'm sure it will be a perfect fit." She leaned close to Bill and giggled. "I don't want you to be cold, you poor dear." She reached her arm over his shoulder and rubbed his back briskly.

Bill pulled away. "Please don't do that. I'm not cold." He pulled up in front of a row of brick houses. "Which one is yours?"

Claudia placed her hand on his knee. "Why you're right in front of it!" Bill got out and opened the car door for her.

"Please come in Pastor Rennie. I'll get the coat for you. I know it will fit you. My Gunther was just your size."

Bill hesitated, "I don't need a coat now; it is springtime."

"Yes, but you could keep it for next winter. I might forget and give it away."

"All right, but I can only stay a few minutes."

They walked into a dimly lit hall. "There's not much light in here," said Bill, looking up at a small light fixture. "Two of the bulbs are out."

"I know. I'm always going to replace them, but I forget. That's what happens when you don't have a man around the house." Claudia led him past a parlor and the bedroom to a small kitchen at the end of the hallway. She sniffed the air. "Can you smell the Chicken soup? It's been simmering since I left for church."

"Yes, it smells delicious," said Bill. "Why is everything so dark?" He looked around at the dark mahogany cabinets and furniture. "It must be all the dark wood. You need a few bulbs in here too!"

"As I said before, I need a man to help me. Sit down at the table and relax, while I get the coat."

She fluffed a pillow and placed it behind his back. "You must be tired after that inspiring sermon."

Claudia placed her hands on his shoulders and started to massage the tight muscles.

Bill started to get up. "I'd rather you didn't do that."

Claudia pushed him down. "Why not? I know it must feel good?" She continued to run her fingers up and down his neck. "Honestly, Pastor Rennie. I never saw anyone get people worked up the way you do." She lowered her hands. "Now, don't you feel better?"

He felt uncomfortable being there. "It's late, I better get home."

"Now, don't rush off." Claudia walked to the stove and ladled the soup into a large bowl. Then sprinkled a few drops in it from a small bottle. She set the bowl in front of Bill.

"I'm going upstairs to get the coat, while you eat the soup."

He took a spoonful. "This is good, it has an unusual taste."

"It's my special recipe. I always put a little almond in my chicken soup, for added flavor. Enjoy it and I'll be right back"

Bill started to sweat. "It sure warms you up."

"I'll be right down," she said, while going up the stairs. Claudia went to the closet for the overcoat and laid it on the bed. She looked in the mirror and applied red lipstick. Claudia smiled and thought, "Pastor Rennie, you're going to feel mighty good when you finish that soup."

Bill's arms were propped on the table, his head cupped in his hands. The bowl was empty.

"Now, isn't this a perfect coat for you?" said Claudia.

Bill stood up, then staggered and grasped the table, for support. His eyes were glassy and his left eye twitched. "I better go home." He started to walk, but fell against the wall.

Claudia grabbed his arm. "Pastor Rennie, are you okay?"

He shook his head and said, "No. I better go home."

"You're in no condition to drive," Claudia pulled his jacket off, throwing it on the chair.

She led him to the bedroom next to the kitchen.

As he entered the room he sneezed. "What's that strange smell?"

She led him to the bed. "Just some incense. I love the fragrance, don't you? Lie down here until you feel better."

Bill's eyes couldn't focus and the mirror over the dresser seemed to swing back and forth. He rubbed his eyes and collapsed on the bed.

"Just relax until you feel better," said Claudia.

His eyelids fluttered as he whispered, "I see an angel!" Then his eyes closed.

Claudia sat on the edge of the bed, waiting for his breathing to slow. When she was sure he was asleep, she slid in beside him. She ran her fingers through his thick, dark hair. Then tenderly traced the lines of his eyes and cheek bones, as she whispered, "You're such a handsome man."

Claudia kissed his lips lightly and he stirred and murmured, "Have to go." Then he woke up.

The moon was shining through the window and he looked around the dark unfamiliar room. "Where am I?" He shook his head to clear the numb feeling.

Claudia got off the bed as soon as she saw him stir. "You're still here, Pastor Rennie. Remember, you weren't feeling well. You laid down and I was so worried about you."

Bill put on his jacket. "I've got to get home, Babe will be worried."

When he got home, the light was on in the parlor. He shut it off and crept upstairs. Jennifer was asleep. Bill turned the light off then crawled in bed.

Claudia banged her fist against the front door when Bill left. "Next time I'll put a little more seasoning in your soup. I want you with me in the mornings."

———————————

As Bill sat down for breakfast, Jennifer said, "You got in late last night."

"Yes I did. Mrs. Runderson asked for a ride home. She told me she had a topcoat that belonged to her deceased husband. I went in to get it and she gave me some chicken soup. All of a sudden, I felt dizzy and she let me lay down for a few minutes. I fell asleep."

Jennifer poured him coffee and asked, "How do you feel now?"

"I feel fine. I was concerned that you would be worried. You were asleep when I got home."

"I never heard you come in. I wonder why you're tired and getting these dizzy spells?"

"I don't know, but I can't worry about it now. I'm late for work. I'll leave it in God's hands." He kissed her goodbye. "See you tonight."

Claudia sat at the kitchen table, drinking coffee thinking about Bill. She knew he would be at church after 4 p.m. "I'll call him then."

At 4:05 p.m., she called him. Bill answered the phone. "Pastor Rennie, this is Claudia Runderson. I finally found the strength to go through my husband's things. Could you come over and help me? I want to give them to the needy."

"I'm very busy. Could we do it another day?"

Claudia pretended to cry. "Every time I go through Luther's clothes, it makes me sad. I could use your support. Besides, you forgot the overcoat I gave you."

"I'm in the middle of a monthly report for the church," said Bill. "I can't…"

Claudia interrupted him pleading, "Please come over. You can pick out what you want and I'll give the rest away."

Bill sighed. It was hard for him to refuse a request for help. "Okay, Mrs. Gunderson, I'll be right over."

Claudia was at the door waiting for him, bubbling with enthusiasm. "Would you like some delicious chicken soup?"

"No, Mrs. Runderson, I don't want anything to eat. I have to get back as soon as possible."

Claudia had a sparkle in her eyes as she said, "You can call me Claudia, after all I do play the piano in church. You know me pretty well." She scooped some soup in a bowl and put it on the table. "Chicken soup always tastes good and gives you energy."

"Mrs. Run…, I mean Claudia; I don't want anything to eat. Please let's get busy with the clothes."

"Well how about a cup of tea?"

"I must insist that we get on with the work. I have lots to do when I go back to church."

"Well, all right." They went upstairs. "Pick out what you want, and then we'll pack the rest in a box."

Bill sorted through the clothes. "I'll take these two suits, this hat, and these shoes."

He piled them on her bed and packed the rest. "I know several men who can use the rest. Thank you Claudia. I'll see you in church on Thursday."

Claudia watched him drive away, then slammed the door. "You should have had some soup." Then she smiled to herself and thought, "I'm glad Jennifer doesn't come to church during the week. Tuesday's and Thursday's are going to be my nights with him."

# Chapter Twenty-Eight

When the children came home from school, Jennifer wasn't home yet. "Let's surprise mama and set the table for dinner," said Margret. When their mother walked in, she smiled and hugged them. "The house is so clean, this is such a surprise. You even put the napkins on the right side of the plate."

"We wanted to help out," said Cassie.

"Thank you very much. Now, I can relax a little before I fix dinner."

The children felt so proud and played quietly, while she dozed off until their father came home.

After supper, Bill went down to the basement to work and Jennifer cleared the table. "Okay kids. Time to do the dishes."

"We set the table. Do we have to do the dishes too?" asked Cassie.

"Mama's tired from working," said Margaret. "That's the least we can do."

Jennifer put her arm around Margaret. "Since you're doing more around the house, I think you should all get an allowance."

"Allowance, what's that?" said Joseph.

Margaret laughed. "That means she's going to give us money each week for helping with the housework."

"Wow! That's great," said Cassie.

"Wipe the stove and don't break any dishes, then I'll help you with your homework."

Jennifer went down to the basement and Bill was reading his Bible. "Are you staying up late tonight?"

"I'm not sure. I'm trying to find a passage to talk about tomorrow night. Then I have to print some flyers. I gave the last ones out today."

"I'm going to help the children with their homework, and then I'm going to bed. If you need anything, call me."

In the morning, Bill was up early and made coffee. The smell of the fresh brewed coffee woke Jennifer.

"Margaret! Wake up. It's time for school." She shook Cassie, and Faith, and then banged on Joseph's door, before going to the kitchen. Breakfast was ready when the children came down. Hot toast and marmalade sat in the middle of the table. A bowl of hot cornmeal sat at each place. Jennifer fixed their lunch of sandwiches and fruit and handed them the bags.

"Come on. Let's go. I have to catch my trolley. You be good in school," she called out, as she stepped on the trolley car.

When she got to Mr. Clancy's house, Roger greeted her at the door. "You're always so punctual. I'm glad. I have an early appointment."

Jennifer smiled. "How's Marsha this morning?"

"She's in a good mood, but I think she's coming down with a cold." Roger put on his suit jacket. "If you need me, you have my number."

Jennifer loved her job and the day passed quickly. When she returned home she relaxed on the couch as she went through the mail. She was surprised to see a letter from her sister Caroline. Jennifer ripped it open and read it.

"Dear Jennifer,

> I'm sorry I haven't answered your letter sooner. Like everyone, we have been in deep despair. Mother is depressed from the loss of our finances. Since the recession hit, we've have to do our own housework and it's hard on her. Believe it or not, Mother says she's sorry she hurt you and wishes she could see her grandchildren. She sits in her room mumbling, "Jennifer, I love you. I'm sorry I treated you so badly." At least something good came out of this horrible mess.

> I've have to work in these hard times and Mother didn't try to stop me. I'm working in, of all places, a speakeasy. Can you imagine! I play the piano and sing. The tips are good and it pays for our food and clothes, but not the expensive ones we used to wear. I still sing and play the piano at church and at weddings, but that doesn't pay much.

> Father is living with us; he sleeps in the maid's quarters. He can't afford a place of his own. He works in the loan department of the only bank that didn't go under. If things don't get better, we may move to Philadelphia. Let me know how you are doing and give the children a kiss for me. They must be big now. I love you and miss all of you.

> Your loving sister,
> Caroline."

Jennifer hugged the letter, as tears rolled down her cheeks. "Mother's not mad at me anymore. They might move here. Oh, that's wonderful."

---

On Friday night, Bill was late in getting home and dinner was waiting on the table. The children could sense their father's mood and were afraid to speak. They finished their meal quickly and went to their bedrooms to do their homework. Bill got up from the table and Jennifer reached for his hand.

"Stay and have another cup of tea with me. I want to tell you about the letter I received from Caroline."

He patted her hand. "I have flyers to print; they're my way of getting the Gospel out to the ignorant sinners."

"What about us, Bill? I'm sure God wants you to spend time with your wife and children." Jennifer put her arms around his shoulder. "You go down to the basement every night. We never go to bed together anymore."

He walked toward the basement door. "God asks us to sacrifice for His love and the love of his people."

Jennifer shrugged her shoulders. "Do we have to give up all our time together? We haven't made love in so long. I miss it."

Bill smiled. "I'm sorry Babe." He kissed her tenderly. "I promise I'll stop early and we can talk then."

Jennifer sighed and went to help the children with their homework. When they were finished, she sent them to bed and started walking down to the basement. Instead, she went to her room and read Caroline's letter again. Tears filled her eyes and she turned the light off and tried to sleep. She was still awake when Bill came to bed at midnight.

"Are you awake?" asked Bill.

"Yes. I thought you were coming up early?"

Bill yawned. "I'm sorry. I got carried away. I didn't realize how late it was."

She reached over and kissed him. "Goodnight, we'll talk in the morning."

"Goodnight Babe, I love you."

On Thursday night, Claudia waited at the door while Bill said goodnight to the congregation. When everyone left, she touched his arm. "Would you mind giving me a ride home?"

"Well, I guess it's not too far out of my way."

Reverend Thatcher pulled Claudia aside. "Pastor Rennie's in a hurry tonight. I'll drive you home."

"But, I'm sure it's out of your way."

"Not any further than it is for Pastor Rennie." He took Bill's arm. "You run along, I know you wanted to get home early tonight."

As Reverend Thatcher drove Claudia home he said, "Pastor Rennie is a very nice gentleman and married to a lovely woman."

"He's so kind and caring," said Claudia.

"I noticed that you always seem to be right by his side."

"He's so devoted to his congregation. It's hard not to admire him."

"As long as you don't get carried away with your admiration."

Claudia leaned close to him. "You don't think I'm… Well, I'm not. I just think he's a perfect gentleman and I want to help him."

"Maybe you shouldn't try to help him so much. It doesn't look proper." Reverend Thatcher pulled in front of her house. "Goodnight, Mrs. Runderson. Think about what I said."

Claudia watched him drive off and then stamped her foot. "Mind your own business, you old fool." She slammed the door and went to the kitchen. "I'll put this soup in the icebox and save it for another night."

"You're home early!" said Jennifer. "Did you have tea at church?"

"No. I wanted to get home before you went to bed." Bill took off his jacket.

"Would you like a cup of tea? I have some made."

Bill put his arms around her. "No, I want to go to bed and make love to you. I hope it's the safe time."

Her eyes sparkled and she put her arms around his waist. "Yes, honey, it is."

———————————

Claudia noticed that Reverend Thatcher was watching her every move. She made a point not to be around Bill. After service was over, she walked over to Reverend Thatcher. "Goodnight. I'll see you Tuesday."

Reverend Thatcher smiled. "Goodnight, Mrs. Runderson. Do you need a ride home?"

"No thank you."

Bill came out later and saw someone standing behind his car. "Who's there?"

Claudia stepped from behind the car. "I twisted my ankle and was resting by your car."

"I'm so sorry. How bad is it?"

Claudia limped toward him. "It really hurt; I can't walk home."

"Of course not. Let me drive you." Bill helped her in the car.

Claudia leaned close to Bill. "You really are a hard worker. You go out in all kinds of weather to help the poor." She placed her hand on his knee and squeezed it. "You are such a caring person."

"Thank you Claudia." Bill lifted her hand off his knee. "It's kind of you to say that. I get great satisfaction from doing it."

"I've been so lonely since my husband, God rest his soul, met his Maker." She pulled out her handkerchief and dabbed her eyes. "I would love to help you distribute your flyers. It would help take my mind off him. Why, I could circulate through the crowd and hand them out."

Excitement rose in her voice as she continued, "I could go into the stores and ask to leave flyers on the counters."

Bill thought for a while before saying, "I really could use some help. Are you sure you want to?"

"Oh yes. I really do."

Bill pulled in front of her house. "Thank you for your offer and we'll talk about it later."

Claudia took his hand. "Pastor Rennie, do you mind if I call you Bill? Pastor Rennie seems so formal. Especially when we will be working together."

"Only when we are alone. In church you have to address me as Pastor Rennie." He smiled and patted her hand. "You are a caring woman. Just full of love for God's children."

She smiled sweetly. "Come in and we'll make plans."

"I think it's better if we talk another time. My wife's waiting for me."

"You said you needed help. If we make plans tonight, I can help you out tomorrow."

"Okay, but I can't stay long."

"Watch your step. It's still dark in here. I never got a chance to replace the bulbs." She led him to the kitchen table. "Sit here and tell me where you plan to go tomorrow afternoon?"

Bill took his coat off and Claudia placed a steaming dish of chicken soup on the table.

"How did you do that so fast?" asked Bill.

She giggled like a school girl. "Here's a cup of my favorite jasmine tea. Now you eat and I'll be right back. I want to change into something more comfortable. This corset is killing me."

"I really don't have time to eat." The smell of the soup made Bill's mouth water and he took a spoonful. "Hmm, this is delicious. I like the tangy flavor." Bill finished the soup and tea and felt hot and sleepy. He leaned back against the chair and closed his eyes.

Claudia walked over to him. Her body rippling beneath the long, white, sheer nightgown she was wearing. She put her hands on his shoulders, "Are you all right?"

Bill reached into his pocket for his schedule and laid it on the table. He cleared his throat, then said, "This is my schedule for tomorrow. Eh, eh, his eyes fell on her sheer gown and the shadow of her massive breasts. The pink nipples seemed iridescent and shone through the sheer material. Bill's brain was too numb to think. His eyes glazed over, twitching rapidly. He staggered across the room and in a husky voice said, "I have to go home."

"You're in no condition to drive," said Claudia. "Come. Lie down for a few minutes until you feel better." Claudia took his arm and guided him to the bedroom. She whispered, "Rest for a while and you'll feel like a new man."

Bill collapsed on the bed as he gazed up. He saw an outline of a woman with silver wings at her sides. He tried to talk, but his throat was dry and he whispered, "My white angel is watching over me." Bill took a deep breath inhaling the strange smell of the incense and murmured, "There are beautiful flowers floating in the air."

Claudia covered him with a light sheet and sat beside him. "Sleep peacefully, my sweet. You won't remember a thing in the morning."

His deep breathing was the sign she was waiting for. She climbed in beside him and kissed him hard on his open mouth. "Your white angel needs you." Claudia smiled and whispered, "That soup really makes you sleep soundly. I like the feeling of a man in my bed."

Bill slept through the night. Waking when the first light of day brightened the room. He sat up. "What am I doing here?"

Claudia walked in the room. "Good morning. Did you sleep well?"

"I'm sorry; I didn't mean to sleep here all night. My wife is going to be worried sick."

Claudia sat beside him and patted his hand. "I'm glad you're feeling better."

"I feel so relaxed." Bill reached for his jacket. "I'd better get home."

"You're late already; you might as well have breakfast. Last night you were so sleepy, we never had a chance to talk. What area are we going to work today?"

Bill stretched. "Let me call my wife first. I want her to know I'm all right."

Jennifer answered on the first ring. "Where are you? I've been so worried!"

"I'm sorry Babe. I drove Mrs. Runderson home last night and we were going over some church work. All of a sudden, I got one of those dizzy spells. I couldn't walk or keep my eyes open. Mrs. Runderson was kind enough to let me lie down in her spare bedroom. I fell asleep and never woke up until this morning."

"Thank goodness! You are all right." Jennifer sighed, "I wish Mrs. Runderson had called me. I was worried. When are you coming home?"

"I'm leaving now."

"I guess I won't see you until tonight," said Jennifer. "I have to leave for work. Will you be home for dinner?"

"Yes, I'll be home early. I'll see you tonight."

When Bill came home, Jennifer was basting a roast chicken. He kissed her and said, "I had a messy job today. Do I have time to freshen up?"

"Of course, I'll call you when dinner is ready. How are you feeling?"

"I feel terrific. I couldn't canvas the streets this afternoon because I had to work all day."

When dinner was almost ready, Jennifer called Margaret and Cassie. "Please set the table, while I go up and get your father."

Bill had bathed and was lying on the bed. Jennifer laid beside him and said. "Hmm, you smell so fresh and clean."

Bill put his arm around her and pulled her close. He kissed her and said, "I love you Babe."

"I love you too."

He kissed her again and said, "Let me lock our door." When he came back, she said, "We haven't had a matinee in a long time."

Margaret was sitting at the table when they came down. "What took you so long? Can we eat now? I'm hungry."

Joseph started to whine, "My stomach is growling. I want to eat."

"All right. I'm putting it on the table," said Jennifer.

After dinner, Jennifer felt exhausted. Bill agreed to help the children with their homework, while she went to bed. When Bill came up, he held her in his arms. "It's not often we go to bed at the same time. Let's cuddle." He kissed her gently and snuggled close to her. "Goodnight my sweet Babe. I hope you feel better in the morning. I love you."

Jennifer cuddled closer. "I love you too."

———————

Jennifer still felt tired when she woke up in the morning. Her nose was running and she felt hot, but she didn't think she had a fever. She prepared breakfast for everyone and called the children. Then, she went back to bed for another half hour.

"Why are you back to bed?" asked Bill.

"I think I'm getting a cold. I feel hot and my nose is running. I was thinking," said Jennifer. "Maybe we could afford to rent a bigger house."

She sat up in bed and said, "This house is so small and the three girls are cramped in one tiny room."

"Well, let me go over our finances and I'll let you know."

"Margaret is going to be sixteen and really needs a room of her own."

Bill sighed, "Jennifer. I said I'd let you know. Not now. I have to get ready for work."

Jennifer returned to the kitchen and sat with the children as they finished their breakfast.

"Junior high school is much harder than elementary school," said Margaret.

Jennifer put her arm around Margaret. "I know you have a lot more homework now. You're also a great help to me."

"I want to help. You're working to help us have nice things."

Jennifer kissed her daughter.

Bill walked in and said, "Okay kids, I'm driving you to school. Let's go."

---

Bill Came home early that afternoon and went over their finances. When Jennifer came home from work, she said, "What are you doing home so early?"

"I went over our bills and I think we can afford a bigger house."

Jennifer hugged him. "That's swell, when can we look for one?"

"Let me ask around and see what's available." He looked at his pocket watch and said, "I have to get to church early. I'll see you later tonight after service."

Since Bill wouldn't be home for dinner, she fixed the children their favorite dinner, hot dogs and beans. She still didn't feel well, but nevertheless decided to make Bill his favorite cookies. She planned to wait up for him and surprise him.

---

After church service was over, Claudia stood at the back of the church waiting for Bill to leave.

Reverend Thatcher approached her. "Can I help you with something, Mrs. Runderson?"

"No. I was waiting to see if Pastor Rennie and you would like a cup of tea."

"Do you need a ride home?"

"No thank you, Reverend Thatcher. I'll catch the trolley."

She walked out of the door and went across the street and stood behind a tall oak tree. Reverend Thatcher and Pastor Rennie walked out together and stood, talking by Bill's car.

"Why doesn't that old fool go home?" whispered Claudia.

They talked for ten minutes before Reverend Thatcher said Good night. Bill got in his car and was ready to drive away, when he heard a knock on the window.

"Mrs. Runderson! What are you doing here? I thought you went to catch your trolley."

She gasped for breath. "I just missed my trolley and ran back to see if you were still here. Could you give me a ride home?"

"Certainly, hop in," said Bill. "Oh! how is your ankle?"

"It's fine, but last night when I went home I heard strange noises. Like someone trying to break into my house. I hate living alone."

"Did you call the police?"

Claudia clutched her hands together. "No, I just prayed to the Lord to protect me."

Bill stopped in front of her house and Claudia asked, "Could you come in and make sure no one's there?"

"I'll be glad to if it will make you feel better." Bill got out of the car and searched every room. "Looks like your safe. Make sure you lock all the doors when I leave."

"Thank you so much. I don't mean to be a sissy. A woman living alone has to be careful." She dished out a bowl of chicken noodle soup. "This is my way of saying thanks for your kindness."

"No thanks, I can't stay I have to get home."

"Don't hurt my feelings; I have to repay your kindness."

"Well, it does smell good." Bill quickly finished the bowl of soup. "That was delicious, now I have to go."

"You can't go yet, I made an apple pie. I know it's your favorite."

She cut him a slice and sprinkled some spice on it. Then she poured him a cup of tea.

He started to yawn. "It looks great, I can't let that go to waste." When he finished, he yawned and rubbed his twitching eyes. "I've got to go, I promised Jennifer I wouldn't be late." He stood up and staggered, grabbing the chair for support.

Claudia could see his eyes were glassy and twitching. "You're much too tired to drive." She led him to the bedroom where he collapsed on the bed. "I'm a little tired too." She crawled in beside him.

He gazed up at her and mumbled, "I see my white angel." His eyes closed and he started to breathe deeply.

"That's it my pet. Breathe deeply and inhale that wonderful smell from the incense." Claudia reached over and kissed him passionately, "You're my man on Tuesdays and Thursdays and someday all the time."

---

After the children were in bed, Jennifer sat in the parlor reading. She dozed off and woke up when she heard the hall clock strike midnight.

Jennifer yawned. "I might as well go to bed." She was still awake at 1 a.m. and she decided to call Mrs. Runderson. No one answered. "Where can he be?" She sat in the rocking chair and leaned her head back. The rocking motion lulled her to sleep. Jennifer woke at 6 a.m. in the morning and saw the empty bed. "He didn't come home again," she thought. "I put up with this when he was drunk, but I'm not going through it again."

---

Claudia was sitting on the bed when Bill woke up in the morning. He grabbed his jacket and started to get up. Claudia put her hand on his arm and said, "Don't hurry off."

"I have to get home before my wife leaves for work." Bill drove home as fast as he could and found Jennifer sitting at the kitchen table. "Hello, any coffee left?"

Jennifer looked at his shaky hands. "Yes, I just made a fresh pot."

His hand shook as he poured a cup of coffee and set it on the table. The over-filled cup splashed on the table and the coffee swirled down the oilcloth and on to the floor.

"I'm…I'm sorry."

Jennifer got a rag and cleaned the table and floor. "Did you have breakfast?"

Bill stirred his coffee as he said, "No."

She took his empty cup and walked over to the stove and refilled it. "Where were you all night?"

Bill spread his hands out on the table and shrugged his shoulders. "When I took Mrs. Runderson home, she told me someone tried to break into her house. She asked if I would look around her house in case someone was there."

Jennifer tapped the table with her spoon. "Yes, go on."

"After I checked the house, she insisted I have something to eat. I finished eating and stood up to come home, then had another dizzy spell."

"Don't tell me. I know. Mrs. Runderson let you lie down and you went to sleep right?"

Bill took a deep unsteady breath. "She really makes good soup."

Jennifer's eyebrows drew together. "I bet she does. Where did you sleep?"

"I slept in a room on the first floor. Why?"

Jennifer's hazel eyes hardened. "What makes you so tired at her house? You stay up all hours working in the basement here."

"I don't know. I'm beginning to worry about these dizzy spells."

"I don't like you being involved with Mrs. Runderson."

"I take her home when she needs a ride. Sometimes Reverend Thatcher takes her home."

"Does he get sleepy and stay overnight too?"

"I don't know. I'm not there."

"Why can't she call me and let me know when you're sick? It's almost like she plans it."

"What do you mean she plans it? Claudia's a God-loving, caring woman. She's only trying to help me. She didn't want me to drive when she saw how dizzy I was."

"Claudia! You're familiar enough to call her Claudia? Why doesn't she call me if she's so caring?"

"I don't know. What does it matter? I'm home now."

The coffee cup dropped from Jennifer's hand and shattered on the floor. "What does it matter? It matters a lot when I'm home worried sick about you. I don't know where you are or if you had a spell while you were driving." Her hands trembled and she hid them behind her. "She should have called me. Years ago I worried myself sick when you were on your drunken binges, but I won't do it again. I won't worry, while you're sleeping with that hypocrite."

Bill's face turned red as he said, "You don't know what you're talking about."

Jennifer sat down on the chair and tried to compose herself.

"I've got to change for work." He went upstairs and pulled on a pair of overalls as he wondered why he kept having dizzy spells. "What make me so tired when I'm at Claudia's house?"

Jennifer grabbed the dishes off the table in such a fury that she dropped them. She felt angry with Claudia for not calling her and mad at Bill for going to her house.

Bill kissed her goodbye. "Calm down, I'm not sleeping with her. I love you. We'll talk about it when I get home."

Jennifer's legs shook as she climbed the stairs and threw herself on the bed. She had been nursing a cold for the last two weeks and it wasn't getting any better. Jennifer blew her nose and wondered, "Is something going on between Mrs. Runderson and my Bill? I love you Bill."

When the children came home, Cassie said, "Mama, can you take us to the store? You promised me new ribbons."

Jennifer looked in the mirror. Her face was covered with red blotches and her eyes were swollen. She looked like a mess. "Okay, give me a few minutes. Wait for me on the front steps."

She washed her face with a cold washcloth and put a touch of rouge on her cheeks. Her nose was stuffy and her head throbbed with pain. She was lightheaded and broke out in a cold sweat. Falling back on the chair, she waited for it to pass. She felt better in a few moments and went out to her the children.

When they returned from shopping, Jennifer felt exhausted. She knew she had a fever and took two aspirins. Jennifer laid on the sofa and dosed thinking, "thank goodness I made a chicken pot pie early today. The children can set the table and Margaret can put dinner on the table."

# Chapter Twenty-Nine

When Bill came home, Jennifer was lying on the sofa. "What's wrong? Are you sick?"

Her voice was a whisper, as she tried to talk. "My cold is getting worse. I think I have the flu." Jennifer coughed so hard she gagged.

"I'm sorry you're sick."

"Margaret's fixing dinner. She is a big help."

"Why don't you go to bed? I'll help with dinner and homework." He helped her upstairs and tucked her in bed. He got down on his knees and prayed. "Dear Lord, keep a special hand on my wife and heal her of the infection. Thank you Lord, Amen." He kissed her and said, "I know you will feel better."

She gagged on the mucus in her throat, then wiped her mouth. "I've tried everything to get rid of this. I feel so weak."

The next morning, Bill got the children off to school and brought Jennifer her breakfast. He kissed her goodbye and said, "Stay in bed so you'll get better. I have church tonight so I won't be home for dinner, but I'll call and see how you're feeling."

"Thank you. I'll call Mr. Clancy and let him know I won't be in."

When Mr. Clancy heard her voice, he said, "Jennifer! I hardly recognized your voice."

"I won't be in today. Can you get your neighbor to help out?"

"I'm sorry you're sick. Is there anything I can do?"

Jennifer coughed again. "No. If I stay in bed today, I should feel better."

"Take care of yourself and get plenty of rest. I'll call later to see how you're feeling."

Jennifer took her temperature. The thermometer read 102 degrees Fahrenheit. She felt weak; it was an effort to pull the covers up. Shivers contorted her body and she fell asleep whispering, "I love you Bill."

After school the children raced into the house heading for the kitchen. "I'm hungry," said Joseph, as he pulled out a jar of peanut butter.

"I wonder where Mama is?" asked Faith.

"Maybe she's upstairs, I'll go see," said Margaret. She was surprised to see her mother in bed. Margaret shook her shoulder. "Are you still sick?' When Jennifer didn't answer, Margaret shook her again. "Mama, wake up and talk to me." Jennifer murmured something inaudible and Margaret felt her head. "You're burning up!" She ran downstairs calling, "Cassie, Joseph,

Mama's sick. I need you to chop some ice and bring it up to me." She got a basin, filled it with water and wiped her mother's face. Joseph brought the ice up and she put cold clothes on her head. After a while, she put dinner on the table for her brother and sister and brought soup to her mother. "Mama, wake up and eat some soup. It will be good for you."

Jennifer never stirred. The children stayed by her side, and took turns placing wash cloths on her head.

"It is 10 p.m. and daddy is not home yet," said Cassie.

Margaret held back the tears, as she wondered what to do. She called the church and Reverend Thatcher answered, but all he could hear was sobs. "Who is this?"

"Is my father there?" asked Margaret.

"Who are you?" asked Reverend Thatcher.

"It's...It's...Margaret Rennie, my mother is sick and I need to find my father."

"I'm sorry, Margaret, he's not here. He left over an hour ago."

"Some nights he doesn't come home."

"What! He doesn't come home at night, where would he stay?"

Margaret sobbed again, then sniffled, "I heard Mother and Daddy talking. He stays at

Mrs. Runderson's house at night."

Cassie and Joseph saw Margaret crying. "What's wrong with Mama?"

"Calm down, honey. Everything will be all right," promised Reverend Thatcher. "Stay with your mother. I'll be right over."

The phone rang as soon as Margaret hung up. "Hello," she said still sobbing.

"This is Mr. Clancy. I'm calling to see how Jennifer is doing. Who am I speaking to?"

"This is her daughter Margaret."

"Oh yes, your mother told me about you." Mr. Clancy could hear the children in the back ground. "Why is everyone crying?"

"Mama's burning up with fever and I don't know what to do!" The phone slipped out of her hand and fell to the floor.

"Hello, hello," said Mr. Clancy.

Margaret retrieved the phone. "I can't find Daddy and I don't know what to do!"

"I'm coming right over," said Mr. Clancy.

Roger Clancy arrived before Reverend Thatcher. Margaret took him to Jennifer's room. He felt Jennifer's head, then gently lifted her eyelids and looked into her glassy eyes. He wasn't a doctor, but his wife had been sick for years and he knew what to look for. Mr. Clancy put his head to Jennifer's chest and heard a wheezing sound.

"It sounds like her lungs are full of mucus and her heart's beating too rapidly."

He went into the hall and Cassie ran after him. "Don't go. Please don't go!"

"I'm not going anywhere, honey." He put his arm around her and said, "I'm going to wash my hands, then I'll call an ambulance. Your mother must go to the hospital."

Cassie let out a wail and grabbed his jacket. "Don't do that! Daddy will get mad and beat us. He doesn't believe in doctors."

Mr. Clancy stared at them in shock. "Beat you! He'll not lay a hand on you while I'm around." He walked to the phone. "Your mother is very sick and needs immediate medical care." The child continued to cry and he patted her head. He held Jennifer's hand while they waited for the ambulance. He heard her mumbling. "Bill, where are you? I love you"

"That bastard," whispered Mr. Clancy.

When they arrived at the Hanamak Hospital, the doctors rushed her to the emergency room.

Mr. Clancy guided the children into the waiting room. "We'll wait here until the doctor comes out to talk to us."

"Will Mama be all right?" asked Margaret.

"She'll get better here in the hospital," said Mr. Clancy as he patted Margaret's hand.

"Daddy says we shouldn't use doctors, that God will heal us," said Cassie. 'Does that mean doctors are sinners?"

"No, doctors are not sinners; they're God's helping hands."

Joseph put his arms around his sisters. "Mama's going to get well. I know it."

Mr. Clancy went to the newsstand and brought the children comic books. He handed them each one. "This will keep you busy for a while."

"Gee whiz, I never had a comic book before. Thank you," said Joseph.

Margaret sat staring into space, and a nurse walked by. "My mother was a nurse," said Margaret.

"Was a nurse?" said Mr. Clancy. "She still is. She takes care of my wife and is a wonderful nurse."

Margaret gasped and was about to say something when Doctor Brewster came out. "Are you her husband?"

"No. I'm just a friend, but these are her children," said Mr. Clancy. "How is she?"

"Her temperature is one-hundred-and-five and she has pleurisy and pneumonia. If you waited one more day, she wouldn't have made it," replied Doctor Brewster.

A look of concern shadowed on Mr. Clancy's face. "One-hundred-and-five! Whew, I'm glad I got her here in time."

"We're working to bring her temperature down. She keeps calling for Bill. I suppose that's her husband."

Mr. Clancy rubbed his unshaven face. "Yes, it is. We're trying to locate him."

"Let's hope we can pull her through." The doctor held out his hand. "She was clutching these in her hands, you might want to keep them for her."

Mr. Clancy took the ivory rosary beads. "When can we see her?"

"She is in a coma. You can go in, but don't stay long."

As they walked in the room, Joseph gasped. "What's that white thing around mama?"

"That's an oxygen tent to help her breathe," said Mr. Clancy.

Margaret held her mother's hand. "She looks so pale. Mama, please don't die! Please open your eyes."

Cassie tried to climb on the bed as she said, "Mama, we love you."

———————

Reverend Thatcher saw Bill's car in front of Mrs. Runderson house and rang the bell. When no one answered, he banged on the door and shouted, "Open up."

"All right, all right. I'm coming!" said Claudia. She was tying the belt on her bathrobe when she opened the door. Her face turned red as she said, "Reverend Thatcher! What are you doing here so late?"

"Where is Pastor Rennie?" demanded Reverend Thatcher.

Claudia stuttered, "He…he's not here."

He pushed her aside, "Don't lie to me woman. His car is out front." He hurried down the hall, glancing into each room until he found Bill lying on the bed asleep. "Pastor Rennie, wake up." When Bill didn't move, Reverend Thatcher shook his shoulder. "Wake up you hypocrite. Wake up now."

Bill opened his eyes and tried to focus on the face in front of him. "What's the matter?"

Reverend Thatcher shook him again. "Get up. What are you doing here? I'm ashamed of you."

Bill recognized the voice and sat up. "Reverend Thatcher! What are you doing here?"

"I want to know what you are doing here?" demanded Reverend Thatcher.

"I drove Mrs. Gunderson home and she offered to help me canvas the streets tomorrow. I was going over the area when I got dizzy and almost fainted. She let me lie down for a while."

"Don't waste my time with your lies, you hypocrite. You walk the streets, condemning others. You're the biggest sinner of them all. Get up! Your wife is sick and you're fornicating with this Jezebel."

Bill got out of bed. "I'm not fornicating with Claudia." He noticed his shoes were off and started to put them on. I knew Jennifer had a cold. Has it gotten worse?"

Reverend Thatcher threw Bill's coat at him. "Margaret called me. She's hysterical, said her mother was burning up with fever and she didn't know where you were. How could you disgrace yourself this way?" Mrs. Gunderson peeked around the doorway and Reverend Thatcher said, "Get out of my sight, you evil woman." He looked at Bill. "You're like an alley cat. Staying out all night fornicating, while your wife and children are home alone. I believe the devil has taken over your soul."

Bill laced his shoes as he said, "Reverend Thatcher, I'm not a sinner. I got very tired and dizzy and came in here to rest."

"You're a disgrace to the church. I'm ashamed of you." Reverend Thatcher's nostrils itched and he sneezed, then sniffed the air. "I know that smell!" He spied the incense burning on the dresser. "That incense is called Devil's Glow. Satan worshipers use it at orgies, and rituals. It's a powerful scent and makes people do unspeakable things." Reverend Thatcher picked up the stick of incense and snuffed it out. "They feed virgins a special spice, an aphrodisiac. They put them in a room where this incense is burning. That's when the orgies or rituals begin." He raised his eyebrows as he looked at Bill. "Did she feed you anything when you came here?"

"She always has chicken soup prepared. Why?"

Reverend Thatcher walked into the kitchen and started to open the cabinets. "It's got to be here."

Claudia grabbed his arm. "You can't search my cabinets. This is my house."

He shoved her aside. "Get out of my way, you harlot." He rooted through her cabinets pulling everything out.

"Are you sure you know what you're talking about?" asked Bill.

Reverend Thatcher laughed and walked over to the stove. "Oh yes indeed, I know what I'm looking for." He spotted a small black bottle tucked in the corner by the stove. "Aha!" he said, unscrewing the top.

Claudia hit him on the back with her fists. "That's mine!" She tried to grab the bottle from him, but the Reverend held it high.

"Oh, no you don't. Bill grab her and hold her away from me." He held a pinch of the powder to his nose and sniffed. "Yep, smells like almonds. This is it. She drugged you with this powerful aphrodisiac. When this powder enters your body, it makes you dizzy and very sleepy. After you are drugged, you go into a trance. You're a willing participant without your knowledge."

"What are you talking about?" said Bill. He pushed Claudia away from him.

She grabbed Bill's arms. "Don't listen to him. He's lying."

The reverend laughed and waved the bottle in front of Bill. "With this powder and the incense, you didn't stand a chance. She could do whatever she wanted with you and you never knew." He laughed again and added, "You were her sex toy."

"No. It's not possible…is it?" He thought for a while, then said, "That's why I always had dizzy spells and was so sleepy when I came here."

Reverend Thatcher put the bottle in his pocket. "Let's get out of here."

"Wait, I'm coming too," said Claudia.

"You're not going anywhere," said Reverend Thatcher. "You're an evil woman, a disciple of the devil. I don't want you anywhere near Mrs. Rennie or the church."

"I'm coming and you can't stop me." Reverend Thatcher slammed the door in her face.

When Bill got home, they searched each room. "Where can they be?" He heard a knock on the door and opened it. "Mrs. Jones! Come in. What can I do for you?"

The neighbor hobbled in and sat her short, thin body on the sofa. She smoothed back her white hair and tucked the loose strands into the knot at the nape of her neck. Mrs. Jones adjusted her glass and said, "I was looking out of my window from across the street. I saw your car and came to tell you, Mrs. Rennie's in the hospital."

"What! Who took my wife to the hospital? Our lives are in God's hands, I prayed that God would heal her."

Mrs. Jones sneered, as she looked him straight in the eye. "When did you do that, Pastor Rennie? You're never home."

Bill lifted his chin and boldly met her stare. "That's not your business. Just tell me what hospital they took her to."

"Hanamak Hospital," she answered still studying him. "Hear you got yourself a fat ass girlfriend."

Reverend Thatcher said, "Thank you Mrs. Jones. We have to leave now. Let me escort you to the door. Come Bill, I'll drive you to the hospital."

As they were getting in the car Mrs. Jones said, "Ha, I always knew you preachers didn't practice what you preach. You're always accusing others of sinning, then you crawl in bed with your Two Ton Tessie." She walked across the street, turned and said, "I hope your wife makes it. She's too good for the likes of you."

———————————

When Bill walked into the hospital, it brought back memories of where Jennifer used to work. They were directed to Jennifer's room and as he walked in, the white oxygen tent shocked him.

The children were at Jennifer's bedside and Joseph ran to him. "Mama's very sick. She almost died."

Margaret had tears in her eyes as she asked, "Where were you? I needed you. Why didn't you come home? I didn't know what to do when I found Mama so sick." Tears rolled down her face as she continued, "Mother thinks you don't love her anymore. If you don't love her, I don't love you."

"Me neither," said Cassie and Faith.

A sharp pain went through Bill. It felt like his heart had been torn out. He never realized words could hurt so much. "I'm sorry, so sorry." He kneeled down beside them and tried to put his arms around them, they pulled away. Jennifer moaned. Bill went to her bedside and looked through the white oxygen tent. She was so pale and thin, his heart ached.

Bill held her hand. "Babe, I'm here. Can you hear me?" When she didn't answer, he sat in the chair beside the bed holding her hand.

Mr. Clancy watched Bill and thought he looks familiar. Then it came to him. He's the man that I gave ten dollars to years ago! I sent food to his house! Oh my God, all this time I was helping Jennifer and her children.

Bill looked at Roger. "Have we ever met?"

"No, we haven't, he lied," offering his hand. "I'm Mr. Clancy. Jennifer works for my wife." Bill ignored his hand. Roger continued, "I brought your wife to the hospital because she was deathly sick."

"How dare you take that upon yourself? Didn't my wife tell you we don't believe in doctors or hospitals?"

Mr. Clancy's face went red, and he stepped closer to Bill. "If you have a problem with me, let's take it out in the hall. Your children have been through enough."

Reverend Thatcher stepped between them. "Bill, don't go flying off your high horse. Calm down."

"I'm taking her home right now," said Bill. "Nurse, where are her clothes?"

"You can't take Jennifer home," said Mr. Clancy. He turned to Reverend Thatcher,

"Jennifer's in a coma. Her fever was 105 degrees Fahrenheit, it's down a little now, but the worst is not over. If you take her home, she'll die."

Bill pushed him aside and went to the bed. "We'll pray for her."

Mr. Clancy shook his head in despair. "I can't stop you, but please think about it. You don't want her to die, do you?" When no one answered, he picked up his coat. "I've got to get home to my wife." Mr. Clancy walked over to Jennifer and patted her hand, and whispered, "Get well soon, Jennifer." As he left he glared at Bill. "She's a very sick woman. You should let her stay."

Reverend Thatcher handed Margaret some money. "Take your sisters and brother down to the cafeteria and get something to eat." When they left, he said, "Bill, let her stay in the hospital"

"What! I can't believe you are saying that."

Reverend Thatcher pulled his chair close to Bill. "I told you before, when someone is seriously ill they should see a doctor. The more I see the work doctors do, the more I understand how important they are." He patted Bill on the back as he continued, "Since the depression, God has many people to help. He's overwhelmed with healing and saving." Reverend Thatcher rested his head on the back of the chair. "God gave no other creature the brain power, to study and learn, that he gave man."

Bill leaned forward on his chair. "That's not what the scripture says," argued Bill. "We're taught that the Lord God will heal and save us."

Reverend Thatcher stood up. "That was written before God let man learn the knowledge of healing. There are so many needing His help. He can't get to them all. Be thankful they brought your wife here in time."

Bill felt bewildered. "What if the doctors save someone he wants in heaven?"

Reverend Thatcher smiled. "When God wants one of us in heaven, no amount of medicine can save him. Now, I want you to make peace with your family and with God." He got down on his knees and Bill followed him in a silent prayer.

The children came back from the cafeteria and Reverend Thatcher said, "I'll take the children home."

"I want to stay," said Margaret holding her mother's hand.

"You'll be more help if you go home and get the children in bed," said Reverend Thatcher. "Bill, will you be all right?"

"Yes, I want to be here when she wakes up."

"When Mother wakes up, tell her I love her," said Margaret.

When Reverend Thatcher returned from taking the children home, Bill was sitting in the corner, a look of confusion on his face.

"What's wrong?" asked Reverend Thatcher.

"Why didn't I realize what Mrs. Gunderson was doing to me? My wife could tell something was wrong. She accused me of sleeping with Claudia."

Reverend Thatcher thought for a while, then said, "Mrs. Gunderson was smitten with you from the first day you joined the church. I could see it. When your wife stopped coming to the weekly service, she was delighted and stuck by you every minute."

"I thought she was just helping out," said Bill.

Reverend Thatcher pursed his lips. "Remember the tea she brought you each night?"

Bill looked at him with an empty expression on his face. "Yes, so…?"

The Reverend's lips twisted into a cynical smile. "That's when she first gave you the drug. Did it have an almond taste?"

"Yes, it tasted strange but good."

"How did you feel when you went home?"

He tried to remember and said, "When I went home, I felt exhausted. Hot and tingly like I had a fever. Then my eyes started to twitch. I remember going into the bathroom, but nothing after that." The next morning, Jennifer said I came to bed and fell asleep instantly." Bill shook his head, "Good grief! Do you think she drugged me then?"

"Mrs. Gunderson is a shrewd woman. I think she was trying the aphrodisiac on you to see if it made you sick. When it didn't, she knew she could give you a heavier dose."

"How long does the drug last?" asked Bill.

"It depends. With a small dose, it wears off in three hours. A larger dose, in twelve hours. The more she gives you, the longer it lasts. To get the effect she wants, it has to build up in your system."

"The first time I took her home she gave me soup and I felt sleepy and dizzy. She said I should lie down for a while. I woke up in the middle of the night. The next time I took her home, she gave me soup and tea and I never woke up until it was morning. After that she always had soup, tea and pie ready for me." As Bill sat quietly thinking, he had flashbacks of things he had not remembered. "Claudia jokingly told me she thought I'd be a savage lover. I didn't understand what she meant. I told her that was sinful talk." Bill paced up and down the hospital room; he felt dirty and degraded. "What have I done? Will my wife ever forgive me?"

Reverend Thatcher smiled. "God will forgive you. What you did was the devil's doings. When Jennifer gets better, you can tell her what happened. Ask for her forgiveness."

The reverend left and Bill sat by Jennifer's bed praying. He heard her murmur and unzipped the oxygen tent. He kissed her lips softly. Tears filled his eyes, as he whispered, "Jennifer, wake up! Please wake up. I want to tell you how much I love you."

His tears fell on her forehead and her eyelids fluttered as she said, "Please tell me you'll love me always."

Bill kissed her cheek and whispered, "My sweet, sweet Babe. I love you so much." He held her hand and Jennifer gave him a faint smile, then drifted off again.

The doctor came in and patted Bill's back. "She's going to recover. Go home and get some rest."

Bill kissed Jennifer's cheek and whispered, "I'll be back in the morning, sleep tight." He shook the doctor's hand. "Thank you and the Lord for all you've done. I'm going home to be with my children."

# Chapter Thirty

Bill walked down the steps of the hospital and as he reached the sidewalk, Claudia grabbed his arm. Her hair was wind-blown and her coat hung from one shoulder. "How's Jennifer? Did she die?"

Bill yanked his arm away. "What are you doing here? We told you to stay away!"

As he walked down the street, Claudia ran after him. She grabbed his coat. "Bill. You're tired, come home with me. I'll fix you some hot chicken soup."

"Let go of me. I'll never eat your food again you...you she-devil." Bill pushed her away. "You drugged me, made me commit adultery. I want nothing to do with you." She reached out for him and he screamed, "Don't touch me."

"Don't touch me. Don't touch me," she mimicked. Claudia's eyes blazed wildly, as she grabbed his lapels and held him. "You loved the way I touched you."

Bill tried to pull away, but she held him tight. She pounded his chest with her fist. Her face looked evil as she screamed, "You're mine and I won't let you go back to her."

Claudia wrapped her strong arms around him and pleaded, "I love you. Come home with me." She grabbed his crotch and giggled as she said, "You love me. Don't you, Billy boy?"

A crowd gathered and a policeman broke through. "What's going on here?"

Claudia heard the officer and lunged at him, hitting him hard with her fist "Go away."

The officer staggered under her weight, and struggled to keep his balance. Then he grabbed her arm. "Calm down, Lady. What's going on here?" He looked at Bill. "Is she bothering you?"

"Yes she is." Bill looked at Claudia as he said, "I want her to leave me alone."

Claudia pulled away from the policeman and swung her fist wildly, hitting Bill in the face. "I hate you." She let out a hideous laugh, "The devil has your soul and he's holding it tight."

The officer handcuffed Claudia and pulled her down the street. "Come with me. The paddy wagons waiting for you."

Claudia turned her head and leered at Bill. "The devil has your soul and you'll burn in hell forever."

Bill trembled and his chest tightened, as a fiery light glowed in front of him. Frightened, he ran down the street and hailed a cab. He climbed in and as it pulled away, he looked back. Claudia was being pushed into the police car. He whispered, "Halleluiah, she is out of my life forever. Thank you God."

# Chapter Thirty-One

Bill got up early the next morning and fixed the children's breakfast. He wanted to get to the hospital.

"Hurry and get ready. I don't want you late for school," said Bill.

"I don't want to go to school. I want to go to the hospital," said Margaret.

"We do too. We're worried about mother." said the other three.

"Your mother would not want you to miss school. Besides, I'm going to need your help with the housework, while your mother is in the hospital. Margaret, I'm putting you in charge. When you get home from school, I want all of you to make your beds and clean the house. Faith, Cassie and Joseph, I want you to listen to your sister when I'm not home." They all nodded their heads.

"They will dad. I'll have dinner ready when you get home," said Margaret.

"I'll cook too," said Cassie.

---

When Bill walked in, Jennifer was sitting up in bed and the oxygen tent had been removed. He kissed her. "How do you feel?"

Jennifer smiled and said, "A little better. They gave me some broth this morning."

"What did the doctor say?"

"He said I'm not out of the woods yet. I still have a fever and my lungs haven't cleared. They just took the tent away this morning, but they're watching me. How are the children?"

"They're worried about you. They wanted to come, but I sent them to school. I want to talk to you about my actions, but I'll wait until you're stronger."

Jennifer nodded her head in agreement, as the nurse took her blood pressure.

Bill patted her hand. "I have to go to work, but I'll be back tonight."

---

When the children came home from school, Joseph picked up his shoe shine box and said, "I'm going out to make some money shining shoes."

"Where did you get that? asked Margaret.

"I made it. Found some old wood up the street," he said, as he started walking towards the door.

"Not until you clean your room and put out the trash," said Margaret. "Cassie, you dust the parlor and dining room. Faith, you make your bed and clean the bathroom."

"I'll do it when I get back," said Joseph.

"No you won't," said Cassie. "You'll do it now. You're just a little kid and have to listen to Margaret and me."

"I'm not a kid, I'm twelve. You're older than me, but I'm taller and I can beat you up."

"Oh yeah," said Cassie, closing her fist.

"Stop it right now!" said Margaret. "Joseph you have to listen to me or I'll tell daddy. Now go clean your room,"

Joseph stomped off to his room mumbling to himself. "I hate girls."

———————————————

Each day Bill went to the hospital for a few hours after church. As soon as he got home, the children were waiting for him. "How's mother?" asked Margaret.

"She's doing much better," said Bill. "Hmm, what's that I smell?'

"I made chicken stew for dinner. I hope it's as good as mothers," said Margaret.

Bill put his arm around her shoulder. "It smells delicious."

"I made the biscuits," said Cassie.

He patted Cassie's head. "You're becoming quite a cook. Oh, I have good news. Your mother is coming home tomorrow."

The children jumped with joy as they said in unison, "Can we come with you to get her?"

"Yes, you can all come. Now, let's eat," said Bill.

Saturday morning everyone hurried through breakfast, then Margaret dusted the furniture. She told the other children to pick up the things that were lying around.

Margaret put the last of the dishes away and said, "I want to make sure the house is perfect for mother."

"Faith and Joseph, make sure your beds are made," said Cassie.

"I already made mine. Hurry! I want to go see mama," said Joseph.

"Where did the flowers in the parlor come from?" asked Bill.

"I bought them," said Joseph proudly.

"Where did you get the money?" asked Cassie.

"From shining shoes. I didn't have enough money. When I told the man I was buying the flowers for mama, he let me have them."

Bill put his arm around his son. "That's very thoughtful. I'm proud of you. In fact, I'm proud of all of you. Come on! Let's go get your mother."

When they entered the room, Jennifer was sitting in a chair talking to Doctor Brewster.

"You're well enough to go home, but you must rest," said Doctor Brewster. "Don't do anything for at least a week."

Bill took Jennifer's hand. "Don't worry doctor; we won't let her lift a finger. We're glad to get her home."

The children gathered around Jennifer and hugged her. "We missed you so much."

The doctor gave Bill a slip of paper. "Get this prescription filled. She needs to take this sulfur drug for another seven days."

The nurse approached Bill and said, "Mr. Rennie, you have to pay your wife's hospital charges before they'll give you her discharge slip."

Bill looked worried and said, "Babe, I'll be right back." He went down to the office. "I'm here to pay Jennifer Rennie's hospital expenses."

"Let's see!" she said looking through the files. "The total is eight hundred dollars."

"Eight hundred dollars! I don't have that kind of money."

The clerk looked at the bill again. "Oh, it's been paid in full."

"That's impossible. Who paid it?"

"It doesn't say. It's just marked paid in full. Here's your discharge slip and a receipt."

He returned to Jennifer's room and gave the nurse the paper. "Babe, are you ready?"

"Yes, I can't wait to get in my own bed." The nurse helped Jennifer into the wheelchair and took her to the front entrance. Bill brought the car around and the children jumped out surrounding her. When they were driving home, Jennifer asked, "How much did they charge?"

"Eight hundred," said Bill.

Jennifer gasped. "What! Where did you get the money?"

"God took care of it," said Bill

"Maybe Reverend Thatcher paid it. Where would he'd get that much money?" said Jennifer.

When they arrived home, Jennifer put her arms around Cassie and Margaret and they helped her into the house. "I feel a bit weak." Jennifer sat on the sofa and looked around. "You children did a great job while I was away. The place looks so clean."

"We're making hamburger stew for dinner," said Cassie.

Bill could see the love and devotion the children felt for their mother and he whispered to Jennifer, "The children really missed you. I missed you too."

After dinner when they were alone, Bill took Jennifer's hand. "Babe, I need to talk to you. I have to explain my past behavior."

Jennifer stared at him for a moment. "I want to talk to you too, but I'm tired. I want to get my strength back first."

"Let me know when you feel up to it." Bill put his arms around Jennifer and gently kissed her. "I love you and want to keep our family together forever."

After two weeks, Jennifer was able to do a load of wash. She had just finished hanging the clothes out to dry when the doorbell rang.

Jennifer opened the door. "Mr. Clancy! What are you doing here?"

"I wanted to see how you're doing. You look wonderful."

"Please sit down. It's so good to see you. Forgive the way I look, I was outside hanging clothes. It's so windy." She ran her hands through her uncombed hair. She sat on the couch beside him. "If you hadn't taken me to the hospital, I would be have died. But little by little, I'm getting back to normal. Thank you for saving my life."

"I'm glad I got there in time. I could see how sick you were. I had to do something. Marsha sends her love and that your job is waiting for you."

"You mean you didn't hire anyone?"

"No. We care about you and want you back. You were the best nurse she ever had."

Jennifer smiled, "That's very kind of you, but I'll need a few more weeks."

"Our neighbor is helping out until you can return."

"Someone paid my hospital bill and I was wondering if it was you."

"Yes. I didn't think you'd figure it out. I knew you didn't have enough to cover it and I didn't want them keeping you in the hospital forever," laughed Mr. Clancy. "Marsha needs you."

"Thank you. That was so thoughtful. I'll pay you back every cent."

"Oh no! You won't. Just promise you'll come back to work. Are you still moving?"

"I was too sick to think about it."

"I have a friend who rents out properties. He has a house that's available and it sounds like something you'd like. I'll check it out and see what he wants for it."

Mr. Clancy stood up. "I've got to be going. Oh! I almost forgot. I wanted to return these." He handed her the rosary beads.

"Thank you so much. I wondered what happened to them."

"The doctor gave them to me." He held her hand and said, "My dear, if there is ever anything you need, just call me."

Jennifer blushed. "Thank you so much. I don't know how I'll ever repay you."

"Just stay as sweet as you are." He walked to the door. "I'll check on you every so often to see how you're doing and I will let you know about the house."

Bill came home from work and gave her a hug. "You must be feeling well. You look so happy."

"Mr. Clancy stopped by today."

"What did he want?" Bill pulled away and sat on the sofa.

"He wanted to see how I was feeling. He said my job is still waiting for me."

"I don't want that man in this house again."

"Why? What did he ever do to you?"

"He had no right interfering in our lives. He took you to the hospital without my permission."

"You weren't around. Remember? If he hadn't taken me, I would be dead. Where were you when I needed you? Hanging around Mrs. Runderson's."

"Don't talk like that. I can explain my actions. Each time I took her home she gave me food with a drug in it. It made me dizzy. Then she'd insist I lie down for a while. When I did, I passed out. Remember the nights I came home from church so tired? Well she had given me tea before I left and it had the drug in it."

"Of course you had to take her home. You had to go in the house and she forced you to eat her food. Ha!"

"When Mrs. Runderson asked for a ride home, she always had a good reason. I hate to refuse anyone a favor."

"I knew something wasn't right! I thought you were sleeping with her."

"I wasn't sleeping with her. I don't know what she did when I was in a drugged sleep."

Jennifer laughed. "Ha! That's a good one."

"That's the truth," ask Reverend Thatcher. "He's the one who figured it out. She fed me this aphrodisiac. It's a powerful drug that's used in orgies. I swear I don't even know if anything even happened."

Jennifer stared at him, not knowing what to believe. Bill took her hand. "Please believe me and forgive me. I wish it had never happened. I'm so sorry I hurt you."

"It's a weird story. I suppose I'll have to believe you. Especially if Reverend Thatcher says it's true." Jennifer leaned back on the sofa. "Did you sleep with her every time you took her home?"

"I honestly don't know. She's acted like a God loving woman when all the time she was a she-devil."

Jennifer shivered at the thought of him with Claudia. "Well let's forget it for now and have dinner. The children are outside playing. Call them in, while I put dinner on the table."

After dinner they sat in the pallor while the children went upstairs to get ready for bed.

Jennifer was knitting and she stopped and asked, "Can we still move to a bigger house?"

"I think so," said Bill putting his Bible down.

"Mr. Clancy's friend has a house for rent. It would be the same price as this ,but bigger."

"Why is Mr. Clancy being so helpful? What does he want from you?"

"He doesn't want anything. He'd like me to come back to work for his wife."

"Just what do you do for his wife, clean house?"

"No, I've been working as her nurse," said Jennifer.

"You what! You were working as a nurse after I forbid it. You've been lying to me."

"I tried to tell you about my job, but you never had time to listen."

"Well I'm listening now. I'm master of this family and you are not going back to work!"

Bill sat down and opened his bible. "Furthermore, we are not taking Mr. Clancy's friend's house. I'll find something else."

Jennifer was furious. She wasn't going to obey his every command anymore, or tell her what she can do! She stood up and threw her knitting on the chair and blurted out, "Let me tell you something Mr. Perfect. I am going back to work for Mr. Clancy. He was the one who paid the hospital and we owe him for that."

"He paid the hospital? Why would he do that?"

"Because he's a kind man who's trying to help us."

"What's in it for him?"

"Funny you should ask that! You're the one always giving away our money. Even when we needed it so badly. How about those coats you gave away?"

"That's different, they were needy people," said Bill.

"And we're not?"

Bill squirmed in his chair and said, "We'll pay him back every cent."

"When I was in the hospital, I thought a lot about our life. I can't live like this any longer. Things are changing. I don't care if you like it or not. From now on the children and I are going to doctors. We will listen to the radio and go to the movies. This one will really upset you. The children and I are going to the Catholic Church. You might think you're the master of this family, but you're not. These are the rules the children and I are going to live by from now on. If you don't like it, leave." She stomped out of the room and went upstairs.

Bill yelled, "You'll do as I say, I'm your husband."

He started to read his bible, but couldn't concentrate, "She can't go back to the Catholic religion, I forbid it. Why is she acting like this?" He thought about their life together. How they changed since their marriage. He'd never seen such fire in Jennifer's eyes! He sat thinking about what Reverend Thatcher had said about hospitals and doctors. Slowly, he climbed the stairs to their room. Jennifer was reading a magazine in bed. He sat on the edge of the bed and stared at her. She was sure he was going to say something about reading unholy scripture.

Jennifer looked at him with fire in her eyes. Don't try to change my mind. I told you how I feel and the terms I insist on.

Bill took her hand. "I've put you through a lot since we've been married. You didn't approve of all the changes, but you went along for the sake of the family. I don't want to lose you. I promise to be a better husband and not so strict with the children." He hesitated for a moment, then said, "Reverend Thatcher gave me a different outlook on doctors and now I agree with him. You can go to doctors, but as for Mr. Clancy…"

Jennifer interrupted, "Don't you dare tell me I can't work for them."

Bill's face went red. "Okay, Okay, you can work for them, but I don't want you to go to the Catholic Church. I can't be pastor of the church if my family is Catholic."

Jennifer patted his hand and simply said, "That's something you have to work out. I told you my rules and that's final."

Bill's voice changed to his dominating tone as he said, "There is no way I can." Jennifer shook her head at him. His voice changed to a softer tone as he continued, "I'll have a discussion with Reverend Thatcher. I don't know how, but we'll work it out."

Tears ran down her cheeks. "I can't believe what I'm hearing. Do you really mean it?"

"Yes I do. Besides I have no choice, if I want to keep my family together."

"It will make life easier and more enjoyable for all of us. She kissed him. I love you."

Bill lay beside her, holding her close as he softly said, "Is it your safe time?"

"Yes darling, it is." She smiled, removed her nightgown and turned off the light.

*The End*